Eastbourne College
A Celebration

Eastbourne College
A Celebration

EDITED BY VAL HORSLER AND ROBINA DAVIES
CONSULTANT EDITORS FORBES WASTIE AND MICHAEL PARTRIDGE

III THIRD MILLENNIUM
PUBLISHING, LONDON

Eastbourne College: A Celebration

© Eastbourne College and Third Millennium Publishing Limited

First published in 2007 by
Third Millennium Publishing Limited,
a subsidiary of Third Millennium Information Limited.

2–5 Benjamin Street
London
United Kingdom
EC1M 5QL
www.tmiltd.com

ISBN 9 781905 942642

British Library Cataloguing in Publication Data
A CIP catalogue record for this book is available from the British Library.

Edited by Val Horsler and Robina Davies
Designed by Matthew Wilson and Susan Pugsley
Production by Bonnie Murray

Reprographics by Asia Graphic Printing Ltd
Printed in China by 1010 Printing International

Contents

Acknowledgements

We received a huge number of contributions to this book in the form of memories, anecdotes, photographs, play and concert programmes and much more. It has been impossible to use everything we received, but it will all, whether as originals or as copies, form a notable addition to the College archive and is gratefully acknowledged.

The four editors would, first and foremost, like to offer huge thanks to their fellow members of the Editorial Board, David Blake, Kim Deshayes, Pam Duffill, Vicky Henley, David Thomson and John Thornley, who uncomplainingly answered questions, never betrayed irritation at intrusion into their busy lives and supported the project unstintingly. Several others on the College staff, from the headmaster down, gave time to talk, correct and confirm facts and stories and help with illustrations. Many of them have their names in the book attached to contributions; but there were others who allowed themselves to be interrogated as well as or instead of writing, in particular Charlie Bostock, Ben Delaunay, Robin Harrison, Jenny Kirtley, Philip Le Brocq, Tim Lucey, David Miller, Brian Prentis, David Stewart, David West, Stuart White and Simon Wood. Derren Gilliam devoted a great deal of time to the scanning of the photographs, and Katie Nye of Radley was also very helpful.

David Burt, publisher of the book, is himself an OE and has been a stalwart from the start; his colleagues at Third Millennium, especially Matthew Wilson and Susan Pugsley, the designers, and Bonnie Murray, the production manager, have put in their usual commitment to high standards and excellence.

PICTURE ACKNOWLEDGEMENTS

Many of the photographs and other material used within the book come from the College archives and are copyright © Eastbourne College. The school photographs on pages 64–5 are copyright © Panora Ltd (top) and Gillman & Soame (bottom), to whom thanks are due for permission for their use. Other images come from contributors who are acknowledged within the captions.

The names of Old Eastbournians are followed in brackets by an abbreviation giving the house to which they belonged and their year of entry to the College; thus (B87) indicates a pupil who came to the school in 1987 and was a member of Blackwater House. OEs of the nineteenth and twenty-first centuries are distinguished from those of the twentieth by giving the year in full, so (B1887) and (W2000). Crosby House is written in full to differentiate it from Craig, and other abbreviations of house names are as follows:

B	Blackwater
C	Craig
G	Gonville
N	Nugent
P	Pennell
Pw	Powell
R	Reeves
S	School
W	Wargrave
Wt	Watt

Fireworks at the 140th celebrations, 2007 (HᴛO).

Editors' Note

A 'bourne' is a place of safety; hence *salus* in Eastbourne College's motto, *Ex oriente salus*. The other words clearly refer to the 'East' element of the name; and the whole is made even more complex by its references to the local stream, the Bourne, and meanings of *salus* other than 'safety', such as 'health' and 'salvation'.

Vincent Allom pointed out the undertones of the motto in his history of the school, *Ex Oriente Salus. A Centenary History of Eastbourne College*, published to mark the College's centenary in 1967. Forty years on, with the school now in the middle of celebrations for its 140th birthday in 2007, we are publishing another book to mark yet another landmark year and the continued onward surge in the development of Eastbourne College in a new century. This is not a straightforward history; rather it is a celebration of a school that has survived and been strengthened by the vicissitudes of those roller-coaster decades that marked the first half of the twentieth century, and has remade itself in order to face the twenty-first with confidence. It consists mainly of the memories and reminiscences, anecdotes and insights, of those men (and later women) who taught and studied here, augmented by material from the admirable school archives and with the benefit of access to Vin Allom's book and other school histories. The earliest personal reminiscence we received specifically for this book comes from the 1920s, but the continuing tradition whereby sons, and now daughters, attended their fathers', and now their mothers', alma mater is evidenced by contributions not just about their own schooldays but about those of their forebears too. It goes without saying that, for the first fifty or so years of the school's history, we have to rely on archival material. But even there we hope that the story will be enlivened by the new

contributions which have flooded in following the announcement about the publication.

Much has changed since the start – not least the presence of girls and women, both as pupils and on the staff. But much has remained constant. Those early Eastbournians would urge on today's successful sports teams much as they did their own contemporaries; they would stand in proud homage to their successors who lost their lives while fighting for their country, and salute with honour those awarded medals for valour. They would certainly not recognise many of the subjects studied today, nor the technology available to help; nor might they feel in tune with the increased informality among both staff and pupils and the breaking down of hierarchical boundaries. But they would surely accept today's Eastbourne College as a true and satisfactory descendant of the school they knew.

Left: Speech Day, 1938 (Derek Wells-Brown).

Below: Speech Day on College Field, 2002.

Right: Rag day on the Cuckmere, 1950 (Richard Browne).

Foundation and early years
1867–1914

It was an Eastbourne doctor, Charles Hayman, who first decided in 1865 that the rapidly growing town would benefit from a new school, 'a Proprietary College… for the education of the sons of Noblemen and Gentlemen [which] would greatly conduce to the welfare and prosperity of the town and neighbourhood.' The Duke of Devonshire, who had major interests in the area, quickly offered his support and made available twelve acres of land already designated for building on what was then the edge of the town. Members of the Council who were to run the school were appointed, as was the first headmaster, the Rev James Russell Wood. The College opened in August

1867 in two houses which had been temporarily leased until permanent buildings could be erected. There were fifteen boys, two full-time assistant masters – a classicist and a mathematician – and two visiting masters who taught French, German, writing and drawing. The fees varied from twenty to twenty-six guineas a year for tuition plus between fifty and seventy guineas for boarding.

By the summer of the following year, 1868, pupil numbers had risen to thirty-nine. But the fledgling school was to face a run of difficulties which nearly saw it go under before it was firmly established, mainly because too few shares had been taken up and there was not enough money in the kitty to begin building work. Matters got worse when the headmaster resigned and announced that he was going to set up a new school of his own in the town, to which many of the parents decided to transfer their sons at the end of the summer term of 1869. Despite this setback, and despite the view of many on the Council that the financial difficulties were intractable, the proposal to close was defeated and Eastbourne College defiantly reopened for the autumn term of that year with a mere five of the original boys and a new headmaster, the Rev Thompson Podmore, who brought four more boys with him. Wood's school was not destined to flourish, and within only a few years it had become a preparatory school.

The financial difficulties were partly resolved by an arrangement whereby the headmaster was not paid a salary but provided with a rent-free house for himself and up to thirty boarders, together with a proportion of the fees and a cost-sharing agreement. A similar deal was soon offered to the Rev George Robert Green who arrived in September 1870 with twenty-one boys and later (in 1873) opened Blackwater House. It was now

Left: James Russell Wood, the first headmaster, 1867–9.

Previous pages: Rugby on College Field, 1957 (A J G Glossop).

remnant of Bird Wood's garden. A gymnasium soon followed and then, in 1874, the chapel. Meanwhile numbers were climbing rapidly – they topped 100 in the summer of 1874 – so more boarding houses and classrooms had to be provided. An early initiative, with an unbroken record of publication to the present day, was *The Eastbournian*, the first edition of which was published in May 1870.

Throughout the remainder of the 1870s and most of the1880s financial difficulties remained, augmented by continuing differences between the Council and the school staff, and further exacerbated by disputes among some of the housemasters. These damaging feuds were rooted in the arrangements whereby housemasters were reliant on their boarders for at least part of their income and were in their turn responsible for the buildings themselves and some of the costs; if one master was seen as keeping to himself

Above: College House (now School House) in 1870, with College Field beyond, taken from the spire of St Saviour's; the roof of the College's first home, Ellesmere Villas (now Spencer Court), can be seen bottom right.

Right: Charles Crowden, headmaster 1888–95.

too that the College acquired Larkfield from the Duke of Devonshire; it had been built by an eccentric retired naval officer, Charles Rawdon, whose equally eccentric gardener, 'Bird' Wood, had laid out the grounds. The duke at the same time offered to underwrite the building of an extension to this house, of which the foundation stone was laid in July 1870. What was Larkfield is now the flint-faced part of School House, which itself is one of the few surviving buildings from those early days, with the Dell a

> *On my arrival, the College consisted of four buildings only: School House, Blackwater House, a portion of the chapel and a rough and cheaply built gymnasium. In those early days we were not too good at cricket, and we played a curious type of football, a mixture of rugger and soccer. The school library was represented by a few books in a cupboard in the dining hall; nothing was done in the way of entertainments; nobody was ever invited to talk to us; no music was ever given us, nor were we at all artistic. But I imagine that all this was common in most schools of the period and, knowing no better, we were happy enough.*
>
> **An unnamed 'boy who was at the school in the 1870s',**
> **written some fifty years later and quoted in Allom**

a majority of the boarders to the financial detriment of another, resentment could easily be aroused. There were two similar cases at this time which became widely known in the town – mainly because the housemasters in question found themselves in debt to the tradesmen – and threatened the reputation of the school. There were health problems too – an outbreak of scarlet fever – which raised questions about the need for a proper sanatorium and also caused pupil numbers to decline. By 1887 the school was running at a loss and, although the problems were not of his making, Podmore resigned. Green was appointed as the new headmaster, but was not to last for long, partly because of his own ill health but mainly because the finances were now so precarious that the only solution appeared to be the appointment of a dynamic new head who could bring with him an intake of new boys – a common occurrence in those days, when a schoolmaster 'owned' the boys in his care and frequently took them with him when he moved to a different school.

The new head was the Rev Dr Charles Crowden, who arrived in the Michaelmas term of 1888 with ninety boys from his previous school, Cranbrook. The College had so shrunk during the disastrous previous years that the new pupils swelled the numbers only to 150. Most of the masters had also left, so there was new blood here too, again mainly from Cranbrook. But old and new bedded in together quickly and well, and there was also money to be spent on buildings when the duke offered to underwrite further financial help.

Wargrave and Gonville Houses opened at this time, to add to Blackwater and School (called at this point College House), and new buildings included a new gymnasium, a chemistry laboratory, a workshop and additional fives courts. The chapel was enlarged to accommodate the higher numbers, and better

provision was made for the day boys. The school quickly became established on a firmer footing, but when once again finances needed for yet further development began to dry up, Crowden decided to leave after only seven years in the job. To quote Vin Allom, 'Crowden was essentially a builder and had not that patience which enables a man to be content in

Above: The first gymnasium.

Left: A lesson in the new gymnasium, 1895.

Above: Corps Camp, late 1890s.

Top right: Big School, pre-1940.

maintaining what others have won.' And although he was 'just the man that Eastbourne wanted at this critical moment in its history,' two pupils of the time were rather more scathing. H M Trouncer, who had come with Crowden from Cranbrook, sorrowfully felt that the high moral tone he had noticed on arrival at Eastbourne did not survive more than a year of the new head's tenure. And L W Wild, who had started at the school under Podmore and survived through Green to experience Crowden's reign, wrote (much later) that, although he had his good points and 'had done a lot to put the College on the map, he was also a charlatan, who got away with it all right with parents, who did not see enough of him to see through him.' Wild was also illuminating about the initial melding of the two contingents – the existing pupils at the College and the incomers from Cranbrook: 'The first impression that we boys got of the newcomers was that they were very rowdy, and the first impression that they got of us was that we were but pussyfoots, and dare not say boo to a goose. However, by the end of the first term we all blended together…'. Moreover, the new boys provided fresh talent which allowed the College to beat other schools at football and cricket for the first time.

The next head, who took office in the autumn term of 1895, was the Rev Matthew Albert Bayfield, who came from Christ's College, Brecon, and brought with him several first-rate members of staff who were to have a positive impact. It was around this time that the Corps was founded and it was also now that school

prefects were first appointed, as well as a senior prefect who later became known as head of the school.

It was during Bayfield's tenure too that the College first acquired a preparatory school, which came about when a formidable widow, Frances Browne, asked to be allowed to run a boarding house for day boys at the school. The existing housemasters objected on the valid grounds that she would be setting up in opposition to themselves, so as an alternative it was agreed that she would set up a prep school for the College, which she called St Bede's; the College agreed for its part to stop accepting boys below the age of fourteen, who were to attend St Bede's instead. The whole venture lasted some seven years, with the relationship between the two schools marred much of the time by financial disputes, before the connections between them were severed and St Bede's went on independently after moving to a bigger site. A lasting result was that Eastbourne College never returned to its previous practice of taking younger boys, but now fell into line with other public schools with an entry age of fourteen. St Bede's flourished and continues to do so to this day on the same site.

Bayfield in his turn fell ill and resigned in 1900, just at the point when the decision to change the school's game from association to rugby football was about to cause uproar, mainly among the old boys. The new headmaster, Harry Redmond Thomson, declined to countermand the decision taken by his predecessor and the change went ahead. It had mainly been at the instigation of Edward Carleton Arnold, later headmaster, who had just arrived at the school as an assistant master and whose devotion to the game was such that he was prepared to do anything he could to convert the rest of the school to his passion.

Thomson was the first layman to be appointed head and – although he too was to suffer from ill health which made his tenure a short one of only five and a half years – his influence on the school was deep and lasting. A tribute paid to him on his death in 1917 sums up how those who knew him felt: 'As a schoolmaster he found his vocation, for he was a born teacher; his forms were always the envy of his colleagues. It is not easy to speak of the work he did, but there can be little doubt that whatever success the College may have attained since, or may attain in the future, it will be based in no small degree upon the firm and solid foundations which H R Thomson so well and truly laid…'.

The Rev Frederick Farewell Sanigear Williams, the next head, was at thirty-six years of age the youngest the school had ever appointed and was to remain in office for the next eighteen years. In 1908, two years after his arrival, he married the sister of one of his prefects, who thus went on to combine his role

The oriel window above the D&T workshop in Blackwater Road commemorates the attempt by an OE to fly a plane from Upavon, the RAF aerodrome on Salisbury Plain, to Canada, reprising Lindbergh's recent solo crossing of the Atlantic but in the far more dangerous westerly direction. Freddie 'Jack' Minchin was a distinguished First World War pilot who would try anything to relieve the boredom of peacetime. A proposal by the Princess Ludwig Loewenstein-Wertheim to attempt this flight, against the prevailing winds and in an aircraft heavily laden with fuel for the crossing, was a challenge he could not refuse. The plane was spotted over Ireland and again in mid-Atlantic from an oil tanker, but was then lost in fog over Newfoundland and assumed to have come down at sea; an aircraft wheel believed to have come from the plane was found on the shore of Iceland some weeks later. The attempt is recorded on the plaque beneath the window:

Frederick Frank Minchin
(School House 1905–8)
late Lieutenant-Colonel Royal Air Force CBE DSO MC and Bar
who on 31 August 1927 with two companions set out
in the aeroplane St Raphael to cross the Atlantic
and passed out of the sight of men

Richard Walder (staff 1992 to present)

as the new head boy with that of being the headmaster's brother-in-law. One of Williams' early initiatives was to restart the fund-raising for Big School, a project that had been started several years previously but had been postponed when insufficient funds were raised for everything that was needed at the time. An appeal was launched in 1907, and building began the following year and was finished in time for a formal opening on Speech Day in 1909. Old Eastbournians were approached to provide chairs for the new building, and Arnold encouraged some of the boys and the masters to take up woodcarving in order to adorn the hall; their efforts over the next twenty-five years were in place until the fire of 1981 destroyed all but one of their wooden panels, as well as the chairs and Arnold's own contributions from his collection of battleship timbers and battle relics.

A new house called Crosby was established in 1914, whose housemaster also assumed responsibility for the day boys whose original accommodation had been a victim of some of the earlier building projects. But the established footing on which the College now appeared to stand was to suffer, with the rest of the country, from the cataclysm that was the First World War.

Left: A boy admires a carved wooden panel in Big School.

My grandfather, William Hay Murray, was first involved with Eastbourne College in 1901/2 when he designed the enlargement of School House and the New Building as part of an extensive development which was to include Big School. That part of the plan had to wait for some years, but he was eventually able to produce a sketch in 1907 which was circulated with the general appeal for funds; plans were approved in February 1909 and the building was finished in about six months. He was also responsible for several smaller developments at this time, including the original cricket pavilion which was built in 1913. Another of his contributions to what is now the College campus was a southward extension to the large house in Old Wish Road called 'Avoca', later in 1931 to be bought by the College and to become the headmaster's house. His last commission for the College was to produce a design for what is now known as the Memorial Building, but sadly he died before the work could begin.

Andrew Murray

Top right: Harry Thomson, headmaster 1900–5.

THE DEVONSHIRE CONNECTION

Michael Partridge (B46 and College archivist) writes: 'The seventh Duke of Devonshire was the early backer of Eastbourne College, without whose generous moral and financial support the College would not have got off the ground in 1867 and whose sponsorship helped to keep it going during the difficult early years.

'By the time of his death in 1891, he had spent over £20,000, with no financial return, on the growing school. Successive dukes have held the post of Council president and have continued to take an active interest in the welfare of the College. Victor Christian Cavendish, the ninth duke, sold the freehold of land and buildings to the College plus a long lease of the playing field on the Links, and the tenth duke, while still Marquess of Hartington, became in 1931 an active member of the Council and its subcommittees, a role he continued while duke until his death in 1950. Subsequently Andrew Cavendish, the eleventh duke, our president for fifty-four years until his death in 2004, became a firm friend and supporter. In 2002 he referred to "your truly marvellous school". "Stoker" Cavendish, the twelfth duke, attended the inagural gathering of the Devonshire Society (the legacy club) in 2006 and in October of that year entertained members of the society to lunch at Chatsworth.'

The jubilee year of the College has, unhappily, been saddened by the loss of many of the most loyal of her sons; to the chronicle of our losses must be added that of the greatest of her former headmasters. That H R Thomson should be so described may seem to some an over-statement; he was headmaster for only five years, and during that time he made enemies as well as friends. But – and I speak as one who was a boy at the College during practically the whole of his regime – it would be hard to imagine a period of more solid and consistent advance in all things that matter most to the fair name of a public school. It was not an easy task that fell to his share, and in his first year Thomson had much difficult and anxious work to do. With firmness and justice, not unmingled with genuine kindliness and sympathy when occasion demanded, he so carried out the work that he may well be said to have left an easy task to anyone who might succeed him. Thus it was that, though he could never have been called a universally popular head from the boys' point of view (his staff were devoted to him from start to finish), before he left he had gained the affection of many and the respect of all. There was nothing small about him, nothing insincere, no suspicion of humbug. His high sense of duty led to frequent self-examination, and some consequent depression; it was perhaps this fact, coupled with the first intimations of the lingering illness which ultimately caused his death, that led to his sudden resignation at a moment when his work had brought the school to the highest level. He never realised the measure of his success.

Gordon Carey (S01, headmaster 1929–38), writing in 1917

Recovery and growth
1914–1940

There were, of course, many privations during the war years and their immediate aftermath, not least the fact that the school's jubilee year, 1917, could not be celebrated properly, with events limited to a chapel service, a lecture and a day's holiday. Moreover the school, like the rest of the country, was badly affected by the influenza epidemic of 1918, which resulted in whole dormitories being turned into hospital wards. Although at some points there were hardly any boys to be seen in lessons, there were fortunately no deaths.

Numbers fluctuated too as the war took its toll – from 200 in the summer of 1914 to 150 in 1916, followed by gradual growth until in 1918 the school had returned to about its pre-war strength. There was

now a rapid increase, until in 1922 there were 300 boys in the school and a new house was opened to accommodate them, named after Theodore Pennell (HB1879), who had practised as a Christian medical missionary on the North-West Frontier of India, habitually dressed as a Pathan and much respected by his patients. He had died in 1912 of blood poisoning following an emergency operation to save the life of a colleague. In his honour, the College maintained a bed in his hospital in India for many decades.

Above: E C Arnold, headmaster 1924–9.

Left: Fencing by the cloisters, 1935.

I was very fond of 'Bill' as we called him [the headmaster, F S Williams]. He was a very gentle man, and a first class classical scholar, but no disciplinarian at all. It was quite obvious to us boys that he and the other staff did not really agree with each other very well because they wanted him to be stricter than he was, so by the time I got there he was rather retiring. However, there was never any question of getting leave off chapel to see your parents or anything like that. I asked him once when my parents came down – and of course they didn't often come down in those days when there were no cars – and he said no but he was very gentle about it.

Among Gordon Carey's innovations in the late 1920s, unusual at that time, was the start of a geography department, but without any funds. It still had no funds when I took over in 1936, but eventually Stephen Foot allowed £10 to buy some maps. I arranged for the flowering cherry trees round the field. Quaife, the College groundsman and guardian of the cricket pitch, wanted the elms out because their roots spread into the outfield. Stanley Sears, the wealthy and generous father of a Blackwater boy, had given Nugee the money for the three trees in front of the bursary, so I continued these round the field. Elizabeth and I planted the (what is now) big cherry by the gym at that time.

John Underhill (S19, staff 1930–71)

Right: The Octagon, the original Cavendish library.

It was now that several significant changes took place in how the school was run. It had been suggested back in 1916 by John Foot (W1898) that an endowment fund should be started, an idea to which the Old Eastbournian Association responded enthusiastically, and a joint committee of the OEA and the Council was set up to manage the appeal and the fund. This increasingly focused on a war memorial to be built next to Big School which would incorporate new classrooms as well as a new gymnasium, laboratory, workshop, armoury and library. There was to be a tower with oriel windows in the centre of the building, and cloisters within which the names of OEs who had fallen in the war would be inscribed. In addition, the original plan included a large dining hall and kitchens to provide a central meals facility for the whole school.

This particular element of the proposal, however, aroused the opposition of the housemasters whose income from providing food, among all the other services at their individual houses, would be threatened. It was therefore dropped; but the opportunity was taken to introduce a new system whereby the school was gradually to take over the houses and all the costs of running them, with the housemasters becoming salaried officials. The completion of this 'hostel system' was to take fifteen years as housemasters moved on or retired.

It was Arnold's energy and enthusiasm that maintained the momentum of what was now the Memorial Fund. A new architect, Geoffrey Wilson (B1900), was appointed to finalise the designs and

The house system was such that we had all our meals by houses and, apart from class teaching, everything we did was relevant to the house; so we tended to have our friends within the house and, apart from games and in class, did not really get to know many boys outside our house. In many public schools of the time day boys were looked down on, and sometimes not admitted if their father's name appeared over a shop in the town. A day boy housemaster I knew found it difficult to overcome the jibe that his house were just the 'townees'. But in the College this was not the case; the day boy population steadily increased, and in my last year the head of school was a day boy.

Michael Girling (P33)

NGDALE
APRAIK
OVEBAND·
IE-SMITH
LYTE
MACKAY
MASTER
CQUEEN

T. L. V.
J. H. M
N. D. F. M
A. H. P. M
T. NEWMAN HALL
A. P. ORDE WARD
A. H. OXLEY
E. G. PASSINGHAM
A. W. PASSMORE
A. F. A. PATTERSON
J. A. PEARSON
P. R. PHILLIPS
S. PHILLIPS
C. F. L. PIERSON
G. L. PITT

Above: Gordon Carey escorts the Prince of Wales, 1931.

Left: The panels in the cloisters commemorating Old Eastbournians who died in the First World War.

oversee the building, which began in July 1923. Money was available for only part of the whole concept at this stage, but the central tower and the south wing were completed by the summer of 1925. Meanwhile the headmaster had decided to leave at the end of the summer term of 1924 after eighteen years in office, and there was little dispute about who would succeed him. Arnold, always known as 'Og', had strong support among both the staff and OEs, he was very much in tune with the recent changes and developments, he had been the driving force behind the Memorial Building and he had the confidence of most of the Council. He himself was not sure he wanted the job, but agreed on the basis that he would serve a five-year term only.

His appointment coincided with the retirement of several long-standing stalwarts among the staff, so he had a number of new appointments to make. He also knew that he had to re-establish a sense of direction, something which had been a casualty of the war years and Williams' rather dispirited final time in office. He was fortunate to have a new ally in Stephen Foot (W&G01), younger brother of the original proposer of the endowment fund, who after a highly successful career in business now changed tack and

The OE Annual Report for 1997/8 announced that School House was to become a girls' boarding house. It so happened that it was seventy years since, in September 1928 with about ten others, I entered that house as a new boy, at which time Stephen Foot was housemaster. There were a number of rules and customs affecting new entrants, some official, some not. I recall that 'first termers' were not allowed to keep their hands in their trouser pockets; 'second termers' one hand; after that there were no restrictions. Stephen Foot, as he subsequently explained in one of his memoirs, kept a fairly vigilant but unseen eye on these initiation customs and very wisely devised his own, known as the 'ringing in' ceremony. A few weeks after the beginning of term, new boys would be told not to attend evening prayers in the dining room (which in those days was in the house), but to wait outside in the vestibule. When prayers ended each boy in turn was to give one hearty ring on the 'Menace' bell, which hung just outside the dining room. The door was then opened by the senior prefect, whereupon the party filed in and stood facing the top table with Foot in the centre. He then gave a short peroration which, to the best of my recollection, went something like this: 'Rudd, Evans, Wyatt, Thomson, Oman, Williams, Campling, Williams, twelve years ago the bell which you have just rung was hanging on the quarterdeck of a ship engaged in one of the sternest fights in England's history. The ship's company, officers and men, would run to their duty by that bell and they were prepared, if necessary, to give their lives for king and country. For you, the ringing of that bell marks a new start in life. It rings out anything in the past which you may have regretted or been ashamed of and it rings in a future for which, God helping you, you, the house and the school may be proud. In the name of School House, of which you are now full members, I have much pleasure in welcoming you.'

Roy Campling (S28)

became a schoolmaster at the College. His business acumen had an immediate effect on the running of the school: he implemented the new house hostel system and managed the finances of the first two houses to which it was applied; he set up a pioneering new careers advice service for the boys; he assumed financial responsibility for the sanatorium and for the recently built house for bachelor assistant masters, for whom he also introduced a pension scheme. It was apparent that he was increasingly taking over the work of the secretary to the Council, a post that had always been held by a local solicitor for whom the school's work was only a part of a busy practice. The Council therefore now appointed him bursar, and the school for the first time had someone full-time and on the premises running the finances and administration.

Aided by Stephen Foot's business sense, Arnold soon made it clear to masters and boys what he expected of them and how he saw the future. As Allom records, he had faults – among which was a tendency to undervalue intellectual ability and originality – but his infectious enthusiasms, his willingness to consult others' opinions and the firmness of his views all meant that everyone knew exactly where they stood with him and recognised that his *raison d'être* was the good of the school. During his five years in office the playing field situation was improved, the chapel was enlarged to accommodate the growing numbers at the school and the Memorial Building was completed with the addition of the north wing. The drive leading up to the tower was straightened so that it became a suitably imposing approach and gates were built at its entrance as a memorial to H R Thomson. These gates were the gift of a group of men whose existence was the result of yet another of Arnold's enthusiasms – the Embellishers' League, later the Arnold Embellishers.

On Arnold's resignation at the end of his self-designated term, the Council once again had no doubt about who was to succeed him. This was Gordon Carey, a distinguished Old Eastbournian who had already played a part in the school's affairs by serving on the Council from 1918 until 1924. He had been

senior prefect and captain of football in his final two years at the school before going on to become Eastbourne's second Cambridge rugby blue. Carey now set about making his mark, continuing many of Arnold's developments but pushing forward in other ways too – notably in the academic and artistic fields. The school had not had a proper art department for some time, and music was practically moribund; he now appointed new masters to take these subjects forward in a much more vigorous way, and himself re-established a choral society (Gillett had set one up in 1889 but it had lapsed) and encouraged the boys to take up musical instruments.

He also appointed teachers of high academic calibre, and reorganised the timetables so that there was a better and more manageable balance between classroom

Above: Cross country, taken from the album presented to Gordon Carey on his retirement.

Below: Ingenious wheel with drawings and facts about the staff, made by Peter Burdett.

Taken from his autobiography A Fiddler Tells All:
We had a French master – not himself French – by the name of Waterfield, who was generally known as 'Bubbles' and who was the target of much ragging. One day when he was writing on the blackboard, a boy took advantage of him having his back to us and climbed up on to the rafters. Bubbles called out 'What are you doing up there, boy?' 'Looking for something, sir' came the answer. 'What are you looking for?' 'Trouble, sir.' Many boys attending his classes took the precaution of padding their trousers.

Ralph Nicholson (G21)

Other memories of 'Bubbles' Waterfield come from Walter (Babe) Woollett (G20) who recalls the merciless ragging, and from Jack Sewell (Crosby31) who remembers 'his gramophone equipped with an enormous horn. It must have been nearly four feet long, with an ever-widening, trumpet-shaped mouthpiece into which Bubbles would put his head. The temptation was too great for the most wicked of us, and small paper pellets would be showered into the mouthpiece. Bubbles never seemed to notice, or if he did he would withdraw his head and say, with a semblance of wrath, "My fine friend, I will put you in detention directly."'

Vin Allom said of Waterfield that 'no small boy could resist ragging him'. Yet he was also 'held in great affection… his was the only surname which many boys had real difficulty in remembering. "Why are you doing that, lad?" one might ask a boy. "I was told to by Mr er… er… er…" "Waterfield?" "Yes sir". He was one of the first members of staff whom an old boy would seek out to visit.'

Above: Cartoon by Rev Ron Johnson.

Right: Beefy Howell at the blackboard, 1934 (Cecil Bell).

work and games. Under his direction the science and languages teaching improved, and the standards achieved in the sixth form became much higher. He had good relationships with staff and boys, and encouraged a more positive rapport between teachers and pupils. He also boosted the numbers of day boys, for whom Arnold had had little time, and gave them their own house – Powell, which bore the name of the member of the Council who had given it to the school. This was one of several property acquisitions during Carey's headship, another of which was the house on Old Wish Road which has, since the school bought it in 1931, been the headmaster's residence. It was not to be long before the school owned all the other buildings on that road too.

One of the legacies of Carey's reign was a general broadening of the boys' interests, including access to a much wider range of sports – athletics, tennis and swimming as well as the continuation of the more traditional team sports – and social activities such as a scout troop and membership of the volunteer charity Toc H. But by the late 1930s Carey was beginning to grow weary of the burdens of the job and announced his retirement with effect from the end of the Lent

I remember two pranks. One was when a boy climbed up on the roof, put a chamber pot on the spire and wrapped a towel round the clanger of the bell. No-one, as a result, went to chapel, so the headmaster, Gordon Carey, summoned everyone to Big School, whereupon the culprit owned up and was led out by the headmaster, no doubt for a caning. I think he became a Spitfire pilot, got a medal and came back to the College a hero. On another occasion, at the house supper before Christmas when Beefy and his guests expected to be entertained, the new headmaster, John Nugee, was present. A boy called Dutton said he was into 'magic' and asked the head to be his assistant. He then stood on a chair with a billiard cue and a cup of water. He pressed the cup against the ceiling with the cue and asked the head to hold it while he got down from the chair. He then walked away. Everyone laughed, and Nugee had to let the cup drop and was soaked. He was not amused.

Kenneth Ohlson
(G37, member of Council 1981–90)

term of 1938. One of his colleagues wrote of him at this time: 'By his wise selection and friendly encouragement, he has welded his staff into a happy and contented family, and it is perhaps to his success in doing this more than to anything else that the very real advance of the school under his guidance can be ascribed. His gift of leadership and his quiet, but obvious and determined, devotion to the welfare of the school cannot but bring out the best in any who serve under him. No headmaster can bring to a school a more valuable quality than that which ensures the loyalty and support of his colleagues. No staff could hope for a headmaster who would listen more sympathetically to their suggestions, or give them more firm or ready support in their difficulties.'

The post of headmaster was now offered to John Nugee, then sub-warden of Radley. He was an engaging and optimistic man who developed further Carey's liberalising policies; though woe betide those who crossed him as he tended not to change his mind once he had formed an opinion of someone. His caring kindness is remembered by Michael Marshall (Crosby38), who received a letter from him in 1944 after he had been wounded in Burma: 'To a nineteen-year-old, far from home and not due to return to England until 1946, this was a great comfort. He had of course served in the trenches, been wounded and decorated and knew in his heart what really mattered.' And Robin Armstrong Brown (W51) has clear memories of his academic standards: 'Short, silver-haired and always wearing a double breasted suit, he carried immense authority. He was a swift and shrewd judge of character, and in a very physical school ruled unquestioned by mental control alone. Each fortnight a resumé of your marks was sent by each teacher to your housemaster. Two or more As, and your housemaster sent you to see 'the Man' as Nugee was

The chapel was very important to the headmaster, Gordon Carey, and every Friday morning the whole school spent an hour in the chapel, under Carey's supervision, practising the hymns for that Sunday. On these occasions most of the boys sat in their usual places in the chapel, but senior boys were allowed to stand at the back. One of them at this time was Woodrow Wyatt (S32), who was in the classical sixth with me and an amusing friend. On one ill-fated morning Wyatt was late for choir practice, and when he came in he had tied a white handkerchief onto his spectacles to make it look like a beard. This greatly amused the rest of us at the back of the chapel. But the headmaster, in the pulpit conducting, saw it and roared out an invitation to Woodrow to visit him in his study. After that interview, I was told that Woodrow had been expelled, which I thought was a bit much. As I was in Gordon Carey's form for English, and thought I knew him well enough, I went to see him and pleaded that Wyatt, although often a foolish clown, was basically an able young man and not a disgrace to the College. He was not expelled. Some years after the war, Wyatt wrote his first book, an autobiography. A review said that he had criticised Eastbourne College severely. I read what he'd said about Eastbourne, that it was a terrible and boring old place, but he actually mentioned my name as being its chief hope…. I think that on the strength of this compliment I took Woodrow out to lunch. But after that, we never met again.

Ruari McLean (Crosby31)

Michael Partridge adds: 'The anecdote about Woodrow Wyatt (later Lord Wyatt of Weeford) has been recalled by other OEs. Wyatt, in his 1985 book Confessions of an Optimist, *was caustically critical of the College and certain of its staff. However he did subsequently fund an annual prize (for an essay on what would make for a happy life) in memory of John Belk, his housemaster, and took pleasure in escorting prizewinners around the Houses of Parliament.' John Thornley adds that, since Woodrow Wyatt's death in 1997, winners of this prize have attended Prime Minister's Question Time following their tour round the Houses of Parliament.*

known, and a single D or too many Cs would send you the same way. The interview in those cases was brief, unpleasant and sometimes harrowing. It was all the discipline that the school needed on the intellectual side. You were not required to be brilliant; but you were required to try. Hard.'

Two initiatives at this time were to have long-standing results. The first was the arrangement of exchange scholarships between English and American schoolboys under the auspices of the English Speaking Union; and the other was the acquisition in 1938 of the buildings of Ascham St Vincent's Preparatory School, which was closing. The College initially allowed the property to be used as a temporary home for another local prep school that had burnt down, and then decided to move both Crosby and Wargrave into it. But the clouds of war were beginning to gather, and Nugee's plans for the College had to take second place to considerations of what was to happen to the school if war broke out.

Preparing for war had been a major preoccupation since the Munich crisis. Masters had gone on courses to train them in building air-raid shelters and protecting those in their charge against poison gases. Boys filled sandbags and came to the rescue when thousands of unassembled gas masks arrived in Eastbourne. Once war had actually broken out, during the summer holidays of 1939, rooms had to be blacked out and timetables reorganised so that most activities took place during daylight. The boys dug up some of their playing fields to use as an allotment and took their turn at the lookout post on Beachy Head. But this was the 'phony war'; and it was not until the spring of 1940 that the perilous position of Eastbourne, on the south coast and close to the action, made it essential to consider evacuation.

During the Easter holidays Norway and Denmark fell to the invading Germans; Holland, Belgium and France followed, and the British army had to be evacuated from Dunkirk. Suddenly the war was very near: explosions could be dimly heard as Calais was embroiled in the fighting, and for many days the sky took on a lurid tinge as the smoke from the burning oil installations floated over the south coast. The Corps came into its own, patrolling the Downs night and day, alert for German paratroopers. But the time had come; Eastbourne had been identified as a landing beach for the German invasion, expected any day. The school had to move.

THE ARNOLD EMBELLISHERS

'Assuming that to make a first-rate school intense enthusiasm must be present and that such enthusiasm is largely stimulated by the possession of really first-rate buildings, the main object of the league should be to remove eyesores and provide the College with bits of first-rate building etc, such as boys and old boys would be proud to point out to their friends and of which they would appear really fond…. The league should never as a body interfere in the politics of the College, but should simply act the part of a fairy godmother towards it, devoting itself chiefly to what the "common-sense" or narrow-visioned brigade would call "wasting money".'

John Nugee, headmaster 1938–56.

At Radley, I remember the dons from Oxford who came to help with the teaching. One who taught geography often forgot what he had written in a book that he'd published, so there was usually a bright spark in the class who would say 'But sir, it says in this book…'. I enjoyed listening to S P B Mais who taught scientists to enjoy English, and I would often turn up at a physics or chemistry set which was not part of my programme to enjoy his inspired lesson. On one occasion when he saw me there he said 'You have already heard what I was intending to say so I will talk about something else.' However, we did not work as hard as we should have done because we would all eventually go into the armed forces and might not survive. A very difficult problem was when a boy had an elder brother who was killed or wounded. What could you say? In the end we mostly said nothing and let him grieve quietly.

Michael Pope (G39)

Almost from the word go we had a good deal of freedom at weekends, particularly in respect of rambles over the nearby Sussex Downs, visiting such places as Og's Wood and the Mere, in groups of three or four, bird watching or chasing butterflies or exploring the beach towards Beachy Head. Another Sunday activity was strolling in groups along the prom and listening to the band. When we met masters or visiting parents and their offspring, we would greet them by removing our straw hats in unison. These were obligatory Sunday headgear together with blue suits.

Philip Venn (B&Pw38)

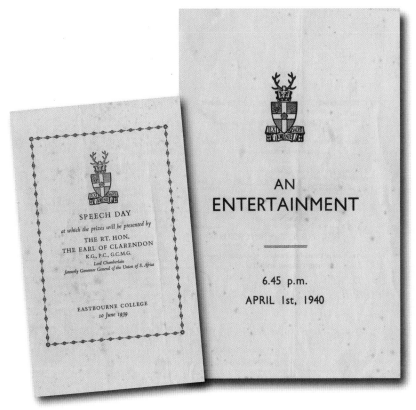

*Programmes
(J Stuart Glass).*

Your 'nurse' had to make sure that you knew all sorts of things, including the traditions to which you had to conform, such as how many buttons on your jacket had to be left done up or undone on different occasions. Other question marks hung over the rooms in the cloisters. One of these was clearly marked 'The Arnold Bird Collection'. A new boy had to ask himself 'Who was Arnold Bird? What did he collect?' Woe betide the boy who failed to find out that it was actually a collection of stuffed birds, and that E C Arnold was a very important former headmaster who loved collecting specimens of all kinds from wrens to eagles.

Peter Burdett (W39)

This was E C Arnold's summing-up of the objectives of the Embellishers' League, which owed its existence to an offer made to Arnold by Stephen Foot in 1917, that he would donate £50 a year anonymously to be spent for the benefit of the school if a number of other OEs could be found to give a similar sum. Membership in those early days was by invitation extended by Arnold to selected OEs and one or two masters, each of whom gave something each year, the amount of each subscription known only to the treasurer. Geoffrey Wilson, the architect of the

Memorial Building, was one of their number, and it was through him and through the bursar, Stephen Foot himself, that the league's projects were put before the school's Council for approval. Some £3000 was spent in the first twenty years of the league's existence, always on decorative projects for which core money could not be made available.

The name was changed to the Arnold Embellishers on Arnold's death in 1949, as a fitting memorial to him. Today, one cannot walk more than a few yards within the campus without coming across embellishments, large and small. From the early years we can number the Thomson gates, the Minchin window, the Bunbury door to the D&T Building and the commemorative pillars at either end of Old Wish Road. More recently, the Dell Theatre has been constructed, the frontage of the Memorial Building floodlit, the Long Room of the Howell Pavilion furnished and the Memorial Arch restored and improved. In May 2005 memorial panels to commemorate the 169 OEs who gave their lives in the Second World War and other twentieth-century conflicts were installed and dedicated at an impressive ceremony. The latest project is the publication in early 2007 of Gordon Carey's memoirs, *Nobody's Business*.

The Embellishers continue to thrive, solely supported by annual donations from members (and Gift Aid refunds from the tax authorities), with a record number of members and a substantial bank balance. The committee is very active and a number of projects, large and small, are in the pipeline.

One summer while we were at Radley, the First XI returned to Eastbourne to play a cricket match on our old field against the Royal Navy which had taken over the College as a training establishment. But there was a difference: the RN had mounted a Bofors AA gun on the tower to shoot at German aircraft which would fly in low over the Channel, strafing the town. During the match the gun would periodically open fire, and it was explained to us that they had to fire it occasionally to make sure that it was in working order. But I began to suspect that it was discharged only at critical moments during the match. I have subsequently played cricket in many odd places round the world, but never again to the sound of gunfire.

George Brown (G38)

The Radley years and the return to Eastbourne
1940–1956

John Nugee had had a long connection with Radley, both as a boy there and later as a master, and had reached an agreement that Radley would provide at least an initial home for the College when it became necessary to leave Eastbourne. The decision to move was taken on 17 June 1940, and the move itself was to happen only three days later. Tom Sewell (Crosby35), who was in his last term at the College and was head boy, remembers that summer term well: 'I was able to pursue my so far unfulfilled ambition to gain my First XI cricket colours – which I finally achieved in the match played on 14 June against the MCC, with Spitfires flying overhead and the guns of Dunkirk clearly audible from across the Channel. A few days later John Nugee called me in. "About this school of yours, Tom" (he had a knack of identifying you with every school crisis), "we have two days to get out." My job was to mobilise the school prefects, and we had a wonderful welcome at Radley. I spent the last six weeks of my school career sleeping on the floor of the Radley gym with everyone else.'

The senior part of the school was to go to Radley itself, while the younger boys would be accommodated at Nuneham Park, the seat of Lord Harcourt on the opposite bank of the river. The two days before leaving were spent in the frantic packing of personal and school necessities, alongside the removal to two of the houses of practically everything else – books from the library, desks from the classrooms, scientific equipment, the contents of the school shop and much else. Many of the day boys, old and current, came to help. An air-raid warning on the final night meant that it was a weary band of travellers who joined the special train the next day; but they were welcomed at Radley by a host of boys and masters who fed them and made them feel at home.

Sleeping quarters varied between the gymnasium, the scout hut, the cricket pavilion, part of the vicarage and the deserted wing of a mansion belonging to the local squire. Classrooms were made available, and many of the senior Radley boys invited their counterparts from Eastbourne to share their studies. Appropriate boxing and coxing allowed both schools to carry on with their sports activities, and members of the Boat Club were delighted to find that they had the straight, wide Thames to row on rather than the meandering Cuckmere. The younger boys at Nuneham Park found themselves being taught under ranges of family pictures and relics of the Grand Tour. Ben Lyte (G39) remembers arriving there, with another boy, two weeks after the rest of the school because they had been confined to the sanatorium at the time of the move: 'There was no special train for Butterfield and me. So far as I recall, we travelled via Reading and Didcot to Culham Halt, and then staggered with our luggage up several miles of drive through the park until we reached Nuneham Park… which had been let to the College at short notice, almost as though the family had just gone away for a weekend. Although most rugs and furniture, porcelain and so forth had miraculously given way to beds and desks and blackboards and all the essential lumber of school, occasional oases of family normality remained. For example, their beautiful music room was still complete with its turkey rugs, shelves of books and scores and in particular a splendid Bluthner grand piano.'

Both parts of the school settled quickly into their new homes and school life went on. The initial arrangement with Radley had been for the remainder of the summer term only. Now thought had to be given to what would happen in September. As it happened Radley – like many other public schools at this point in the war – was down in numbers and was consequently threatened with the possibility that the premises would be taken over for wartime needs. To

Aerial view of Radley College, 1944.

28

My two older brothers and I escaped from Germany four months before the start of World War Two as refugees. That word is significant because Eastbourne College did in fact become a refuge for all three of us. Oldest brother Walter was in School House from 1939–40, and Wolfgang and I went to prep school in Eastbourne and then on to the College in 1941 and 1942. Like most of us of that era, what we learned was not as important as the fact that we learned how to study; and I also learned how to get along with people. I was still pretty new at this English language and when I didn't communicate as I should, there was always someone to help me. Of course, after I moved to the United States in 1947, I had to learn another new language. I

remember that when the College returned to Eastbourne, School House spent the first year in Wargrave and we had those cold walks down the hill. There was that absolutely terrible (for me) thing called 'the run' which paradoxically included running along a street called Paradise. Never did a street have a worse name for the activity on it. And then there was the shock when at breakfast one morning we were told that our housemaster, John Belk, had suddenly died in the night. A kinder, gentler man I never encountered at Eastbourne. The College was a refuge in the best meaning of that word. It was not just a place of education, but a place where we learned how to really live. Long may it prosper.

Peter Homburger (S42)

> *When I read* The Old Eastbournian *now it comes as a shock to realise that when the date of an OE is given as perhaps '88 it refers to 1988, not 1888 as it would have been in my time. I also remember Vincent Allom telling me that as I had blond hair I would be bald by the time I was thirty. But I'm not doing too badly and still have a good head of hair.*
>
> **Michael O'Neill (B49)**

avoid this, they offered to house the whole of Eastbourne College on a more permanent basis, and this offer was accepted. So when the schools returned in September, it was to better and more considered arrangements.

Teaching was fully integrated, to the benefit of both schools which had lost many masters to the forces. Sports and games, on the other hand, remained separate, as did accommodation. Some of the Eastbourne houses had to be located away from the school, though as the war proceeded declining numbers meant that they were able to move closer. Eastbourne had inevitably lost its day boys, and new admissions continued to fall as time went on – few parents would choose a school in exile. From 296 boys at the beginning of the summer term of 1940, and 241 who made the journey to Radley, the complement at the beginning of 1944 was only 145. Nevertheless, the two schools combined were much larger than the buildings could easily take, so timetables had to be ingenious and many allowances had to be made.

Philip Venn (B&Pw38) recalls: 'The move was a masterpiece of organisation, and in retrospect it seems that the integration of Eastbourne and Radley took place with a minimum of fuss, though goodness knows how the staff of both schools achieved this. Their traditions were very different to ours. We had a headmaster and they had a warden; their boys wore short gowns, we didn't.' Other traditions differed too, such as chapel services: Radley took a more formal line than did Eastbourne, so it was not long before the College approached the local church to ask whether they could use it for Sunday services. Rules had to be adapted: wireless sets, previously permitted, were now forbidden because Radley did not allow them. And uniform fell victim to the privations of rationing: blue serge jackets and grey flannel trousers gave way to tweed jackets and corduroy trousers which required fewer coupons. Some innovations took root: a permanent legacy of these years was the Eastbourne College Dramatic Society, formed under the influence of the strong acting tradition at Radley; drama as an activity had never previously established itself firmly at Eastbourne.

Like the fiftieth, the College's seventy-fifth anniversary in 1942 also took place under the shadow of war, though a small celebration was managed: a two-day cricket match with Lancing was arranged, Arnold came to preach at Matins and messages were received from a number of well-wishers. But the exile was beginning to threaten the very existence of the school. The town of Eastbourne was awash with

> *I was destined for Eastbourne College because I had an aunt and cousin, Nan and Betty Foxley, who lived at 12 Grange Road (now Watt House). I was to live with them and be a day boy in Powell House. But when I joined the College in the Michaelmas term of 1941 it was at Radley and I became a member of School House under Henry 'Aggy' Belk, our housemaster. When I left I became an Old Eastbournian who was never at school at Eastbourne. My son Michael (S78) followed my footsteps in School House years later.*
>
> *At Radley, we were taught in classes together by either a Radley or an Eastbourne master, supplemented, as we were near Oxford, by lecturers from the university. S P B Mais, a well-known author, taught us English and was renowned for the broad minded outlook that he had on life (and for his brightly coloured waistcoats). He gave us James Joyce's* Ulysses *to read and discuss, as well as* Tropic of Cancer/Capricorn *and other controversial books; they were banned at the time but for us schoolboys great to read. Dr Alden was in charge of music and organist in chapel, and I was lucky enough to be taught musical appreciation by him.*
>
> **Anthony Foxley (S41)**

> *Betty Foxley also remembers her connection with the College through her ownership of 12 Grange Road. In the belt-tightening 1950s the Council took a lease of the top three floors of this house while Miss Foxley continued to live in the basement. As she recalls, 'I have happy memories of my Eastbourne home, watching rugger from the wall, cricket from the dining room windows, hungry boys buying sandwich loaves from the tucker and having them to lunch on Sunday.' Miss Foxley has kept up her interest to the present although, as she now writes, 'Owing to the sudden closure of the Eastbourne home, with poor sight (now 98) I have not applied for next year's magazine.' And she signs off 'Good luck, College.'*

When I arrived at Radley in 1943, both schools had settled into a satisfactory modus vivendi. We combined for work, but the layout of the buildings and the smaller number of boys in both schools because of the war allowed us a separate dining room and use of the chapel at different times of day. This meant that one made one's friends very much within one's own school, although some friendships were made in the classroom. Beyond the classroom, the staff must have found discipline difficult. Looking back one feels one was able to wander at will around the country, and certainly to cycle into Abingdon with a pass from one's housemaster, whose signature was easily forged. Quantity rather than quality was, as ever, the most important factor in feeding boys, and the problems created by wartime rationing must have been considerable. Hall was a long way from the kitchens, and once or twice a term one was detailed off to form part of a team of three – one house prefect, one middle room boy and one prep room boy – for 'school serving'. This was a misnomer for forming a team of general skivvies for the whole of one day, excused from all work and games.

The weather on D-Day was fine and PT outdoors was accompanied by a never-ending stream of aircraft overhead – bombers, gliders on tow and fighter escorts wending their way to the continent. That evening the warden invited his form to come to his house to hear the 6pm news. There we sat in his drawing room, cross-legged on the floor, while Mrs Vaughan Wilkes ate a boiled egg and toast off a tray on her knee. This in front of twenty hungry boys who went empty away! The end of the war in Europe, VE Day, was rather less exciting because by then it was expected. A whole-day holiday was announced and we amused ourselves as we thought fit, but the day ended with a gigantic bonfire, on top of which was a figure of Hitler stuffed with thunderflashes, round which the entire school, staff and villagers assembled and made merry. It was the end of an era.

Godfrey Milton-Thompson (B43)

sea. He also recalls 'one questionable benefit from the German air activity, that candidates taking exams were subject to the invigilators' reports on the "fear factor" caused by concurrent air attacks.' Patrick Attenborough (W47), who joined the College as a nine-year-old day boy in 1943, has clear memories of wartime Eastbourne: 'Apart from not being able to get onto the beach, it was heaven for a ten-year-old boy. Windows to be broken in bombed buildings as no-one minded. Tail fins off incendiary bombs to be collected from down our back lane the morning after St Anne's church went up in flames. But less happily, lunch spoilt by glass in the rice pudding from the windows blown in when a bomb tore through the living room of a house near us; only a parrot in its cage survived.'

The Blitz spirit prevailed. Despite frequent warnings about the danger of picking up objects found on the ground, periodic raids on lockers found hoards of the detritus of war; and one football match due to be played in the afternoon of a day when there had been an air raid had to be delayed while the teams were organised to sweep the field clean of all the metal

Right: Memorial tablet in the cloisters to those who ensured the survival of the College in the Second World War.

rumours that the College was likely never to return, so the decision was taken to reopen a day boys' branch there, which in the event – in order to attract sufficient numbers – also took boys of preparatory school age. Kem Bagnall-Oakeley as headmaster was supported by Vin Allom and David 'Teddy' Craig in what was known as 'Eastbourne College, Eastbourne Branch', with Miss A R Howlett and a part-time master recruited for the younger boys. Michael Clark (Pw42) remembers the vicious air raids – 'at least thirty while we were at Gonville; the town was judged to have been subjected to the most air attacks on the south-east coast' – and also the fear engendered by the doodlebugs towards the end of the war, and the noise of the anti-aircraft units set up on the coast to shoot them down over the

In memory of all
who made it possible for
the College to survive
the Second World War
by taking us to Radley College,
under the leadership of
Headmaster Francis John Nugee MC,
and, when peace was returned,
bringing us safely home
1940–1945

Cross country run, 1948 (John Knapp-Fisher).

objects that were littered all over it. A further delay occurred when a boy came up to the master overseeing these operations with an unexploded cannon shell from which he had unscrewed the cap; it was placed on a nearby flower bed and blown up by a naval officer. It was only then that the match could start.

The main College buildings, meanwhile, had become HMS *Marlborough* under the command of Captain T G Jackson. As the end of the war approached, discussions began as to when the Admiralty would agree to release at least some of the buildings. With the return of more peaceful conditions, Radley's numbers had started to rise again and they were anxious to see their guests depart. Eventually an agreement with the navy about most of the buildings was negotiated, and the way was open for the school to return for the Michaelmas term of 1945.

The low numbers of the College in exile had been boosted by the far-sighted decision to establish the branch at home. Now, when the future of this branch had to be decided, it was agreed that the preparatory department would continue in existence as the new Eastbourne College Preparatory School,

Ascham – a decision made easier and justified by the fact that all but one of Eastbourne's pre-war prep schools had left during the war and were now declaring their intention to stay in their new quarters. Moreover, members of the Council were now prepared to open their doors to 'any boy who would benefit by an education thereat', despite Arnold's continued antipathy towards the admission of the sons of Eastbourne tradesmen; as Allom says, this was the final breaking down of the social barrier which had for too long excluded them.

The success of the Eastbourne branch was evident in the numbers: seventy-eight boys in attendance and about 150 future entries, plenty with which to re-establish Powell as a day boys' house and to form a prep school. So the College reopened in its original home with 214 boys in the main school and ninety-three in the prep. School House was still retained by the navy, as was Ascham which was intended for the younger boys, so it was initially quite a squash. The laboratories had to be housed for a time in a series of Nissen huts, and much toing and froing between the houses that had been released by the navy ensued.

I joined School House in September 1944, during the last year of evacuation at Radley. When we returned to Eastbourne in autumn 1945 we found a town that was looking very much the worse for wear – a very different environment from that of Radley in the depths of the country. I also recall that the College acquired one of the nameplates of the steam locomotive 'Eastbourne' when it was scrapped in 1961. It had been commissioned in the 1930s by Southern Railway as one of forty to be used for secondary main line duties, all of which were named after public schools. Does the school still have the nameplate or was it lost in the fire? The school was also presented with a large framed photograph of its locomotive; that for Eastbourne was unique in that it was the only one to be autographed by the chief mechanical engineer and designer, R E L Maunsell.

Ian Dawson (S44)

John Underhill was a legend in his own time. I was fiddling under the desk in the evening geography class with some newly acquired gadget, when there was a shattering crash: an iron tipped arrow was quivering in the desk less than a foot in front of me. He hated inattention! Juggins Storrs was not an eccentric at all, but a well liked housemaster and science teacher, and certainly a character. His nickname came from his very gentle, deep-voiced reproach – 'You are a silly juggins!' He was an unusually tall man, with a taste for very long black overcoats. I can still remember his demonstration of sodium lighting. On a gloomy winter evening he turned out the laboratory lights, then simply sprinkled salt onto a wire mesh above a Bunsen burner. Under his faded black teaching robe his body almost vanished, but floating high above the orange flame his long cadaverous face was flickeringly lit from underneath, his nostrils flared, and above the dark shadows beside his nose there were little orange sparks where his eyes were almost sunk in their deep sockets. Hammer Films would have paid good money for that effect!

Robin 'RC' Armstrong Brown (W51)

In September 1944 I was left at Paddington Station to catch the school train to Radley. As the train pulled away from the station my eyes swelled and fear set in as I had never been away from home before. When I arrived, I was shown to my dormitory and told to take the bed by the window next to the original main external entrance doors. So far so good, except that these doors had a two-inch gap between their bottom and the stone flags beneath them which had been worn away over the centuries. The room was cold, uninviting and badly lit; and one night in December we succumbed to a heavy blizzard and I woke to find the dormitory by my bed under an inch of snow and the foot of the bed covered in wet snow. But as the months went by I began to enjoy life among the wonderful surroundings, buildings and facilities of Radley College. I shall never forget the candlelit Christmas carol service in their magnificent chapel with both schools attending.

John Vinnicombe (S44)

John Underhill, writing in 1993, recalls the return to Eastbourne from Radley in 1945: 'Elizabeth, baby Martin and I arrived back in Blackwater the afternoon before VJ Day in August 1945. All the shops were shut for two days, but our old friend the chemist in South Street opened up and supplied us with tins of baby food and rusks to keep us going until things returned to normal and we could buy our rations. We at once discovered that the private side of the house was full of fleas, the walls of the kitchen in the basement had to be scraped with garden spades to get the fat deposits off, cockroaches swarmed everywhere and, as we realised after suffering a series of shocks, several electric plugs had been cut off and the wiring left live. No help was available, because the only woman who did come in left at once on seeing what a filthy state the house was in. That first term there was no hot water in the changing rooms, no central heating and hot water for baths only after three weeks of term; as it happened, this was the healthiest Michaelmas term we ever had – no epidemics and almost no colds. The housemaster did the stoking of the boiler and the boys cleaned the dormitories and the day rooms themselves.'

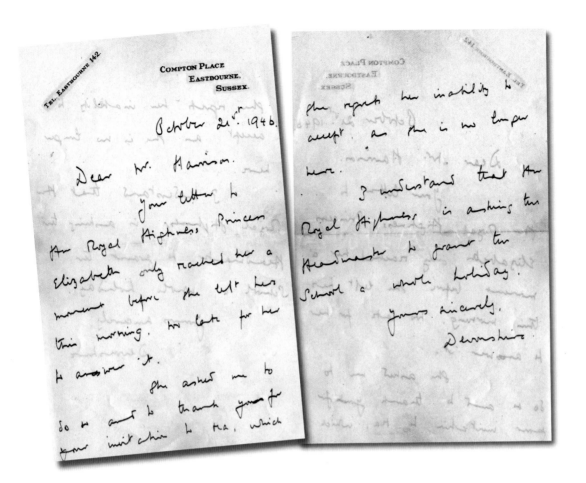

Left: Robin Harrison's letter from the Duke of Devonshire on behalf of Princess Elizabeth.

Below right: Old Blackwater.

Elizabeth Underhill's memoirs, written in 2005, record the same period: 'We had heard a bit about the bombs over Eastbourne but none of the stories had prepared us for the shock as we came out of the railway station. The taxi driver drove us down Grove Road explaining the reasons for the various gaps, holes and piles of rubble that we passed. Once we had arrived at Blackwater and John had collected the door key from under a brick we had to get ourselves ready for the night. Torn blackout curtains hung from every window and the place was dim and dank. There was no electricity but there was some coal, so we lit a fire and were able to boil water and cook the emergency rations

Things I remember from Eastbourne College at Radley: buying a fresh egg at a local farm on a Sunday; swimming illegally in the Thames on a free day, with the prefect who caught us preferring to join us rather than hand us in; Dr Alden trying to teach me the piano and giving up saying I'd better try an instrument with only one line of music; being told by the headmaster when duty prefect to clear up the vomit recently deposited at the chapel entrance (good training for fatherhood, I suppose)…!

John Oecken (S41)

When Princesses Elizabeth and Margaret were guests of the Duke of Devonshire at Compton Place, the Pennell prefects decided to invite them to tea. When I mentioned the idea to our housemaster, 'Juggins' Storrs, he never turned a hair… though much later he admitted to great misgivings because he could not imagine how we could ever sort out the chaos of our study and banish the unique and lingering smell of burnt toast, rancid milk and old socks into a fit setting in which to entertain princesses. As it happened they did not accept the invitation, but they did respond to our other suggestion that they should ask the headmaster to grant the school a whole-day holiday. Nugee was rarely willing to grant such a thing, and was clearly somewhat mystified, slightly annoyed and felt that it was all quite unnecessary. But when two senior housemasters told him that he couldn't refuse a Royal Command he gave way, and the school gained its extra holiday.

Robin Harrison (P42, staff 1953–2004)

Ex Oriente Salus; well, if not safety perhaps enthusiasm. Between the September of 1944 and the end of the summer term of 1949 I had five very enjoyable years in Blackwater House. During those far off days there were no such things as exeats: half-term was a day off work, when we would be given a packed lunch and expected to take ourselves off for a good day's walking. But in the main, at the start of each term our parents dispatched us to school on the school train from Victoria, and at the end of each term we were dispatched on the school train home. For my last two terms I was appointed head boy – a travesty of justice in some people's minds – but it was a time I enjoyed to the full. Nugee was a terrific headmaster to work with: prepared to listen to my wildcat schemes, open to suggestions and very conscious of how the post-war world was changing. So during those two terms, with his permission, we introduced a debate with Moira House, a dance with Battle Abbey and visits to the cinema ('improving films' only) and the Devonshire Park Theatre. Each of these may seem small beer in these enlightened coeducational days but in the 1940s they represented giant leaps of faith. Some years later my son went to Eastbourne and, indeed, to Blackwater. On one of our old boy reunion visits during his time there, a contemporary of mine was taken round by my son. Later on he remarked how he had enjoyed the experience: 'the one thing I noticed was how enthusiastic your son was about everything in the school.' Well, I think that sums up Eastbourne.

Dermot O'Shea Hoare (B44)

we had brought with us. Once we'd got VJ day out of the way so that shops were open again, John discovered a workman at the headmaster's house who knew how to restore our electricity, and things began to get better.

'Miss Fox-Harvey, who had been the Blackwater House matron with the Burtons before the war, offered to come back and help us and a very nervous lady cook answered one of our advertisements. John then wrote to some boys who had been with us in Powell House at Radley, asking if they could come back early to help put up beds, sort out blankets and move furniture. We now began to order food, though rationing was still of course in place. To begin with the bursar sent me a

It was the end of the Michaelmas term and, as was the custom, the pupils put on a show. Seated in the front row was our housemaster, John Underhill, with his family. On the stage was Maestro Ponke and his performing fleas. He demonstrated what the fleas could do – jumping through hoops, over bars and so on. The star flea was Alphonse who could perform astonishing tricks. Then consternation – Alphonse had leaped into the air and disappeared. 'Where is Alphonse?' the Maestro asked the audience. He went round the room calling for the flea until he stopped in front of Mr Underhill. 'Ah, there he is,' he said, taking something from Mr Underhill's hair. 'But… this is not Alphonse!' Mr Underhill took the joke in good part and laughed loudly along with everybody else.

John Arnold (B51)

As a youngster I was very interested in printing, and while at the College I attended a lecture and demonstration on 'italic handwriting' which absolutely captivated me – the writing was so graceful and elegant, and it was as though the letters were expressing something beyond the words. It was only years later, by chance, that my interest in calligraphy was rekindled, but I have now been making my living in that field for nearly thirty years. I often say a quiet 'thank you' to the College for starting me on that successful path.

Peter Joyes (B51)

In my first term the First XV was awful, and after we had been beaten 34–10 by Radley the headmaster called the whole school into Big School on the Monday and announced that we were losing because the school was asleep. Therefore with immediate effect there would be pre-breakfast prep starting at 7.15. I can remember thinking at the time that the decision was the biggest non-sequitur one could imagine. But it went on for two years.

Alfred Glossop (G52)

At Radley, with all the younger masters away at the war, we were taught mainly by older men who included a fair number of temporary staff with no teaching experience. One of these was a small, shortsighted and highly academic Irishman who taught history and had no ability to control a class. One ingenious trick played on him was to invent an extra, fictitious member of the class who was duly blamed for all bad behaviour and was frequently sent to the headmaster for punishment. Essays of a deplorable standard were prepared by the class on his behalf and sent in for marking, and the master even wrote a termly report for him.

John Lock (S43)

One of our quartet in the Gonville Middle Room, who must have had access to a great deal more money than the rest of us, had spent a proportion of it on Gordon's gin which he kept locked away in his tuck box. One evening we were visited by a house prefect – a macho man, a Stag of proven bravery and a cricketer of no little skill. His chosen seat was the tuck box loaded with gin, and he proceeded to give us a lecture about how we were puny layabouts, lacking in all the attributes we should possess, lazy and unlikely to be able to recreate Gonville's golden years on playing field and running track. In short, he told us, 'what this generation lacks is spirit!' How we longed to tell him that if he would only stand up and open the box on which he was seated he would find a substantial quantity of the stuff he thought we lacked – and we could only mumble that we would promise to put more spirit into our activities immediately, starting as soon as he had left the room.

David Atkins (G49)

The winter of 1946/7 was particularly cold, and we had a couple of weeks of snow. A couple of fellow Wargravians and I decided we had to build a sled to take advantage of the snow on the downs. There was a room in the cellar at Wargrave which was used for storage, but was out of bounds. Nevertheless we managed to gain access and found the necessary material to build the sled (I hate to tell you what we took apart). Then wearing football boots for traction and in shorts, we headed off for the Downs towing the sled to conduct trials. On arriving on site at the top of the Downs we all piled on the sled, one on top of the other facing forward, kicked off and went careering down the hill at breakneck speed, totally out of control, shouting at the top of our lungs for people to move out of the way. The frozen ground took a tremendous toll on our bare knees, but we continued with several hair-raising runs until a side runner collapsed and the three of us went hurtling into space. Happy days!

Ian Sacré (W46)

menu at the start of each week, but when I realised how unbalanced it sometimes was I asked if I could rearrange things as long as I didn't spend any more money, so I put up an old blackboard in the kitchen and wrote up two days ahead what we were all to eat.'

Robin Harrison recalls: 'An anti-aircraft gun sat on top of the tower, the cloisters were all bricked up as an air-raid shelter and concrete gun emplacements and two huge water tanks scarred the sacred turf of College Field…. The amenities were meagre… but still it was

OTC at Radley, c1943.

home and we were glad to be back, though not a single boy remained who had been at the College before the evacuation. We even had to ask our way to our houses when we arrived at the station for the start of term.'

The finances of the College had benefited during the war from low rates of interest and other concessions made by the organisations to which money was owed. The bursar, moreover, had regularly submitted over-gloomy budgets which were now queried, and more realistic rates of interest were demanded. A result was a rapid expansion of admissions – from 214 at the start of the school year in 1945 to 375 a mere three years later. A further result was the decision taken by the bursar and the Council that the debts must be liquidated as soon as possible, which was creditably achieved while carrying out a considerable building programme. Moreover, the Old Eastbournians stepped in at this point to remedy the long-standing deficiency in playing fields. This

The father of one of my friends had commented to him that our generation of schoolboys were a dull lot when he remembered the escapades he and his school friends had got up to. Stung by this, four friends from Gonville and two from School House decided to found the Japers Club. Our first two japes were the most successful, but after that we rather ran out of ideas. For our first, someone produced a large skull and crossbones flag which we ran up the flagpost at the top of the main school tower in the early hours of the morning, as well as decorating the school façade with lines of CCF navy section signalling flags draped from attic window to attic window. These made a great stir but were quickly removed. Our second jape lasted well into the following day. At about 1am we moved the entire furniture of one of the ground floor classrooms to the far side of the cricket pitch, complete with master's desk and blackboard. The master whose classroom it was may not have had classes that morning and the rest of the staff must have assumed he was planning a nature study class, as the furniture was not put back until the afternoon to make way for cricket practice.

David Pope (G49)

End of term at Victoria Station, 1952 (Richard Browne).

initiative was a memorial to OEs who had lost their lives in the Second World War, and the subscriptions raised enabled the association to buy the grounds and remaining buildings of what had been St Cyprian's prep school. Further work was done on the property to provide athletics facilities and a shooting range, together with a lych gate designed by Sir Hugh Casson (S24). The whole splendid gift – Memorial Field – was formally opened in July 1956.

By the summer of 1946 the navy had relinquished all the remaining buildings, and also handed over the surplus funds from the NAAFI canteen at HMS *Marlborough*, which were used to endow two mathematics prizes. Numbers were growing, encouraged by the Council who believed that the decades following the war might take the same shape as those following the First World War, when a period of prosperity was followed by a crippling depression. This was another element in the decision to give priority to paying off the debts, but as it turned out the feared depression did not happen, and the school was eventually faced with the 'baby boomer' period following the upsurge in the post-war birth rate. The complement topped the 400 mark in the early 1950s and never reduced below it thereafter.

The late 1940s and early 1950s saw Eastbourne College growing and consolidating, putting its roots down in the town ever more strongly and developing its outreach. In 1948, a party of boys from the Ecole St Martin at Pontoise arrived for a visit, shepherded by their Anglophile teacher; this led to a long-standing liaison between the two schools, with boys and masters regularly exchanging visits. In 1949 for the first time senior boys attended dances with girls' schools, firstly with Battle Abbey School and later with Moira House. Building, altering and refurbishing went on apace, with accommodation extended and improved both at the main school and at Ascham. John Nugee was proving to be one of the longer serving heads; but his tenure came to an end, after over seventeen years at the helm, at the end of the summer term of 1956.

We fled from Austria after the Anschluss, and many of my family died in concentration camps, including my only grandparent who was seventy-eight when she was taken to Auschwitz. My mother divorced my father for being anti-German; her two brothers served in the Wehrmacht. So I was a square peg in a round hole when I came to the school at Radley, constantly in trouble and not infrequently at the end of Mr Howell's cane. But he and Mr Bagnall-Oakeley, with whom I went from Gonville to Wargrave as a very unlikely prefect to help him to restart the house, were two marvellous men who changed my life. After waiting for naturalisation, I went on to do national service and then a degree. Most importantly, thanks to Eastbourne College, no longer a square peg!

Dick Dynes (G&W44)

I came to Eastbourne from the mythical American public school, St Grotlesex – a term that stands for a group of American private schools, founded in the nineteenth and early twentieth centuries and typified by St Paul's, Groton and Middlesex, that were established by Anglophiles who espoused 'muscular Christianity' with born-again fervour, and who took as their model their belief of what a proper English public school should be. The form seemed to involve a great emphasis on the classics, appalling food and harsh discipline, and so when I arrived at Eastbourne, to the extent that I had any expectations at all, I assumed that I'd be spending a good deal of time and effort on obscure Latin poets with little emphasis on sports which would of course be the province of those proficient enough to represent the College in the first teams. But when I arrived at Blackwater in 1947, I was surprised and delighted to find no vestige of St G in the house or in the College. No one babbled in Latin or Greek. Instead, I became involved in mathematics and physics classes much more challenging than those I had faced and easily aced at my former school. I found, despite continued strict rationing, better food than my previous school could ever have managed to put on the table. And perhaps most important, this immigrant from the west found salus in the east in the skilful balance of academics and sports. John and Elizabeth Underhill set the welcoming tone, and I could not have been more fortunate in my study mates. The College's greatest gift to me was teaching me, through the medium of three unfamiliar games – rugby, fives and cricket – that as good as it may feel to win, the sheer joy of playing is incomparably better. I discovered, in looking back in later years, that this experience freed me completely from St G's emphasis on being a 'super jock', on making the first team and from the dogma that 'winning isn't the main thing – it's the only thing.' The College taught me that the main thing, the only thing, is simply the physical playing – and this joy, this freedom, have stayed with me throughout my life, and have given it a balance I'm sure it would not otherwise have had. I'll be grateful as long as I have breath to the College for that gift; and may salus continue to be found there for the next 140 years!

Peter Albrecht (B47)

I was teaching a third year set in my fairly early days, at a time when first names were hardly used; in any case, I liked to use French versions of the boys' names. One boy I called 'Fusil' which I spelt out for him – masculine, rifle or gun. He smiled. His next test was good – eighteen out of twenty. 'Well done, Fusil. But you have made a mistake – you have misspelt your name.' 'Mistake?' he said in an innocent voice. By now you could have heard a pin drop. 'Yes. You have spelt Fusil with two ls.' 'Oh no, sir,' he said, quietly but very clearly; 'I have not made a mistake. You see, sir, I spell Gunn with two ns.'

Christopher Kirk-Greene (staff 1949–86)

I have been associated with Eastbourne College all my life – born in 1933 when my parents were living in the flat next to the headmaster's house in Old Wish Road before taking over Gonville House in 1937; then at the age of four going to live in Gonville, hearing the boys as a distant sound on staircases and in the large rooms, with the smell of food coming up from the kitchens in the semi-basement. At the age of six in 1939 going with my parents and brother to Nuneham Courtney by train with all the other boys, full of a deep uncertainty about all this and why it was happening; and then in 1947 I came from Gonville to Pennell as a new boy, welcomed by my housemaster, Robert Storrs, a man of great understanding and enormous kindness. Because I was who I was, ie a son of one of the masters, life could have been difficult but it wasn't. I lived in the school, term time and holidays. I still love to come back and see it all and remember the people who tried to get me to absorb knowledge. Now the school has girls in it. My father said, 'It makes the chapel choir much better.' Then you could only raise your straw boater or cap and wait to speak to them in the holidays.

Stephen Howell (P47)

It was 1945 and I was arriving for my first term at School House, complete with trunk, tuck box, bed blanket and various articles of clothing specified but never worn (a trilby hat comes to mind…). Gun emplacements had not yet been removed from College Field, and signs appertaining to officers and ratings etc were everywhere. Shortly after my arrival, I heard that if you belonged to a 'society' you would be able to have time off to engage in the activities, so I got together one or two friends and founded the 'Historic Expeditionary Society'. We went by bus or bicycle to explore places like Pevensey, and also to the Downs where we had fun at an old disused quarry, pushing a truck up a railway track and riding down it at breakneck speed. Very educational!

John Knapp-Fisher (S45)

Lionel Rees's medals.

ACTIVE SERVICE

Eastbourne College's twentieth-century war record is a matter of pride as well as poignancy, as is so clearly obvious on the panels in the Memorial Building which record the names of those who died. At the start of the First World War many members of the College were among those who enlisted in the patriotic fervour of the autumn of 1914, and many others joined them during the ensuing four years. By November 1918 886 OEs had served in the forces, of whom 164 had been killed, 192 wounded and eleven taken prisoner. As Roger Holloway (P47) wrote later, 'The school's record in the Second World War equalled or perhaps exceeded that of the earlier war – a fact of which we were reminded at the recent dedication of the panels bearing the names of our fallen. No school in Britain, allowing for size, can compete with it, and our record in the armed services more than equals that of the well-known "services" schools: we have only to look at our current list of generals; or to note that it was, so recently, an OE who was the first-ever British Supreme Commander Atlantic, in command at Norfolk, Virginia, the heart of America's navy; or that the British multinational commander in Afghanistan was until recently an OE lieutenant-general.'

During my year at Radley, Gonville was housed in what had been, I think, the vicarage. Our dormitory was on the top floor and the means of escape in the event of fire was one of those slings into which you harness yourself and then, jumping out of the window, are slowly lowered to the ground. We decided that it should be tested, and all went well until, as I was half way down, matron appeared in the drive. Result? Six of the best from the housemaster, Beefy Howell.

J G Mighell (G44)

When I started at the College in September 1945, all those who had been at Radley were effectively 'new boys' too in that they did not know the geography of the school. For a few weeks boys would turn up in the middle of classes after searching for the right room – or so at least they said! I remember one incident when a boy who had not deposited any money in his pocket money account at the beginning of term was found, shortly before half term, to have about £40 in it. When the housemaster investigated, it emerged that the boy in question was always ready to 'trade' – for a price. He would supply a replacement copy of a text book, picked up when someone else had left it carelessly lying around; he would run errands, look after kit, supply sweet coupons and clothing – it was the age of the 'spiv' and he was a younger version in our restricted world. Details of his adult career are not known! Looking back, it occurs to me that there were several 'wounded' boys in my intake: there had been a huge war, with evacuation, bereavement, upheaval of all sorts. I am aware too that my father, who was at the College until about 1913, never attended OE days because there would be so few of his lot there – most had been killed and it would be too painful for him. He did come one year and met a few of his old mates, but it was with a very heavy heart.

Duncan Symington (P45)

As David Thomson (G55) writes, 'Old Eastbournians have won large numbers of military awards during our first 140 years, including two Victoria Crosses. The first of these was awarded to Capt Henry Singleton Pennell (B1887), a distant cousin of Theodore Pennell for whom Pennell House was named, who earned it for his valour during an operation against hostile tribesmen on the North-West Frontier in October 1897. The second was won by Grp Capt Lionel Brabazon Rees (B1898) who was the first fighter pilot to take part in aerial combat and destroy an enemy machine; by October 1915 he had already been mentioned in despatches and awarded the Military Cross. His VC came when, on the opening day of the Somme offensive in July 1916, he single-

In January 1945, aged fourteen, after four miserable terms at another school, I came to Eastbourne-at-Radley and to School House with John Belk as its housemaster. I found myself welcome – welcomed by Mr Belk who made me feel understood and warmly welcomed by boys of my own age. No more rules about whom you could or could not look at or speak to, no rules about jacket buttons or hands in pockets, no more fagging, no more tormenting or bullying. The warmth of the welcome was only matched by the cold of our day room, with its stone floor, high ceiling and ill fitting double doors. John Belk was a quiet, gentle man who spoke softly and hesitatingly, his 'ummm' much imitated. He was not a sports lover, but once astonished everyone by appearing on the frozen lake at Radley and skating in brilliant figures of eight. Then back to a strange school we had never seen at Eastbourne, with divinity lessons with Bishop Carey who could always be diverted from theology to rugby. 'Are the Ten Commandments like a sort of touchline, Bishop?' and in no time we would be hearing his philosophy of successful back play, and how the inside centre must make the crucial break if tries are to be scored.

Patrick Parry Okeden (S&W45)

When the boys of Blackwater were about fifteen years of age they would get a summons individually from John 'Pot' Underhill on, perhaps, a Sunday evening after supper. There he would be sitting at his desk with a warm, disarming smile on his face. 'Sit you down and tell me what you know about sex, girls, babies and things.' Should I tell him what I knew and show my ignorance, or just say that I knew nothing? I am not too sure how we survived the allotted half hour, but full marks to him on tackling such a sensitive subject. All boys and no girls at the College in the 1950s. Did this make a difference? Was the absence of girls responsible for boys fancying each other? One year there was a bit of an epidemic of that sort, which Pot tackled with his usual smiling thoroughness, never shirking his responsibility as a housemaster.

Richard Browne (B49)

handedly attacked a large force of German aircraft near Loos. He remains the most decorated OE, and the school still has his medals.'

Francis Whaley (S10) was a pupil at Eastbourne College at the outbreak of the First World War. In an article written for *The Eastbournian* during the early days of the later war, he described what it was like to be a schoolboy at that time. Appropriately, as it seemed, he was at an OTC camp on the day war was

CCF inspection, 1957; sailing party on shore (Roger Blackburn).

declared: 'At the outset I cannot remember a single thought or rumour of war, but in a few days events moved with startling rapidity. First the regular cooks left at short notice and were replaced by volunteer cadets. Then the early break-up of camp was announced, and on the last morning cadets of leaving age were invited to give in their names for immediate service, and a number did so. We were then treated to a striking foretaste of a troop train journey, relieved by the ovations we received from people at stations *en route*, who believed us to be the expeditionary force travelling to some Channel port. When the school reassembled for the winter term of 1914, it was to find many unexpected absentees, both from the staff and from seniors who had left to join up. One never knew who would leave, or when. One day a senior would be in school; the next he would go out and come back proudly in a uniform and a Sam Browne. Inside the College the changes of war were felt more gradually. It was not until after I had left in 1915 that the food shortage became acute; but I remember the business of darkening windows owing to Zeppelin raids, when the headmaster tackled the job in person and mounted a ladder in the School House prep room to paint the windows black. The biggest effect was, of course, in the Corps where stripes and efficiency badges assumed an importance equivalent to athletic colours.'

The sense of adventure permeated the thoughts of a group of day boy reprobates who planned what was to be a fated canoe trip out to one of the Royal Navy ships that was visiting Eastbourne. Three boys would man two canoes while two others would hire a rowing boat at the pier which was to act as the 'safety boat'. Everything quickly went wrong: the sea was choppy, the distance out to the ship had been underestimated, there was a delay in getting the rowing boat and the two canoes were exceedingly unseaworthy. The smaller one, single-manned, sank about half a mile off-shore and the larger one was shipping water rapidly and about to sink. Fortunately our plight was noticed and there was a speedy rescue – but we had to endure a great deal of ribald comment back at school when our 'intrepid five' escapade was made public.

Alistair Cuthill (Pw52)

Paul Hirst taught me pure mathematics maybe for only a year or two – absolutely brilliant. Rather a dandy – used to ensure his shirt cuffs extended precisely two inches below his suit cuffs. Used to call people 'darling', which caused a bit of a stir! Ralph Simpson taught art, but also ran an excellent course on philosophy for sixth formers. He had trouble with the letter s – his Mercedes was pronounced mur-shee-deesh. Coffee bars and juke boxes made their appearance in about 1957. There was one very popular one in Terminus Road to which prefects were allowed to go to while away an hour or two over a single cup of espresso coffee. It was made much more interesting by the music and the presence of girls from the Eastbourne School of Domestic Economy – known to us as 'cookers'.

Keith Dawson (B53)

In 1947 the College organised a skiing trip to Switzerland, which was the first from the UK since the war so we had our photo on the front page of the Daily Sketch. About twenty or so of us, I think, went by boat and train, and as I was the smallest I slept on the luggage rack. On our first day there the master in charge broke his leg, so we boys were on our own; I don't think we got into much trouble, though I seem to recall giving the German waiters a bad time. As a matter of interest, Rita Hayworth was on her honeymoon at our hotel!

Alex James (W46)

My 'socius' was a boy in his second term whose task was to prepare me for the fags' test. Some of the information was of personal benefit such as the location of the various classrooms, playing fields and tuck shop, but I also had to know how to identify the ties worn by my elders and betters – school and house prefects and those who had excelled in major or minor sports. In my spare time I helped run the College press, printing Speech Day programmes, carol sheets and notepaper for the staff on two ancient printing presses located beneath the wooden stage of Big School. My future career and interests must be attributed very largely to Brian Mulvany, who taught me to write English essays which he called 'journals', to Robin Harrison who opened my eyes to the geography of the world and to John Underhill who introduced me to a love of countryside and in particular to the geology, landscape and natural history of the South Downs and the High Weald. When I left the College I took with me a tatty text book called Downs and Weald which I still treasure, and a thirty-seven-year career in town and country planning followed.

A FESTIVAL OF NINE LESSONS AND CAROLS

Eastbourne College 1957

John Templeton (B55)

We used to have bath nights in the basement, where there were about eight baths in one bathroom, four down each side with an aisle down the middle. We used to splash water into the aisle and then slide on our backsides from one end of the bathroom to the other. Our housemaster, Mr Bagnall-Oakeley, had a cat, and one night we heard a caterwauling outside our dormitory window, and the boy nearest the window picked up a loose tile and threw it aimlessly. The noise stopped, and next morning at breakfast Bags announced that he was sad to find that his cat had died during the night. We never knew whether he associated it with the throwing of the tile, but the cat is buried under the window from where the tile was thrown.

Ian Caulfeild Grant (W47)

By my final three terms I was eighteen and so legally entitled to drink, though the College did not recognise that fact. A few of us would cycle off after chapel on Sundays to the Tiger at East Dean for a few beers before lunch back at the house. On one occasion I opened the pub door only to see a master – Tony Henderson – sitting at the bar. I turned swiftly and told my friends to scatter, but Tony had seen me and called us back. We were apprehensive, but – knowing we were all eighteen – he merely said 'Gentlemen, what would you like to drink?' and we heard no more of the incident; naturally his reputation was enhanced as a result. The 'general sixth' was formed for me and a few others who were not regarded as up to the normal sixth form work. It was run by Brian Mulvany, who summed me up in one of my reports as follows: 'He sits in my class with an air of oriental profundity – but knows nothing.' However, I found on leaving the College that financial reward was an incentive to work, and my successful and pleasurable life owes a great deal to the grounding I had during my formative years at Eastbourne.

David Winn (S54, member of Council, chairman and now president of the OEA)

I have mixed feelings about my time at the College. Starting with the negative side: even while being fitted in the school shop for a blazer before actually starting school, I was picked on by its other occupant. However, I survived the bullying and general atmosphere of terrorism, the homosexuality, the lack of normal sex education, the lack of education about the important topic of evolution, having to wear a silly 'basher' on Sundays, the Christian indoctrination – which I am happy to say has resulted in me being a confirmed and militant atheist. Anyway, enough moaning; on the positive side, I was a member of the choral society and a member of the school orchestra, and I can claim to have won the house music competition for Powell by my efforts on the oboe. I became captain of fencing, and took part in the novices' boxing quite successfully until they found someone who could knock me out; also I managed to get my A levels, in spite of being told that I would never pass biology. Occasionally, when in Eastbourne, I come and wander around Old Wish Road and reminisce, so obviously my time there made an impression on me in my formative years. However, when I went to medical school I was surprised by how 'nice' everyone was, which says something about the type of people I was obliged to consort with at school. Sorry to sound so jaded; I have decided I am a cynic. I doubt if you will publish any of this.

Reg le Sueur (Pw54)

I recall two reports I received for mechanics, algebra and trigonometry in 1950/1. The first read, 'It is rather difficult to judge his present standard because he is too fond of obtaining the right answer by fair means or foul. He must sometimes admit he can't get the right answer.' The second was more encouraging. 'Satisfactory work. He seldom "cooks" the answers these days.'

Colin McKerrow (W47)

When I was a new boy at Wargrave one was well advised to keep the lowest possible profile. Unfortunately I was not very good at this and so frequently fell foul of the system. But one source of interest and solace in this daunting world was a fascination with the working of clocks; studying them was an escape, and with the aid of books and broken examples I was soon able to supplement my pocket money by repairing watches for other boys. Spare parts were a problem, but I gradually got to know a local jeweller and watchmaker, Geoff Lee, who after a while suggested that I might like to help him with some of his work. It was a risk, but the offer was tempting and as I got more confidence and was higher up the school I soon found myself spending afternoons at the shop. It was idyllic, working in the workshop at the back while listening to test matches on the radio, brewing tea and in summer eating strawberries and cream. My absences did not go unnoticed by my Wargrave comrades, but hard experience had taught me that the only sure way to keep a secret is not to share it, so none of them knew where I went. There was a heart-stopping moment one afternoon when I recognised with horror the voice of my housemaster, Mr Rodd, in the shop. The relief when I realised that he had come in to bring a clock for repair! I even managed to let Geoff and his wife have a fortnight's holiday in Spain by taking on some of the repairs while a temporary staff member looked after the shop.

Anthony Randall (W52)

Ascham – Eastbourne College Preparatory School

ASCHAM

The College's first venture into founding its own prep school had ended in the early years of the century when the link with St Bede's was severed. The successful establishment during the Second World War of a branch of the College in Eastbourne for day boys and younger pupils was the stimulus for the decision made after the end of the war to continue with the preparatory school. The College had acquired the buildings of Ascham St Vincent's prep school when it closed in 1938, and it was now intended that the new prep school would use those premises. But the navy was still in occupation, so it was housed for the time being in Powell House, with Henry Collis as its first head; he had taken over from Kem Bagnall-Oakeley who had opened and run the wartime branch of the College in Gonville, and it was not long before the school was able to settle down in its permanent quarters when the navy released Ascham in May 1946.

Michael Ross (S52), son of Guy Ross, housemaster of Granville, summarises the school's history: 'The first headmaster, Henry Collis, was still at the War Office when the school was opened in September 1945 in Powell and Reeves with boarders accommodated in Wargrave. It moved to Ascham and Granville in 1946 and 1947, and Collis was succeeded in due course by Guy Hepburn and Michael Keall. The school flourished, accommodating up to 250 boys and providing a constant stream of pupils to the College as it recovered after the war. By the mid-1950s about one-third of College boys had come from Ascham. As Nugee testified, "Not only is the ordinary boy taught well but they have sent us some real scholars, and also some good games players. Although character cannot be assessed in terms of scholarships and colours, they have sent us some sterling boys." Ascham won many awards to the College during the period, and apart from sport there was a particularly strong tradition of music and drama.

'In 1977 the College Council took the decision to close Ascham. The dependence on a feeder school

Below left: Ascham (Vera Ross).

Below: Ascham boys by the sea after saluting HMS Eastbourne as it passed Beachy Head (Vera Ross).

Ascham staff, drawn by S Y D Jordan, 1955 (Vera Ross).

had diminished and there were problems in administering the schools together. The prep school merged with St Andrews which absorbed the pupils and most of the staff who remained, and the buildings, together with the playing fields and grounds, were sold for development as a residential estate. The proceeds of the sale provided valuable core funding for the College at a time when money was needed to begin the programme of capital development which has continued to this day. Three Aschamians currently serve on the College Council.'

Guy Ross's wife, Vera, remembers the challenges and excitement of being part of the birth of a new school: 'Henry Collis believed that there should never be a dull moment. Terms were long by today's standards, with no exeats, so activities were numerous – games, scouts, cubs, clubs, lectures, films and plays, weekend expeditions when the whole school embarked on buses to places of interest. During hot summers the boys were constantly asking to swim off the beach, which would not be possible among all the crowds – until brainwave! Breakfast on the beach before the crowds arrived! Cooks and matrons only were alerted in case of a change in the weather, but when a Sunday dawned with perfect conditions, everyone galvanised and we descended on the beach with no-one else in sight. Swimming was organised in groups and a hearty breakfast was devoured. Then we returned to Granville to find John Nugee in the front hall with the Chairman of Governors whom he had brought to visit. A hesitant explanation was followed by silence; and then: "Vera, when the boys have forgotten all their Greek and Latin they will remember breakfast on the beach."'

There are many fond memories. David Smith (Pw77) writes: 'I was at Ascham from 1972 to 1977 before coming on to the College. The more I thought about contributing to this book, the more I really wanted to focus my remarks on Ascham. Now a Cambridge don and a historian, I am prompted to say

Left: Ascham boys and staff by a miniature steam train, 1947 (Vera Ross).

Below: Famous Old Aschamians drawn by Derek Thorpe.

how much I feel I owe to Ascham in setting me on the path which has led me to this. The school stays very vividly and fondly in my memory and I cherish my memories of its friendliness, warmth, enthusiasm and family atmosphere. It embodied an ethos of concern for others and a sense of purpose in developing whatever talents one had been given. This went together with an atmosphere of great kindness and support, and real care for each pupil as an individual. It was, to me, the formative and most crucial phase of my education, and the one to which I feel I owe the greatest debt.'

Ian Forbes (Pw60) remembers Ascham as a very happy school, as does David Thomson (G55), who arrived in 1953, aged twelve, from Hong Kong for his first experience of boarding: 'It could have been a terrible shock, especially as I knew that I would not see my parents again for the better part of three years; but thanks not least to the kindness of Henry and Betty Collis, it proved to be a very happy period in my life, and many of my friends from those times are still friends to this day.' He has less happy memories of swimming in the cold English Channel and the uninviting swimming baths after the lovely open-air pools in Hong Kong, but he remembers fondly being inculcated into the pleasures of both rugby and history by Guy Ross. Michael Fish (R58) has a mixed bag of

Celebrating the diverse careers of boys who passed through the gates of Ascham Preparatory School

TOP ROW: Nick Estcourt: Mountaineer, John Wells: Actor, David Smith: Cambridge Don, Chris Older: Farmer.
MIDDLE ROW: Christopher Leaver: Lord Mayor of London, Edward Lewis: Hotelier, Graham Boal: Judge, Angus McIntosh: Police Officer.
BOTTOM ROW: Patrick Coulcher: R.A.F. Pilot, Ian Forbes: Royal Navy Admiral, Andrew Macintosh: Priest, Ian Parsons: Photographer, Michael Fish: Meteorologist, David Thomson: Army General.

memories, including being taken in an open-top bus on a cold damp day to London to see the Coronation decorations, and of 'standing under the clock' for the whole school to see while waiting to be punished after being naughty. Christopher Leaver (B51) 'has lost count of the many schools I had trying to educate me, while I was evacuated to the USA and the West Indies, before arriving at Ascham barely able to read, write, add up or even tell the time. I was happy there. As a day boy who lived across the road opposite Ascham's back gate, I would lie in bed in the morning listening for the school bell for chapel, when I would dress at high speed and dash across the dual carriageway via the bushes. To ensure speed I cut a tunnel in the hedge which divides the two roads; it is there to this day.' Peter Estcourt (Pw57) remembers 'Ken Hay always throwing our homework exercise books back at us, and opening the classroom windows in the hope that they would sail out to the wide blue yonder and we would have to go and collect them.' Patrick Coulcher (R50), who was one of the group known as the 'Three Musketeers' (with John Wells (Pw50) and Peter Brown) because of their exploits, writes that he was always known as 'Chuck' after his appearance as a hen in a school play, and retained the nickname throughout his College and RAF career. He tried to revert to Patrick when he was on exchange with the USAF, but they had somehow found out what he was known as and continued to call him Chuck – a favourite name in the USA, of course.

Far right: The three Terry brothers in Ascham uniform (Richard Terry).

Below: Fire practice.

Into the present
1956–2007

The new headmaster was Michael Birley, whose appointment at the age of only thirty-five was a forward-looking initiative that would, over the next fourteen years, see Eastbourne College established on increasingly firm foundations and spreading its wings to embrace the rapid changes of the post-war world and the second half of the twentieth century.

Birley came to the school after six years teaching classics at Eton, inheriting a school that had been at grave risk during its exile but was now well and truly on its feet again. In an interview with Forbes Wastie he paid generous tribute to his predecessor: 'I did realise that I was succeeding a man who had absolutely heroically managed teaching elsewhere in the war and maintaining the right of Eastbourne College to exist, though it was at Radley. He then took it back to

Above: Gym on College Field, 1958 (Keith David).

Below: Michael Birley, headmaster 1956–70.

Eastbourne and managed to get it going again. So by the time I arrived he'd got the place in proper order and one could really start looking at the future; whereas he had been pretty well clearing up the past.'

He did not feel that the Council had given him a particular brief to modernise the school, but that is nevertheless what happened. In reply to a question as to how he dealt with the 'swinging sixties', he said: 'I do think that if you are going to run a school the main thing you've got to do is to get to know the kids in it. To go with that you do not impose what people think of as discipline, you don't have a set of rules and see to it that everybody observes the rules. You get them to want to like to have space, to

> *I consider my days at Eastbourne College the happiest in my life, and the education I received held me in good stead through medical school, thirty years of medicine, over ten years in the army, two wars, marriage and five children. I was inspired by Mike Birley and Mike Young with their optimistic outlook towards all people. Dr Pennell's example was the inspiration for me to go and help those in need of medical care. I was at the College during the transitional period, with the ending of fagging and beating by prefects and the introduction of coeducation. I believe I hold the dubious title of being last boy to be beaten by the head of house and the last boy to be beaten by Mike Young, housemaster of Pennell.*
>
> **Jo Shubber (P65)**

Above: A divinity class, summer 1956 (Roger Blackburn).

Right: Michael Fish and classmates, c1960 (Michael Fish).

Far right: The 1957 appeal booklet and its accompanying letter (Keith Pinker).

like to have choice – they need to be choosing what they are going to do themselves because if people have done that they are going to do it a great deal better than if you've just told them what they've got to do; they need to have not orders but encouragement. You've got to get to know them and you've got to know why things sometimes go wrong.'

Birley paid generous tribute to the staff of the College, and regarded himself as very lucky to have had so many supportive colleagues. One or two regarded his apparent liberalism as worrying, but most of them went enthusiastically along with an attitude that was

increasingly seen as good for the staff and pupils and for the school generally. He allowed the students a degree of freedom and expected them to behave well; and most of them responded by doing so. His views on academic work were similarly robust: 'It was important that people should be interested in the work they did and that we should get them to do it as well as they

The staff all wore gowns – Beefy Howell's was so old that it was green in places and the sleeve had been repaired as he used it to clean the blackboard if he could not find the normal eraser. Once, when a bell went for the end of a lesson, one boy shut his book and we were reminded that the bell was an indication merely that the class might now end and we would now be there for a further ten minutes.

Robin Scott (S58)

Beefy Howell – a legend in his own time and much revered (and mimicked) by his pupils – had an invariable habit as he entered class of addressing us with the greeting 'Good morning, creatures', following which he would stride (with gown flowing) to the blackboard. Arriving there he would select a chalk and, with a stylish flourish, draw a horizontal mark across the board accompanied by the exhortation 'take a straight line'. So predictable was this performance that a wag decided one morning to remove from the blackboard shelf all but one stick of chalk. At the tip of the remaining stick he drilled a small recess into which he carefully inserted two Swan Vesta match heads. We sat in hushed expectation as Beefy entered the room. 'Good morning, creatures' he called as he strode to the blackboard and grasped the chalk. There was the customary flourish followed, on this occasion, by a loud crack and a flash of fire. Wholly unperturbed, Beefy calmly turned to address us: 'Excellent,' he said without a moment's hesitation; 'at last, a bright spark in the class.'

David George (Pw60)

Left: Joanna Birley presents a bouquet to the Queen on her centenary visit in October 1966.

Right: Beefy Howell.

could. And we were lucky that we had somebody very good at the top of pretty well every subject. There were some remarkable results – Kenneth Hindley one year had six open awards in mathematics – but we were not simply there to teach academic boys; we were also there to do our best for people who might be much better at other things. I tried to see to it that non-scientists would get a little scientific teaching even if it was only a small amount; and we developed general studies to get people thinking about life outside school and the world they were living in.'

His headship saw much new building – new science blocks, new classrooms, better facilities for the arts and music – and strong pastoral care from the various chaplains combined with out of school social involvement initiatives. His relationship with the town grew much stronger too, and he found many members of the Council extremely helpful with financial and other advice. Fund-raising was, as ever, one of his priorities, which fostered his links with the OEA. And he also oversaw the beginnings of the end of fagging and beating. 'I may have beaten one or two to start with. But I still remember when I had stopped it, the head of School House saying "We haven't beaten anybody this term and we're not going to." And that really was pretty near the end of it anyway. It just died out. It was quite clear that it was a silly way to try and deal with any problems – it just made them worse.'

The writer of the following account of his time at the College in the mid-1960s wishes to remain anonymous, and indeed found it easier to write in the third person; but it is important to record his particular experiences – and his unhappiness – as part of a rounded picture of the school as it weathered the increasingly rapid changes taking place within society as a whole and within the world of public schools at that time. As he writes, the power of hierarchy within the school was still alive and well during his time: 'The somewhat stunning opening is when at thirteen years old he, like several of his age, waited in bed in the dorm for the house prefects to do their round on the first night. Three of them came in, one of whom brandished a swagger stick, which interestingly is how such a person was portrayed in Lindsay Anderson's film *If….* He is applauded by his housemaster for "being an efficient and hard-working fag whom I will look forward to getting to know better." He never did get to know him, and how could he respect someone who allowed fagging to take such a prominent place in these young boys' lives? So he learnt to survive, to keep his head down, not to be emotional or at least not to show it…'. It would indeed be some years before the ethos of schools generally, and perhaps boarding schools in particular, changed to allow values different from what was regarded as the norm to flourish as strongly as they now do. But it is clear – despite some setbacks, as this pupil found – that attitudes were changing.

Birley presided over the centenary of the College's foundation in 1967, reaching a landmark that, twenty years earlier after exile at Radley, might have seemed unattainable. As the special centenary edition of *The Eastbournian* records, 'In many ways we are lucky to be celebrating at all, let alone contemplating the future with confidence.' Not only had the low numbers and huge debts of the early 1950s been reversed first by Nugee and then by Birley, so that the school now numbered nearly 500 and was in a much stronger financial position, but also the wonderful success of the centenary Development Appeal meant that the College had the capital resources for expansion and continued consolidation and growth. The celebrations started with the visit of the Queen and the Duke of Edinburgh in October 1966 and continued with an educational conference in April 1967, an Arts Festival Week in May and a series of events for current pupils and their parents as well as for Old Eastbournians, including a centenary ball and dinner.

Michael Birley also made the forward-looking decision to admit girls to the College sixth form from 1969. His own account of this innovation comes in his interview with Forbes Wastie who himself was involved right at the start because he was housemaster for the first six girls. As Birley says, 'We started by inviting some of the local girls, actually the girls in Moira House, to see if they would like to join our sixth form classes…. There was some point at which I was ringing up a few headmistresses to see if they were interested in joining up a bit more. It was after one of those conversations that, as I've told people often, there was a burn in my carpet which was the result of my telephoning this woman and her reply was not in the least favourable! But I think it was a well worthwhile improvement; I still remember the girl whom I met walking up to lunch, and I said "Well, what's it like being in a boys' school?" "Oh," she said, "it's wonderful. They don't mind when you wash your hair." It's unnatural not to have girls being taught with boys, really.'

By the time he left – after, in his own words, 'fourteen years of enormous enjoyment' at the helm – the College was a very different place. He himself, writing in one of the 1969 issues of *The Eastbournian*, defined his philosophy: 'Many Old Eastbournians must wonder sometimes what is happening at the College. You see editorials extolling our "progressive" policies, or castigating our academic inadequacy; and now you hear

I had taught myself guitar and we formed the school's second group. The first had been called 'The Dynamics' so we called ourselves 'The Statics' because there was a maths book then in use called Statics and Dynamics. *Suitably, our title tune was 'Walk Don't Run', a tune then popularised by the Ventures. This was of course all pre-Beatles. In 1962, at the revue* On the Rebound *we played in the interval and got a mention in the local paper. By the time of our final appearance in Big School in December 1963, we had gone vocal. The Statics were Nigel Richards, David Willoughby and myself on guitars plus Keith Ross and later Matthew Williamson on drums. There was also a dance band run by Mr Foad, although I cannot remember ever playing for a dance – there was no-one to dance with in our day. When I accompanied Reeves on piano at the house singing competition the adjudicator warned me that with my honky-tonk version of 'There's a Tavern in the Town' I would end up in a sleazy nightclub. Anyhow we came second and got the most applause; Reeves normally came last. I also founded a cookery club as a relief from school meals and the tuck shop. We had cooking lessons at the hotel run by the Charlton family whose three sons – Timothy, Martin and Clive – were all at the College. I recall we cooked a gala meal for Mr and Mrs Birley but I have no idea what it was. Both interests have remained with me to this day.*

Martin Swain (R58)

My lasting memory of the College is taking biology O level in the gym. On the table were three gooseberries which we were all supposed to dissect and discuss for question 1. One of us sat down, ate all three gooseberries, then read the question and without hesitation wrote 'delicious' as his answer. It is still one of my best after dinner stories, and I know Simon Cornford (the guilty party) won't mind if you print it.

Rufus Voorspuy (R63)

I had borrowed a bicycle from one of the day boys, and intended to take a picnic and cycle out to Willingdon for the day. For some reason I decided to cook some baked beans as part of my picnic, and placed my tin in water in a saucepan on the gas ring. Suddenly I heard the short interval chapel bell, flew out of the door and got to my seat just in the nick of time. When I arrived back at the house there was pandemonium. I had forgotten to pierce a hole in the can before putting it in the water, the saucepan had boiled dry and the subsequent explosion had blown a pane of glass out of the conservatory roof and covered the wall with baked beans and tomato sauce. What was said was less than complimentary and culminated in my being presented with a bucket of soapy water and a cloth and told in no uncertain terms to clean it all up. So that was how I spent Ascension Day.

Michael S C (Sam) Hill (W57)

The memories of Michael Fish (R58) and David Stone-Lee (R57), collated over a pleasant lunch in May 2006: The food (at school) was ghastly; jugged hare was not a favourite – 'every house ended up with a couple of eyeballs and some fur' – and the spread of myxomatosis in the late 1950s led to a clear and sudden increase in rabbit for lunch. Supper was better as it consisted of toast and jam. Chapel was attended every day and twice on Sundays, wearing a blue suit. Day boys had to attend all services including those on Sundays. MF commented that compulsory chapel put him off religion for life and made him a confirmed atheist.

MF remembers pranks played on Eric Northcott, housemaster at Reeves. He had a Morris Minor which six of the boys managed to lift and turn by 90 degrees so that it fitted sideways inside his garage, and a bike which the boys managed to hoist up the flagpole on the top of the Memorial Tower. MF also noted that the curriculum was very regimented and this restricted the combination of A levels he could do; he wanted to do maths, physics and geography but had to do chemistry instead of geography. About teachers: 'John Underhill brought the Classics alive' (DS-L); 'I wouldn't be where I am today if it hadn't been for Donald Perrens' (MF); 'Teddy Craig put me off history for life' (MF); the head was God; you only saw him if you were in real trouble.

Michael Fish (R58) and
David Stone-Lee (R57)

My housemaster at Blackwater was John Underhill (above) who was avuncular for the most part – he would put his arm round your shoulders in class and address you as 'My son' or 'My poppet' – though he could be fierce enough when necessary. He was not a snooper, though I believe little escaped his notice, and in my experience he was tolerant of misdemeanours provided you were discreet. Once, when some of us attended a party at the house of a day boy whose parents were away, and were spotted by the Wargrave head of house who reported us, his response – far more lenient than that of some of the other housemasters – was to gate us for two weeks. I like to think he shared our contempt for the boy who shopped us! And on another occasion after an ambitious Blackwater leaving prank about which the headmaster took a hard line, he beat the culprits as ordered, but not before congratulating them on their planning and execution: 'You'd all make good staff officers.'

Michael Barber (B56)

that we are going to teach girls in the sixth form…. [My line of action] is to provide a situation in which boys may become accustomed to working out their own answers to moral problems, and making responsible choices about what they do…. There are risks and difficulties involved in trying to educate in this way… but I believe this is the way to help boys to become mature and independent individuals, and only if we do this shall we be serving both our pupils and the society of which we are members.'

As Tony Henderson wrote, in an article published just after Birley's retirement from the headship in the autumn of 1970: 'Above all else, Michael Birley is a doer…. A detailed catalogue of the material achievements alone which he inspired would make a splendid tribute to him, but it would leave no space for the most important things of all – a picture of the man himself and of the inspiration so many boys and men drew from his example and personality…. For fourteen years Mike's inexhaustible powerhouse of energy has driven the College on. One must confess that there have been times (though rarely) when one has felt like clinging, weak and punch-drunk, to the nearest support and crying feebly "Stop the College, I want to get off!" But what he has done needed badly to be done, and it is unlikely that anyone else could have done it in the time, or done it half so well.'

There were to follow three difficult interim years under a new head who neither built on Birley's modernising initiatives nor gained the support of staff and pupils. Although he went on to a successful headship at Wellington School, Somerset, John Kendall Carpenter did not make his mark at Eastbourne and survived a mere three years, the last of which was spent in a sabbatical induced by ill health. During that year, Donald Perrens was acting headmaster, and then in the autumn of 1973 Simon Langdale joined the school as the new head. In his own words: 'Diana and I were very conscious that there had been a difficult period at the College, and that it was now time to look forward again. As one boy said to me, "You are my fourth headmaster in my five years here." Happily the College Council was led by a wise and committed chairman, Derek Empson, there was an extremely competent bursar in Bernard Alder and there was an intrinsic loyalty to the school among those involved with it.

'Every school has its challenges, and to a newcomer to Eastbourne two stood out. First, because few parents nowadays want to send their offspring to

In a bid to be a part of the hip sixties, three Blackwater boys (their stage names being Drew, Eugene-Reg and Dijon) decided to form a rock group, the catalyst being the playing of tennis racquet guitars and singing along with pop records in the Blackwater Nook. The slight disadvantage of not being able to play any musical instruments was never regarded as a drawback to our vision, although we did know that another Blackwater boy (stage name Toni) not only knew how to play a guitar but actually had one… and so

he was drafted into the fledgling band as the lead guitarist. As Drew was a member of the CCF Drums squad, he became the band's drummer (with a borrowed set of drums). Eugene-Reg insisted on playing the rhythm guitar and Dijon was left with the bass guitar. After many aliases, the band became 'The Purple Clan' and, following much practising with three-chord songs, got its first date in the summer of 1966 to play in front of the whole College (sans masters) in Big School.

As the date approached we became more and more nervous. On the actual night, about an hour before the concert started, Eugene-Reg suggested that a few sips from a bottle of vodka (that he happened to have with him) might ease the nerves… and we complied willingly. Any form of spirit was a novelty at the time and the first few sips appeared to have no impact on the nervousness, and so we had a few more… until the bottle emptied. After changing into our costumes, we made our way to Big School and the assembled masses. What happened next was mostly a haze until the evening came to a premature end. John Lush, who happened to be passing Big School during the latter part of the concert, looked in, saw that things had got a little out of hand and, probably very wisely, decided enough was enough! Needless to say, the band never played again.

Jon Thompson (B62)

Above: Simon Langdale, headmaster 1973–80.

Above right: Chris Saunders, headmaster 1981–92.

schools more than an hour or two away, the College suffers from the disadvantage of having half its potential constituency in the English Channel. Second, the school lies in an attractive but physically restricted site which makes further development difficult, although successive regimes have done wonders to make the most of the limited space available; one could not help casting wistful glances at Devonshire Park across the road. There were the inevitable crises; but what I remember most was the achievements by boys and girls, individually or collectively, of things beyond what was expected of them – an exam result, the mastery of a skill, an award, a sporting success – something in which they could take pride and which lifted their potential and horizons to new levels. Surely much of what education is about!'

Simon Langdale took on a bruised College, but his tenure put it firmly back on track, though he had to take

the sad but necessary decision to close the preparatory school, Ascham. When he left in December 1980 he was succeeded by Christopher Saunders, who came from a highly successful career as a housemaster at Bradfield. As he recalls, 'My headship started somewhat dramatically with the burning down of Big School in the early hours of 19 November 1981. A positive outcome of this unexpected catastrophe was that it enabled me to quickly cement close relationships with OEs, past and present parents and other College supporters. An added bonus was being able to spend many happy days in David Winn's sleek Rolls Royce visiting Eastbournians and asking them for financial support. David was a huge character in every sense of the word and a quite marvellous chairman of the OEA. He worked tirelessly for the College and was extremely kind and generous to Cynthia and myself in so many different ways.

'It was well known amongst members of the Senior Common Room that I was not keen on bureaucracy, and I found the majority of the missives from the DFE pointless and depressing in the extreme. But thanks to my delightful PA, Sue Davies, anything important was rescued from the waste paper basket and passed on to my long-suffering and superb director of studies, Andrew Boxer. I must have been the only head of eighteen years experience who was never formally inspected, but I did undergo various social service visits. I recollect taking vigorous issue with the lead inspector when she and I strongly disagreed over whether it was permitted to put a comforting arm round pupils when informing them of a family bereavement. The other people-centred job that was in my view of paramount importance was the appointment of good quality young staff. Fortunately the College had them in abundance and my time at Eastbourne was made so enjoyable just because I was constantly supported by so many energetic, loyal and committed colleagues. I also had two wonderful chairmen of Council, Sir Derek Empson and Sir Christopher Leaver, and a quite outstanding deputy head, Forbes Wastie. Cynthia and I have a host of happy memories and the College will always have a very special place in our hearts. Happy 140th birthday!'

Cynnie Saunders has her own memories: 'When I look back at our years at Eastbourne my immediate

memory seems to be of the sun shining, the seagulls mewing, the sound of leather on willow on College Field and the conviviality of gentle chat while watching the cricket. I can only think how lucky we were to live in the middle of a town, within walking distance of the sea and the shops, with a lovely garden on one side, College Field on the other and beautiful country within easy reach. Of course it wasn't always sunny – in every sense of the word! We watched Big School reduced to ashes in our first year, endured a hurricane, walked the children to St Andrews through deep snow and, sadly, attended several funerals for pupils and young OEs under twenty-one. I remember how nervous I felt

Above: School prefects, 1974 (David Sibree).

Far left: 19 November 1981.

when we first arrived. I was fresh from pushing my babies round a country school campus wearing my jeans and wellies, and I found the Eastbourne housemasters' wives all looking incredibly smart – so much so that I felt I had to rush out to buy some new skirts. But the warmth of the welcome we were given by them, and others, was typical of the College and we enjoyed laughter and friendship from countless people. We were able to witness so many different activities of the school. Wonderful choral singing in the chapel culminating in memorable carol and Speech Day services; excellent productions of school plays and musicals (our children trod the boards for the first time in one of them); house concerts and plays; Victorian evenings; staff pantomimes; and a host of different sporting activities. We encountered so many lovely people – staff, bursarial staff, pupils, parents, prep school contacts, governors, old boys and townspeople. It is all remembered in a rosy haze of busy activity, fun and happy days. I count myself fortunate to have experienced it.'

The fire that devastated Big School in Saunders' first term was a traumatic start to his tenure; but neither he nor anyone else allowed themselves to grieve for too long. The next *Eastbournian* may have had an image on its cover of flames licking up a building, but its editorials talked firmly and positively of the chance that had been unexpectedly bestowed on the College to build a new cultural centre at the very heart of the school. 'We will never have this chance again and must make sure that the final product is better than just a replacement, by being both bold in its design and adventurous in its financing…. Do not expect the entire magazine to be itself a commemoration of Big School. For the pupils, the year stretched ahead of them and they got on with what there was to do to fill it.' The energetic fund-raising that ensued was led with huge enthusiasm by David Winn who had become chairman of the OEA in April 1981 and been elected to the Council on 18 November – the day before the fire! Such was the support and the response to the appeals that the headmaster was able to announce on Speech Day in July 1983 that the total had reached £400,000; the final figure was £650,000.

The fire was nevertheless a momentous event. Philip Le Brocq recorded his feelings, both at the time and later: 'It was an appalling night…. The telephone shrilled me awake and Cynthia Saunders' carefully controlled voice warned me that there was a fire in Big School and that School House might have to be evacuated. I scrambled some clothes on, donned gumboots, grabbed my camera and quickly found that it was no small blaze, but a bustling, devouring, enveloping dragon of a fire. I had never realised how noisy a really big fire is! The brigade's sirens cut through the roaring flames, though their hoses had less effect. "Drench the main buildings and the Music School – the Hall is a lost cause…".' But a year later he was looking forward with keen expectation: 'I no longer have nightmares about the towering inferno of that November night, but only about a lost opportunity. Nostalgia will only serve to convince prospective parents that our school is rooted in the past. Its growth must be for the future – the phoenix to aim for from those ashes will not be a crow of ill omen but a bird of paradise.' The loss was not just of the building but of all those adornments with which E C Arnold had embellished it, including the carved panels; one of them survives, memorialised now behind glass. And after only two years the new Big School boasted a magnificent, purpose-built theatre, its opening commemorated by a plaque in the vestibule carved by David Kindersley.

The sudden closure of Beresford House girls' school at the end of the Christmas term of 1992 precipitated a major decision for Chris Saunders and his deputy, Forbes Wastie. Anne Williams, head of modern languages at Beresford House, describes how 'the plight of the girls who were about to take mock exams was particularly acute, so when the College stepped into the breach and offered to accommodate these pupils, the offer was greeted with a huge sigh of relief. I was offered a post teaching French and German, along with the specific pastoral role of helping the girls to settle in. Watt House, then in the charge of the housemaster Alec Deighton and his wife Joyce, was reorganised to provide study rooms, and the Christmas break was spent scrutinising the different syllabuses and organising courses so that the girls returned in January to a full timetable of lessons and activities which would prepare them for their forthcoming examinations. The initial trepidation felt by some members of the Common Room at the advent of fifth form girls into the exclusively male bastion of the lower school was swiftly dispelled and the College community embraced the new arrivals with characteristic warmth and understanding. For the girls it was an intimidating experience too, but they soon adapted to the new regime and made an active contribution to College life in academic, artistic, dramatic, musical, sporting and of course social

Above: Brochure for the Big School appeal following the fire in 1981 (James Young).

Left: Ronnie Corbett with Chris Saunders.

spheres! The success of coeducation in the College owes not a little to these pioneers of January 1992, who in many ways were instrumental in convincing the community that girls and boys can work and thrive on equal terms in the College environment, gaining mutual benefit from the association.'

Chris Saunders left at the end of the 1992/3 school year to return to his own alma mater, Lancing, as its head. His successor was Charles Bush, a mathematician and Marlborough housemaster, and it was early in his tenure that the College went fully

> I remember stone floors and large Victorian baths that drained via gutters in the floor… getting a serious telling off for smoking out Philip Le Brocq's study as we started a remote control aeroplane engine in his basement one evening while someone else was practising something by Status Quo far too loudly on his guitar… a paper dart hitting a guest in the back of the head at the 'Revue' after the head had specifically instructed that they should cease, and the evening being cancelled as the curtain opened for the start…!
>
> Roy Budgett (S73)

coeducational. He had been a colleague of Michael Birley at Marlborough, and recognised the innovatory force of his decision to admit girls to the Eastbourne College sixth form in 1969; it was clearly now logical to extend coeducation to the whole school. He describes his own involvement in the process: 'By the early 1990s independent schools faced challenging times as negative perceptions of boarding and rising costs affected the prosperity of the sector and hastened the need for change. Sussex schools adapted gradually as business-conscious governors and forward-thinking headmasters saw the time ripe for merger and full coeducation. Local prep and all-girl schools were worst affected with the stronger, originally all-boy, HMC schools more able to adjust and weather the recessional storm.

'My arrival was the right time to complete the process, modernise the school's approach and thereby coincidentally redress any issue of declining numbers. The move was in line with all the local prep schools successfully becoming coeducational. It also met

The Boyfriend, 1986 (Philip Le Brocq).

My recollection of the time commitment that day boys made to the College in those days is as follows. Monday to Friday: 8.15am arrive for chapel or assembly; 8.40pm leave for home after doing prep unless you were on fagging duty, in which case you might not leave until 10.00pm. Saturday: 8.15am start, home around 4pm after sport. Sunday: compulsory attendance at chapel in the evening, wearing a blue suit. This last requirement seemed particularly harsh. A large group of us used to go on sixty-mile cycle rides into the Sussex countryside on occasional Sundays. The Bexhill contingent could take their time – they were excused chapel attendance. Those of us living in Eastbourne had to leave the others early in order to get back in time for chapel. Home life? It was little more than bed and breakfast.

Mike Scott (Pw64)

Whilst having a business meeting with Mr Hart (the current bursar at Tonbridge School) I mentioned that I was an Old Eastbournian; he gave a knowing chuckle and explained how his favourite First XV game of the season was when Tonbridge played the College in Eastbourne and – as he described it – 'half the town would be hanging over the wall, intimidating the opposition.' I think rarely has a member of staff from any school enjoyed watching their own teams terrified by a rival quite as much as Mr Hart.

Brendon Mitchell (S94)

Having arrived back late after shooting on the Crumbles, and missed tea, I went straight over to the kitchen at Wargrave to try and find a bite to eat, and instead stumbled on a fire in the dailies' sitting room. I rang the fire alarm, and returned with an extinguisher and put the fire out. Up to this point there had been no reaction at all to the sounding of the alarm, but then a friend and fellow prefect wandered over to see what was going on and whether someone was mucking about. To his surprise he found me emerging out of the smoke and – never one to miss an opportunity – promptly produced a packet of cigarettes. My father was subsequently surprised to receive a letter from Michael Birley: 'I thought I ought to write and thank you for having a son who is sufficiently on the ball to have stopped Wargrave going up in flames the other day.... There is, of course, quite a lot to be said for burning down Wargrave, because we could rebuild it much better, but it would have been an inconvenient moment to choose, and we are very grateful to him.'

Terry Lugg (W60)

changing parental expectations for daughters' education; the question most asked by prospective parents was why the College did not provide the same style and quality of education for daughters as it did for sons. They were keen that girls too should benefit from the all-round academic culture, the extra-curricular strength, games, CCF, music and drama that were not perceived to be on offer at other local schools. Discussion on the possibility of change had been engaged in by governors through the optimistically named Way Forward Committee under the inspiring chairmanship of Richard Wainwright, vice-chairman of the College Council. No assumptions were made, and the consideration of alternatives was comprehensive and thorough, although ideas had been widely raised within the Common Room through a series of meetings during 1993 to assist the governors and the new headmaster. In truth the announcement, when it came in March 1995 at a special Common Room meeting in Big School on a Saturday morning immediately after the end of the Lent term, had become a poorly kept secret. After four years of discussion and debate, with an opportune change of headmaster midstream, no-one expected any other outcome and the momentum for change was very strong.

'Even though the issue had been well considered over the years by the governors, when the decision was finally taken there was a moment of potential farce in that, due to a number of unavoidable and unrelated governor absences, there was the possibility that the meeting might be non-quorate. However inauspicious this might have seemed at the time, the detailed consideration proved to be right on all counts even if the announcement that Blackwater House was to be demolished and its boys spread around the other houses took everyone by surprise. The cost of refurbishing and rebuilding a building that was fundamentally flawed was considered too great a risk and the new Blackwater became the "statement on the corner" that coeducational Eastbourne needed. Nine intrepid thirteen-year-old girls (a number that increased to eleven by the end of their first term) started as junior members of the existing sixth form Watt House in September 1995, with four girls boarding out locally and Charlie Bostock as the first housemaster. One year later he moved the day girls from Watt House to the new Blackwater, generating a warm pastoral community with typical style. The tone

1960s, as a gangly fourteen-year-old, I found myself at a school in a strange seaside town, not knowing anyone and wondering just how the next few years of my life would work out. Very quickly I realised that I was not the only pupil to have exactly the same thoughts and it wasn't long before I struck up real friendships, which forty years on are still going strong. I suppose if I was honest I'd say that it was for the sport and other social activities that I most remember my time at EC. Playing hockey or rugby on College Field were real highlights and the First XI hockey tour to Holland with the girls from Moira House was especially memorable. Our Dutch hosts looked after David Gould and myself so well that to this day there are still a few moments I can't account for. Then, of course, there was the school skiing trip with Mr King to Brand in Austria. We travelled across Europe on a train which was full of various school groups, and along the way we managed to acquaint ourselves well with a number of fellow students, most of whom seemed to be female. The fact that we were able to acquire a bottle of rum on the journey certainly made us quietly popular. For some unknown reason one or two of us were banned from the nursery slopes the following day. The school dances were a wonderful sight. Boys one side of the dance floor and the girls from Moira House on the other, eyeing each other up and down with a Beatles song blasting out in the background.

David Burt (G66)

John Mico and Alison Townley on their way to the Cornflower Ball, 1972.

Fund-raising after the fire: the float made by Forbes Wastie and Ian Markland (Forbes Wastie).

exasperated police, Bomb Squad, Fire Brigade and the long suffering people of South Street.

Other memories: Chris Evert complaining when the Corps of Drums struck up 'Sussex by the Sea' during her match in Tennis Week, putting her off her stroke and causing her to lose; having to ask Martina Navratilova not to use College Field for her training runs; and being told by Chris Saunders that, on the night Big School burnt down, he and Cynnie had had a bit of a tiff and when he went to tell her what had happened her immediate reaction was 'Go away! Don't think you are getting around me with a story like that!'

Forbes Wastie (staff 1961–98)

One afternoon I was in my deputy headmaster's office when the headmaster's secretary, Sue Davies, came in to tell me that she had a very irate police inspector on the telephone saying that they had had to close the whole of Grove Road in which the police station is situated because a suitcase with BOMB on the outside had been reported in an alleyway close by. The Fire Brigade was in attendance and the Bomb Squad had been called from Aldershot. Two suspicious characters, purported to be College boys, had been seen leaving the scene. Miraculously, I was able to identify them because the witness had noticed the colour of their house ties and a quick phone call to the house revealed two likely names who had authorised passes. They were quickly apprehended and despatched to my office. 'It was a prank, sir, we were just playing a joke…'. But we still had to deal with the

In 1972, with three young children and a dog, Forbes and I inherited Blackwater with its seventy boys, along with the resident matron, Olga Jensen-Humphreys, who was well connected and grandiose, with, despite a fearsome appearance, a soft heart. She demanded good manners from the boys and in her domain she ruled with a rod of iron, instructing me in the clearest of terms on covering surgery, sick room and laundry when she was off-duty (or watching the racing on television). One hot summer night Olga appeared at our bedroom door in a long cream dressing gown and her hair in curlers: a bat had flown into her bedroom at the very top of the wooden stairs and she refused to return to bed until Forbes had caught the offending animal in a towel.

Diana Wastie

was set and further girls were recruited with ease for September 1996. Housemistress Fiona Donaldson then initiated a wonderful junior girls' boarding atmosphere in Watt House and then School House, living for one year only side by side with existing boy boarders (years 9, 10, 12 girls; years 11, 13 boys). David Hodkinson (housemaster) and Fiona Donaldson (housemistress) made the union work extremely well. School House (girls) were encouraged

to take on the 130-year-old traditions of School House (boys) and the house thrived and grew to full capacity in a short time. Soon Watt House reopened as the second day girls' house with Gwen Taylor-Hall in charge, followed by Nugent, with Linda Salway as housemistress, as the second all-age girls' boarding house after building a major extension in 2006.

'The College effected this irreversible change with speed and caution, care and consideration, and with the interests of pupils paramount. It was possible because of the enthusiastic motivation of the members of Common Room, who underwent special INSET training in preparation for teaching junior girls, and the near universal support of pupils and parents. It should not be overlooked that all three boys' day houses were totally refurbished between 1995 and 1998, including a major extension and development in Craig. As the girls became equal citizens, as their calm confidence confirmed, so the boys were not forgotten. A head girl, Lucy Grime, was appointed for the first time in 1999 and solo head of school Joelle Meakin held office most successfully in 2001–2. It is typical of Eastbourne's attitude and meticulous planning at all levels that such a potentially troublesome time passed without hiccough. The College has been immeasurably changed and, in my view, for the better. It is well set and prepared to face the future as a stronger and richer community. It was the greatest privilege to be living in the headmaster's house as this successful metamorphosis unfolded.'

Further insights on the move to full coeducation are provided by others who were involved: Charlie Bostock writes: 'In September 1995 a core of seven existing parents recruited two others to provide the first group of nine girls in the first term. They became "the pioneers" and house assemblies through the first

Do I have fond memories of the College? Well, at the time I was not that happy about it all. It seemed to be all work or sport and no free time. I rather expected to have to work at school, but a seven-day-a-week school? I didn't like PT every morning break; I didn't like having to do sports, especially on Saturday afternoons (if a First XI wasn't playing, for if so we had to watch), particularly running Paradise. And I missed not being able to go to the pictures. As a day boy, I had to stay to do homework and not leave Reeves before 8pm Monday to Friday which, since I lived in Bexhill and commuted by train, meant that I didn't arrive home until after 9pm. We also had to appear at chapel on Sundays. But now I look back and think how fortunate I was. The College gave me as good an education as I was able to assimilate and I went on to make a good living.

Geoff Reynolds (R57)

year were invariably characterised by their pioneering feats: involvement in junior plays, in the choir, in the first junior girls' rounders, netball and tennis teams, playing in boys' hockey and cricket teams and scooping nine academic prizes at the end of their first year. The pioneer team blended in well in the first half of their first term and could easily be mistaken for sixth formers given that the junior uniforms did not arrive until after half term. The change of dress prompted concerns from a variety of sources: the girls

The first nine year 9 girls, 1995 (above) and (left) the seven girls who were still at the College in 2000.

Right: CCF, 2006.

Far right: Reeves common room, 2006.

were not keen on the ties with the bright yellow stripe nor were they happy to change into the distinctive kilts. However, the first modelling of the kilt material came in the form of a pair of trousers that I sported in a bid to empathise, as well as to initiate the rumour that this was set to be the uniform for the junior boys. The disquiet amongst the boys left the girls in good humour and punctured their anxieties nicely.

'The excitement in the growth of our number of junior girls was matched by that of the development of Blackwater House, the new day girls' home from September 1996. Its large, airy, two-storey common room together with balcony provided an inspirational focus for most of us to move into. The pioneer group split at the end of the year, with two of the original nine remaining in Watt as part of an embryonic boarding house led by Fiona Donaldson; she, as the College's first housemistress, inspired our mathematically minded headmaster to create the "hsm", the English spelling-rule-defying title for a housemaster or housemistress in our new climate of equal opportunity. Then Blackwater mushroomed to begin life as a house of fifty-one in four year groups; three senior girls buried a time capsule and planted a tree at the official opening of the house by Virginia Bottomley and chairman of governors, Sir Christopher Leaver.'

As commander of the Royal Navy's Surface Fleet, I was visiting HMS Endurance in the Antarctic. As part of the trip, I had to embark in a small two-seater aircraft of the British Antarctic Survey that launched by flying off a glacier edge. The large, bearded pilot, resplendent in red flying suit, gave me confidence. We hurtled off the glacier, and climbed across an icy wasteland to 10,000ft. The view was glorious. Clearly a man of few words, the pilot suddenly turned to me in the cramped cockpit and said, 'Am I right in thinking you are Ian Forbes from Eastbourne College?' He registered my surprise, and said with a smile, 'I'm David L–, we were in the same geography class at the College.' The years fell away as we spent the two-hour flight at the bottom of the world recalling boyhood memories of Eastbourne. We agreed our time there had been the best of days, and served us well. It was a special moment, epitomising the College fraternity and spirit. I know neither of us will ever forget it.

Ian Forbes (Pw60, chairman of Council since 2005)

David Hodkinson adds: 'School House was the original Eastbourne College: the classrooms, the pupils' accommodation, the staff accommodation and the headmaster's house. Around it were fields! As the College expanded School House remained the senior house and firmly at the heart of the College community. The house was spacious but antiquated, and by the time of the late 1980s and early 1990s it was in need of refurbishment to take it into the twenty-first century. The work started in 1987 with the opening of Tenby Lodge, the annex, and continued through the 1990s. And then the momentous decision was taken to consolidate the boy boarders into four houses and move the girls from the crowded Watt House to the spacious School House: after 135 years the original house was to become a girls' house.

'The change took place in September 1998, but those boys who were due to take public examinations in the summer of 1999 were given the option of staying in School House with Tenby Lodge as their "house within a house". Fiona Donaldson moved into the annex to act as housemistress to the girls who lived in the main house and I remained as housemaster to the boys. So started the one and only year in College history when a house was truly coeducational. The senior boys looked after the younger girls as brothers would look after sisters, and the experimental coeducational house was a real success. The ability to put on a house play or concert without having to persuade boys to put on dresses was a real bonus, and the atmosphere within the house was civilised in the

Eastbourne College above 1961; below 2006.

extreme. Unfortunately this was only a temporary experiment, and in July 1999 the last "School House boy" left the girls to feminise the corridors of what had been the home to the first ever "School House boys" back in the early 1870s.'

After twelve successful and innovative years at the College, Charlie Bush decided to move on with effect from the end of the 2004/5 school year. His successor is Simon Davies who took over in September 2005. It was his decision to commission this celebratory book, not just because 140 years of history are worth commemorating but also because we are in a new century, with new challenges facing us and new stimuli to which we need to react. His vision for Eastbourne College is set out in Part Three.

Dave Mitchell, Doug Wicks, 'Tub' Bathgat___ I decided that we should celebrate the e___ our College days in style. Our primary m___al was to be white blanco, as used for so___y years to whiten our gym and cricket s___ and pads. Following a few glasses of liqu___ refreshment, we started late at nig___ abseiling with feet dipped in blanc___om the third floor of the old Pennell Hou___ Grassington Road. During break___ the following morning our housem___r, 'Deany' Hindley, said in a perplexed m___r: 'Someone walked across the road and u___e wall to the top of the house!' We then___ed on to the cloisters. Dave and Tub ser___s blanco replenishers. Doug and I h___ed side by side on our left feet, and with___ right feet dipped in the blanco we placed___iscellany of right-footed patterns along___entire length of the cloisters. I planted m___otprints on each side of Memorial Arch.___ng his end of year speech in Big Sc___ Michael Birley referred to the white foo___s. He applauded the amusing n___ but expressed concern at the effort th___uld be required to remove the paint___ed up to the prank and explained tha___co, not paint, had been used. This c___d him up, and he said: 'I should have ___ssed it was you, Morris!' The floor was duly ___ashed, but the pale white outline of my right footprint remains to this day on each side of Memorial Arch. Fortunately my son Louis (P97) did not follow in all of his father's footsteps.

Tony Morris (P59)

This is a condensed version of the speech made by Ted Young (B74) at the retirement dinner given for Forbes and Di Wastie in 1998.

'"Dear boy". I think those were the first words Forbes ever said to me as I arrived for the new boys' tea party at Blackwater House in the Michaelmas term of 1974. It was a phrase often used by my contemporaries during our five-year stint at Eastbourne College. Of course, when Forbes uttered the phrase, the meaning could be interpreted in any number of ways. A "What are you doing, dear boy?" fired off as you were caught standing, pillow raised above your head, in Masefield dormitory, sounded distinctly icy. A "Dear boy, where have you been?", employed as you returned from a First XV social evening, had a tone very similar to that of Her Majesty's constabulary. When, some years after leaving, I was awaiting the arrival of my first child, who should walk into the delivery room but old Blackwaterian Emery Cooper, who turned out to be the duty paediatrician. How else would we have greeted one another? "Dear boy" we both exclaimed, to the bemusement of my wife and the midwife.

'It is fair to say that Forbes has devoted his life to Eastbourne College – obviously as a housemaster but in so many other fields as well. I am delighted to hear that four new scholarship awards have been named in his honour – "after the ultimate all-rounder, and made annually to candidates who make a significant all-round contribution to College life." I can't think of a greater tribute. It's just rather unfortunate they're to be called "Wasters". But make no mistake, Forbes is the ultimate all-rounder: there is Forbes the rugby referee; Forbes the cricket coach; Forbes the biology teacher – the bomb disposal expert; the fireman; the deputy headmaster; the shares guru; the gardener; the commanding officer of the CCF. But it strikes me as amazing that nobody has thought to mention the supernatural qualities of one Forbes Wastie who – just as you were having a particularly vivid conversation about what you intended getting up to at the Moira House disco – would be there, like a flash, standing behind you. No footsteps, nothing. I suspect, around the world, there are hundreds of former Blackwater boys who look over their shoulders before saying something indiscreet "just checking if Forbes is around".'

I am one of those people (as was my father, interestingly) who annoyingly claim at dinner parties that school was the 'best days of my life'. I did not even mind fagging from what I recall; there was a terrific spirit amongst us Prep Room boys, and we were confident that it would be our turn one day, as indeed was the case. Of course there were personal high spots: leading the First XV out on to the pitch as captain for the first time – that feeling of sheer pride in the team and that we were representing the school in the way that, at that time anyway, mattered more than anything else. The chants of 'Collay, Collay' from the crowd and the roars of approval when we scored a try stand out in my memory. I was also lucky enough to be head boy, but it coincided with the arrival of girls at the school for the first time. Stand me up in front of 500 boys and I would have no problem; but stand me up in front of fifty girls and I went tongue-tied and inarticulate. The first time

I had to do it, to greet them, I turned quickly to my deputy to continue the briefing, and fled. As he had only come along to cast an approving eye over them and was unprepared for anything else, this took him by surprise; he became a clergyman and I sometimes wonder if I had something to do with it. Today, as I confront the complexity of senior command in places like Afghanistan where my daily routine is taken up with meetings with senior politicians, ambassadors and a few less respectable types, I look back on my time at Eastbourne with affection and considerable nostalgia. Life was straightforward and lived within a caring community that sought to do the right thing, individually and collectively. I have no doubt at all that that broad education is one important reason why I am at ease in the pressure-filled life I live today. Thank you, Eastbourne College.

David Richards (W65)

A number of us boarders were always working on excuses to frequent the town's numerous pubs and cafés. One of our favourite wheezes was to request a cinema pass, whereupon a gang of us would dive into one of the many pubs that weren't frequented by prefects or masters. I can't begin to tell you the numerous films we never saw! I'm sure that most of the masters and prefects knew what we were doing as they would come into our dormitories at the end of the evening and question us about the movie that we hadn't seen, so we had to pretend to be asleep. In my last year I remember one Saturday night in a pub some distance from the school, where we were celebrating a rugby victory. We had been spotted, or perhaps several school prefects had decided to search us out, and when they arrived in the pub everybody just poured out trying to avoid punishment. But we decided there was no point running away as we were 'bang to rights', and I think the only reason we weren't reported was that most of the First XV were in that pub that night, and numerous suspensions might have affected future results.

Peter Burt (G70)

I have to admit that starting at the College after spending the previous ten years at Beresford House was quite a shock. Socially, I was relatively shy, but looking back on those years it 'did me the world of good'. Even on the other side of the world, I am still in touch with several students from all those years ago and have attended a couple of OE reunions in Sydney. At Nugent House I will always remember the camaraderie – and the smell of toast for those afternoon snacks. Memories and the people from the time I spent at Eastbourne College are an important part of my schooling years, not to be dismissed or forgotten. I congratulate the College on its 140th anniversary. As my eldest son prepares to start high school here in Sydney next year, I hope his schooling years are remembered as fondly as mine are.

Sally Clark (Edwards, N74)

During my time at Pennell, the new housemaster, Culain Morris, wanting to inject a little pride into the house, found a collection of silver cups for a boxing competition and various other sporting events that had long been discontinued, and displayed them in a glass cabinet in the library. Boys being boys we – myself and John Henshaw – started to turn the cups upside down. After we'd done this several times, Culain decided to lock the cupboard – but by simply running a penknife between door and frame we could push the bolts open top and bottom, turn the cups over and, using string hooked over the bolts, close the cupboard again. By now we had started to perpetuate the school-wide myth that every boarding house had a ghost, and Pennell's spectre was having a laugh. But the joke did not stop: Culain went to increasingly desperate lengths to stop us getting access to the cupboard, and we resorted to increasingly ingenious ways to foil him, including eventually, after he'd locked the library door, climbing down the drainpipe and through the window. Our last hurrah was to replace the lock. Culain was now stuck: upside-down cups in a locked library with a cupboard for which he didn't have a key. I can't remember how the situation was resolved but it gave us weeks of entertainment.

Paul Browne (P77)

Double study period on a Saturday morning in the summer term of the sixth form was the ideal chance to escape to the beach for a sneaky pint or two. Unfortunately, on my return from one such morning, I found out I had been advanced to the Second XI cricket team, and worse still that I was opening the bowling as those above me had been advanced to the firsts. My first three balls were 'headbeamers' with a few more being called wides. Taken off fairly rapidly, I was sent in disgrace to the boundary to field – only to let a simple ball go straight through my legs for four! My younger brother was once told in a French lesson by Mr Gardner, 'Simon Richards – you are quite possibly the worst French student I have ever had the misfortune of teaching… since your brother.' Neither of us were really known for our academic brilliance.

Jim Richards (B83)

My fondest memories are of my English teacher, Nigel Wheeler, cycling into the classroom on his bike reciting Shakespeare. He would take us down to the seafront where we would learn poetry and we once even acted out the first scene from The Tempest *balancing precariously on the breakwater of the beach. His eccentricities were great as they helped you to remember what you were learning. Other memories include racing back from town on a Saturday night in time for the curfew at 10pm; hearing the bells chiming and praying that you were going to get back in time to report to Mr Cantwell was scary to say the least!*

Catherine Clifford (Bowker, N89)

We had a shortlist from which to select an establishment for the next stage of Anna's (Alexander, S99) education, and Eastbourne College was near the top. We asked Anna what she thought. 'Eastbourne,' she said, 'because it has boys and I liked Miss D, and the girls invited me into the galley for some toast.' Eastbourne it was then, and we got to know the road from Battle extremely well for the next five years. We remember Eastbourne with affection and gratitude. We gave them a gawky, mischievous thirteen-year-old, and five years later the College gave us back an independent, polished – well, almost – young lady, ready to face the world head-on – a young lady who had completed the Duke of Edinburgh gold award before the end of her last term, as well as achieving academic results good enough for her to secure a place at Portsmouth University to read criminology and criminal justice.

Marcia and Simon Alexander

Pennell leavers, 2005.

One particular memory is of my French teacher who, after just two weeks of teaching me A level, asked me not to hesitate to come and find him should I wish to give up French. Other happy times were singing and being part of the school musical, My Fair Lady, *champagne breakfast in the Dell on Speech Day, dyeing the water in Mr Cantwell's water tank red with food colouring, and making lifelong friends and having fun at the College.*

Sarah Chu (Wright, N88)

Lucy Evershed (de Moraes, N88) *has the same memory of dyeing the water red, which 'horrified Mr Cantwell when he turned on the taps the next morning to run his six-month-old baby her bath. We were soon found out, as nobody else had access to those tanks.'*

Charlie Allison, my maths teacher, gave me this report in 2002: 'Tarquin's top button is inevitably undone and his tie is correspondingly loose. He enters the class like a city broker who has just enjoyed a substantial lunch and is rather reluctant to do any serious work. He will look at it and ponder, but he is never to be found leaning over his work, scribbling furiously. As exams loom I hope to find him concentrating harder and accomplishing more in the lessons. However, he does do some fine pieces of homework though they occasionally have been done in collaboration with others. Working together is fine insofar as both parties think about what they are writing; as the summer looms, Tarquin should feel worried if he is unable to complete work by himself.'

Tarquin Glenister (W2000)

Working in the language lab, 2006.

I have many memories. Tit Ryder, Latin teacher, saying to Dave Short 'Are you cheating?' 'No sir, just checking,' which caused the teacher to stop looking stern and roar with laughter. Monty Young in a CCF inspection catching someone trying to hide his long hair in a hairnet: 'You'll be wearing suspenders and stockings next.' The senior swim team sharing all the races out between the four of them and all in psychedelic Bermuda shorts. Being captain of the First XV in the first match that Robin Harrison had ever lost to Brighton as player or coach. Liz Harrison, his wife, advised me not even to speak to him, and the team started winning again when Robin got rid of me from the centre of things out to the wing. I came into Gonville at the end of fagging and there was never any unpleasantness. I was happy to make toast for my superheroes – and even on one very cold winter night to be awoken from sleep right at the top of the building to be told that John Gosden required me to slip past matron and go down to the basement and sit on the toilet; it's my claim to fame that I warmed the seat for one of the world's greatest racing trainers.

Peter Henley (G68)

Eastbourne College in the late 1960s exuded creativity and encouragement – and the odd prank, such as the early morning discovery of moles on College Field. The head groundsman almost had a heart attack gazing at the earth mounds that had popped up on the hallowed ground of the cricket square. Apoplectic, he calmed down once it became apparent that the pranksters had simulated the molehills with soil. Personally, I gained the confidence and discipline to take on the world. I read and I learned how to think. But above all I learned how to use my initiative and not be intimidated by anything or anyone. My win over Jo Shubber (see p95) taught me a key lesson: the biggest and strongest don't necessarily always win. Nobody ever remembers how fast you get the job done – just how well. You have to stay confident and believe in yourself if you're ever going to achieve anything. Thanks for the memories!

David Gould (B66)

I often refer to my time at the College as the best two years of my life. It was like being in a huge adventure playground that you were encouraged to explore. I have a thousand memories of my time there. Vociferously supporting the First XV rugby team on College Field; standing on the boundary clutching a pile of books that I had no intention of studying while the First XI cracked the ball around the ground and down the cloisters; singing loudly in chapel; being taken to London to see fantastic plays; forging life-long friendships. I practically wore out 'the boards' of Big School, I trod them so often. I particularly remember the foot-high flood in the dressing room on the opening night of South Horrific *(sorry,* Pacific*), and the 'away' match to Tonbridge with* Antigone *– arranged on an exeat, probably because we'd laughed so loudly at their production of* Blood Wedding*. And naturally all of my year remember the tragic and untimely death of John Le Brocq. We were all deeply shocked and clung to one another for support as we struggled to come to terms with his death. He was a good friend and we all mourned long and hard for him.*

Fiona Bottomley (Caffyn, N79)

The late 1970s saw Simon Langdale ask a newcomer to the SCR to be the College's master-in-charge of discos. Twenty-three-year-old John Thornley, keen to gain some street cred, eagerly accepted the post in the hope that it would lead to more prestigious extra-curricular responsibilities. Regular minibus outings for groups of lower school boys (the sixth form had their own girls) on Saturday evenings to Roedean and Benenden were arranged, and JT had the unenviable prospect of spending the evening drinking sherry while his charges boogied the night away. This position led on to the dizzier heights of being involved in monitoring the last night of the summer term when Susie West and JT were paired up to go round all the Eastbourne nightclubs to check that no pupil was in there. Free entry to TJ's and all the other trendy joints made this pair the envy of the SCR. Moreover, as one of the least sporty members of the SCR, JT was given the task of running the cricket junior leagues, a competition for those boys who failed (or did not wish) to gain a place in a College team. At the beginning of his fifteen-year tenure of this position, keen to impress, he organised some away fixtures. One notable outing was to Hurstpierpoint College, where the master in charge of junior leagues knew even less about cricket than JT. At the end of a nail-biting match, neither JT nor his counterpart knew which side had won and it was only during supper back in College in the Bachelors' Common Room (as it was then called), when Nigel Wheeler clarified the rules, that Eastbourne realised that they had won.

John Thornley (staff 1978 to present)

My memories of Eastbourne College: walking down Old Wish Road laden with books; the trudge up to Summerdown playing fields; Mr Langdale behind the rugby posts on Saturdays watching the First XV; army helicopters landing on College Field; exploding iron ore with Doc Ed; sitting for hours in the bay windows with a pint of milk and packet of custard creams trying desperately to learn the relevant passages before my next divinity lesson with Mr Comyns; the peace of the school library; the ice cream after tea whilst wandering around the Devonshire Park Tennis Tournament with one of the girls from Nugent; the clatter of the cloisters; having 'waffle' written across my geography homework by Mr Harrison; calm hours spent watching the cricket; fraught hours spent doing tests and exams; above all, the camaraderie and beauty of the College and College Field in the sunshine each summer.

Matthew Honey (R79)

I was a boarder in Nugent and have many happy memories of my time there (after I'd got over being so homesick for the first half of the first term – thanks to matron, Mr and Mrs Harman and making lots of nice friends). We had lots of fun and I remember amongst many things pillow fights with pillows flying out of the windows onto a very displeased Mr Harman's balcony, and hiding in wardrobes in friends' rooms as matron came round to check we were all in bed trying not to snort with laughter at the same time and get caught. Even lessons weren't too bad – obviously the best being one biology lesson when Mr Bostock arrived and announced that did we all think he was daft or something as there was no way he was teaching us on his thirtieth birthday: 'Leave your books, I'm taking you all out for an ice cream at Fusciardi's to celebrate.'

Catherine Fellows (Mitchell, N94)

Graham Greene said, 'There is always a moment in childhood when the door opens and lets the future in.' Mine was at EC. I went there as a rebel without a cause; I left with one. The motivation and encouragement from authority figures such as Forbes Wastie, and opportunity combined with peer pressure, set me on the right path. Some say we have a rosy perspective on the transparent images of youth. As adult life obscures and masks many aspects of living, I find that the motivation fostered at EC still cuts through this. I spent the next twenty years flying planes, operating as an orthopaedic surgeon, starting a family and building research collaborations across Europe. It would not have happened without the beliefs and self confidence that the College instilled within me. Best thing of all about Eastbourne – it was fun, as it should be.

Simon Grange (C82)

I remember in particular Mr Hodkinson, and Mr Pendry who taught me to row and play rugby in the third form, but who were both also inspirational teachers in the classroom. All 'Hoddy' asked was that you tried your best every time and if you did he had all the time in the world for you. Mr Pendry would always answer my questions – and boy, did I ask questions! He also told me I wasn't allowed not to do A level maths, something I would have lived to regret. There was also Mr Bostock teaching third form DT; it wasn't his subject but he gave it a go and his enthusiasm took him and us through it. The College found things that you could succeed in; in the third form I couldn't catch a ball, so I rowed; more to the point, I capsized – one time it was in the notoriously unstable 'blue boat', which was so bad it was never named. To my rescue came the fourth form crew who took my oars off me and, using me as a tow rope, hauled my boat the full length of the home straight. I was encouraged by Mr Hodkinson and later Mr Alcock to persist, and eight years later I was coaching at Headington School. Another memory is of the expedition to the Himalayas in 1997, run by a very special teacher in her first year of teaching, who also ran the rowing and taught me geography. Miss King went beyond the call of duty, as so many Eastbourne teachers do, when three of us became ill and had to come back off the mountain before we attempted the pass, and she came with us. I have spent much of my life since in India and Nepal after she opened my eyes on that trip.

Nick Sankey (P93)

Canoes on a flooded College Field, 1961 (Peggy Hindley).

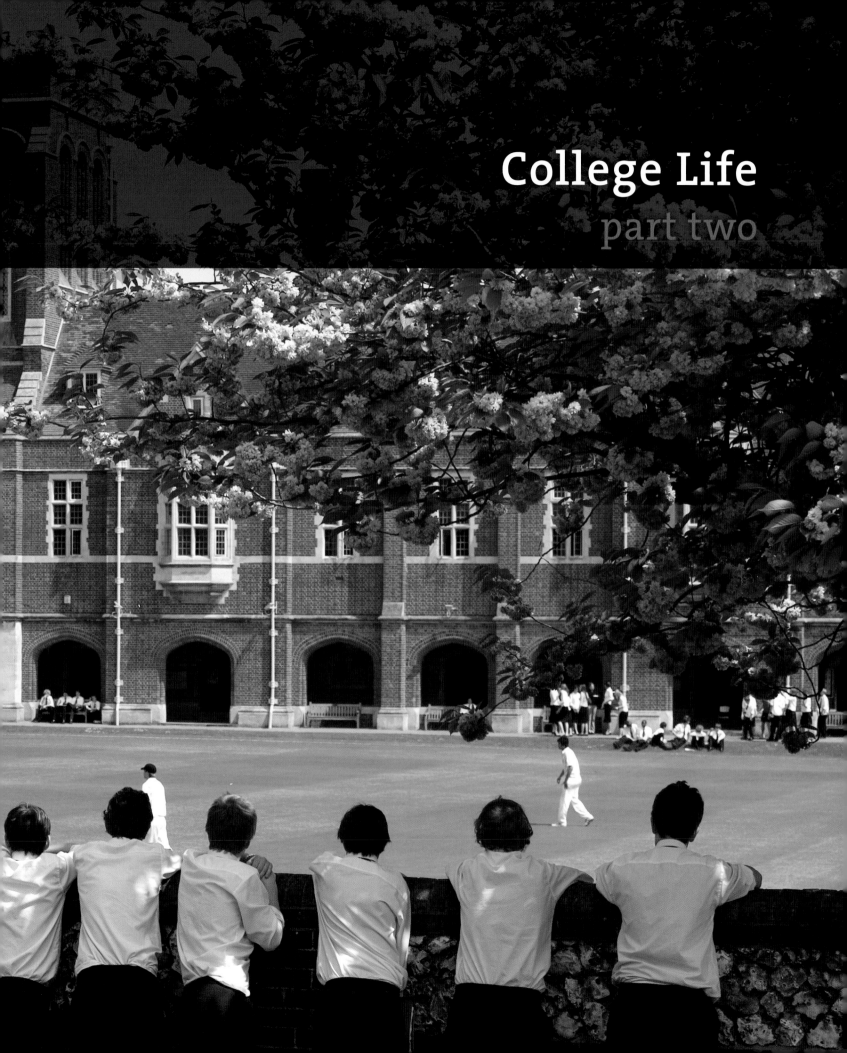

College Life

part two

Academia

It is perhaps not surprising that the majority of the contributions to this celebratory book concern extra-curricular activities; the bread and butter of school life – lessons, exams, qualifications – often fade in one's memory in contrast to sport, friends, pranks and the general hurly-burly of a busy community. Moreover, in common with most other schools throughout the first century of the College's existence, the curriculum was standard and unchanging: strong emphasis on the classics, little science, at some points nods only towards artistic and musical studies. What is remembered is stimulating teaching: Tony 'Barrel' Henderson, for example, writing wonderful poetry in English, Latin and Greek while also running the CCF, and Andrew Boxer, inspirational history teacher and drama director.

Today's academic standard is consistently high. Stuart White, deputy head academic, believes that 'the academic profile at the College is stronger now than it was five years ago. Most of the pupils go on from GCSE to A level, and then on to university or college. Eastbourne draws strength

Below: Below: School reports from 1933 (Keith Pinker) and 1988 (Nick Richards).

Below left: Cavendish Learning Resources Centre, 2006.

I had become entirely settled in my own mind that there was no such thing as an external deity, and out of respect for those who thought that there was it might be better if I were to stop going to the normally compulsory chapel services. The chaplain said he had no problem with that, but that I would have rather more difficulty persuading the headmaster. Birley was indeed none too impressed, and was particularly keen that I should not get away with anything. After some thought, he proposed that I should use the time that I would otherwise have spent in chapel (together with a fair bit more, as it turned out) learning philosophy. Each fortnight he would set me a topic: What were the key differences between the philosophies of Locke and Hume?; Evaluate Spinola's proofs of the existence of God; Where are the weaknesses in Descartes' cogito ergo sum?' and more of that sort of thing. The deal was that if I ever failed to impress him with my understanding of each assignment, then I was headed straight back into the pews. I worked extraordinarily hard, and once a fortnight I had to survive a vigorous cross-examination, which typically took place in his kitchen on a Sunday morning as he ate his breakfast, or by his side as he strode around the school. I managed to keep my end of the bargain, just; at any rate I was never sent back to chapel. Over the following years, I forgot most of the detail of the philosophy. But I never forgot the adrenalin rush that came with those oral tests. With the benefit of hindsight, it would have been much easier for me to go to chapel like everyone else. But not nearly so much fun.

Robert Fenwick Elliott (W65)

from its dual role and its fifty/fifty balance between boarders and day pupils; it is both a Kent/Sussex boarding school and the town's virtual grammar school. It is big enough to be able to offer lots of choice and to be ambitious, but not so big that individual needs get swamped. It is busier than many similar schools, and we have managed to implement the requirements of Curriculum 2000 – the need to study four subjects at AS level, for example – without cutting down on our wide ranges of extra- and co-curricular activities. We aspire to be a school which does as much as possible, and we believe that the academic side of things benefits and is hugely energised by everything else we offer.

'The curriculum is massively wider now than it was even thirty years ago. We still do all the traditional subjects including classics, for which there is high take-up at both GCSE and A level. Our language options now include Mandarin, and we offer relatively new subjects such as history of art, economics and business studies. Our religious studies teaching includes a strong philosophy element, and we also offer an AS in critical thinking. Art, design, music and drama are all taught at both GCSE and A level, and IT is everywhere both on its own account and as an aid to other subjects.'

This book cannot and ought not dwell on individual academic subjects *per se*; but here are a couple of elegant reports on their subjects from past and present members of staff.

An English class in the Dell Theatre taken by Christy Hawkins, 2006.

ENGLISH

Philip Le Brocq describes his time at the College from 1962 to 1988: 'I arrived at Eastbourne College fresh from my finals at St Catharine's College, Cambridge, to be met for tea by the long-standing, snuff-taking head of English, V M (Vim) Allom. He had a degree in chemistry. The A level results had been abysmal. Vim's comment was "We have good years and bad years. This was a bad one." The teachers' responsibility was not an issue. Three years later I was made head of a department of two teachers. Michael Birley's inspirational motto to staff was "If you have a good idea, try it!" So I did, and instituted a number of simple practical ideas. The department met for a weekly lunch on Thursdays at the New Inn for a "hammy-cheesy-eggy-thingy" and beer, to mull over the successes and failures of the week. I established a system of weekly lectures for the sixth form, given by different members of the department, so that the whole year would see that we could differ in our interpretations of literature and yet still be passionately committed to the subject. The department grew from two A level sets to five, with seventy pupils and seven staff. We eschewed mock exams and took our sets out onto the Downs to write poetry or read plays all morning, or went to London or Brighton for a theatre outing. Every Michaelmas half-term we took a coach load to Stratford to see three plays in two days. Walks at 6am with the mist rising over the Avon remain a mesmerising memory. As a department we toured the local prep schools with versions of Hamlet or Dickens, and were entertained royally by slightly surprised but exhilarated headmasters. Then there were the departmental "bangs", when we all combined to lecture, sing, act and show slides on topics like Tragedy or The Romantics – exposure for us and for the pupils. We invited help from expert colleagues in other disciplines.

The large door was thrown open. And there he was. A man larger than life, his energy confronting us, making it difficult for us to stand there idly. He commanded attention, our full attention. He stood there looking at us, a mixed bunch if ever there was one. We were nervous. He had one of us read the poem 'Leda and the Swan'; and then he looked at us and asked us what the poem was about. We looked at him, a little gormless. After a few feeble attempts, one of us said gently 'rape. It's about rape.' Philip repeated the word 'rape', but loudly and forcefully, again and again... and then he stood on one of the desks and shouted at us. 'Say it... rape....' And there we were shouting 'rape' in our first English lesson at Eastbourne College. For me this was the beginning of the most fabulous adventure. Having come from a very strict girls' school, I felt that I had arrived. I walked out of that lesson with a feeling of exhilaration. Somehow Philip had carte blanche. We followed him around the garden, eating rose petals, trying to get a feeling for the Romantics. He arranged picnics, outings, plays. Philip Le Brocq was and is an inspiration.

Claire Locher (Payne, N78)

I was a sullen youth, with no idea what I was for, why I was trapped in this system, what I wanted to do or be. It all seemed to be inflicted on me, rather than my choice. So I drooped around the place, with occasional flashes of sarcasm and resistance. One afternoon when I was in the fifth form, I was confronted by my form master and house tutor, John Hargreaves. It was about my French. Monsieur had told him that I wasn't working. Other staff had told him that I was doing as little as possible, toying with subjects instead of studying them. Why was that, he asked. I didn't have an answer. He went through my last French translation in detail, and finally said 'Next time, you'll show your French prep to me before you hand it in.' I left his study with a half-hearted curse. Who did the interfering sod think he was? Why exactly did he get involved? Why would he bother? Who was going to be impressed by this very private bollocking? No-one, after all, knew about it except him and me. He hadn't given me any extra work. The only extra work was what he had done. So why? And slowly I worked out that he didn't spend all his energies, like me, trying to avoid spending any energy. He did things because he thought them worth doing so long as they were done well. He worked hard at them, and as a result he achieved things he could be proud of. He'd put himself out, I had to conclude, not for his sake, but for mine. Not because he owed me anything, or because he had to, but because he cared about me and what might happen to me. The French was not the significant thing to either of us; it was an example. In future, it would be easier for me to get it right than to get it wrong, because I would have to show my work to him. So I began working hard and found out how rewarding it could be in itself. Le Brocq took me on and began to show me some of the works of literature that still mean the most to me. The best term I ever had at school was my last, my seventh in the sixth form, when A levels were over and I was studying only English for my Cambridge exams. Le Brocq, Brezicki, Budge and Cathy Taylor each taught a tiny group of us about the writers they most loved, and we had a wonderful time. I am grateful to them all. But most of all I am grateful to John Hargreaves for teaching me that they were giving their best for me. And I am proud now to say that, as well as for my own sake, I gave my best for them.

Jim McCue (S77)

Top right: History with Teddy Craig.

'We set up a lecture system for the last term of A levels – a visiting lecturer each week on our eight set texts, with seminars instead of lessons, and an in-form timed essay, marked by the department – each essay twice – by supper time so that the results could be posted on the then Room 20 door to make or break hearts on a long-shadowed summer evening. "Oooohh! I can't have only got a C grade!" We toured English conferences at other schools and demonstrated the Le Brocq "bounce around" which I had started as a way of getting the newly arrived sixth form girls to integrate with their arrogant but awkward male colleagues. We used trust exercises, bits of set texts and wild improvisation to break down barriers and build up confidence. Different members of the department took it in turns to run this for the first double period every Saturday morning. It was an amazing commitment. Our colleagues complained about how hyper their students were for period three. It was a time of experimentation, of vision and of delight – and the results were amazing, considering that we took all-comers. My best year was eleven A grades out of a set of sixteen. After A levels it was sherry, smart hats, dresses and suits with chocolate gateaux at the Grand, later followed by an informal picnic on the Downs, to celebrate. We were known as the "mad department" and that meant we could break all the rules as long as we kept our results excellent. We did. I hope that philosophy remains my lasting legacy.'

Colin Polden brings the story up to date. 'Today's student is dominated by examinations. The lower sixth year of leisure has become part of the module treadmill. Teaching styles have had to change: in a system where how a question is answered is more important than what is said, much emphasis has to be placed on giving the examiners what they want. Most students accept that there are rules for the Assessment Objective game, just as there are for rugby and cricket, and play along without too much cynicism or loss of passion.

'Passion for the subject is at the heart of all good teaching and it cannot be measured, though it can be recognised. It was heartening to come across the first inspector of the department ten years on: he immediately recalled Nigel Wheeler's lesson on *Death of a Salesman* where pupils (and inspector) huddled on the floor under lowering piles of classroom furniture

Chemistry, 2006.

An alien from outer space might have surmised from reading a College magazine of my period that the education of humans revolved mainly around chasing balls of different shapes around a field. He would have been surprised to learn, however, that there were some humans (but don't mention it) whose minds were on other matters. I have strong memories of standing freezing on a desolate rugby pitch daydreaming about whether it was a good day for the propagation of short wave radio waves by reflection off the ionosphere or how many tons of wheat you could grow on the pitch or would it be possible to wheelie a Suzuki TS250 along the length of the cloisters. You will rightly deduce that sport was not the highlight of my time at Eastbourne. However, I hold some happy memories. The Technical Activities Centre (TAC) was a haven for a small but dedicated group of enthusiasts who were interested in technology at a time when calculators had only just become available to the masses and 'technology' was far from being considered a mainstream career. The inspirational teaching of the physics department led me to take a degree in electronic engineering. At the top of the College tower we had a meeting room for the Radio Club, where we could listen to and transmit short wave radio around the world. In the internet age, this does not perhaps sound as exciting as it was then! Pennell House, under Mike Young, was considered an anarchic or eccentric house (I was there with Eddie Izzard!).

William Reid (P72)

to experience the urban claustrophobia felt by Willy Loman. Nigel's pupils will remember that as well.

'Perhaps in a decade today's students too will recall the awesome impact of Canterbury Cathedral on a Chaucer experience day, the scabrous delivery of a scrupulously prepared lecture by Richard Palmer, the satisfaction (as well as the financial reward) of creating a Dobtcheff project of original work, maybe just a stimulating lesson where the merits of a piece of literature were hotly debated because people were involved at a visceral level. Literature matters; it's fun, it's serious and it defies measurement.'

SCIENCE

Forbes Wastie arrived at Eastbourne College in 1961 to teach physics, chemistry and biology: 'I quickly found that biology, as in most schools, was the Cinderella science. It was taught by that great character Peter Phillips, "the Brute", with a little help from "Percy the persuader" (a squash racquet handle), and from time to time by Kem Bagnall-Oakeley, "Bags", who was first and foremost a chemist. Just one lab, B1, was set aside for the subject at the top of the stairs in the old Science Labs in the New Building (now the D&T Centre). Although I was appointed to teach all three sciences, my real interest was biology. I had been at King's College, London, in the late 1950s when Maurice Wilkins and Rosalind Franklin established the X-ray crystallography patterns of molecular DNA, for which the former received the Nobel Prize. The subject was developing fast and the frontiers were being expanded. I was soon able to concentrate on it, and despite limited facilities we achieved much success with A level candidates, particularly those going on to study medicine. My enthusiasm led me to explore curriculum development, stimulated by the Nuffield Science Teaching Schemes launched in the early 1960s, and in 1965 I persuaded Michael Birley to allow me to take a sabbatical term in order to explore the scheme prior to possible implementation at the College. With his blessing I spent a busy term at Portsmouth College of Technology, where we quickly became absorbed with the new teaching methods which involved learning by discovery largely through practical exercises.

'On my return I was able to introduce the scheme into the College curriculum, and at that point biology became both popular and a compulsory subject up to O level. As a result lab space and facilities were inadequate, until after much lobbying Michael

Top: *Physics with David Hodkinson, 2006.*

Above: *Physics, 1962 (Tony Ling).*

Birley and the Council were persuaded to build a brand new Arnold Biology Centre, named after Og, the great naturalist headmaster of the 1920s. It was ready for use by 1973, housed in prefabricated buildings with a life span of twenty years. The school was now expanding in size, with more sets to teach and a growing uptake at A level, and of course staffing levels also increased. The life span of the building was well exceeded, and so thoughts turned to new buildings for all the sciences. To the great joy of everyone involved, the new Science Centre was completed in 2002. It is a centre of excellence and the realisation of a vision, brought into being by the generosity of many Old Eastbournians and friends of the College.'

After starting teaching at the College in 1975 and becoming head of maths in 1985, I decided in 1994 to take on the new challenge of learning German. Chris Waller, who had come to the College in 1991, said I could attend his year 10 GCSE classes as long as I was treated like all the other pupils. So it was that I made my way nervously to the Michelle Pfeiffer suite, his name for his classroom. Bizarrely, Roy Orbison's 'Pretty woman' was playing on the cassette. Pupils arrived breathlessly, sat down silently and listened reverentially. Posters of Clint Eastwood – looking uncannily like Dr Waller – and Michelle Pfeiffer dominated the walls. I realised I'd entered an alternative reality. When the lesson began difficult grammar was made as clear as crystal, then a poem's beauty was revealed, then questions on the last homework were fired off around the room at machine-gun speed. There was a heightened level of consciousness and sense of expectation. There was no place for anything but total concentration. To give less would have been an affront to both the subject and the teacher. As the lesson ended Dr Waller explained solemnly that he was going directly to Heathrow Airport to collect Michelle Pfeiffer and take her to her next engagement. He would be late home and he would be staying up all night to catch up on his correspondence and on his marking. We blinked and nodded and filed out in silence. I couldn't wait for the next lesson and I asked the pupil next to me on the stairs how the lesson had been for him. 'I'm exhausted but I learned loads. I think Dr Waller may be late for Miss Pfeiffer's plane; he'll definitely stay up to do the marking though – he always does.'

Chris had a clear mission as a teacher: to fire the imaginations of young minds so that they would come to have the highest possible appreciation of the riches of both language and literature. He used his exceptional intellect, imagination and drive to achieve that aim. He inspired generations of pupils with a love of learning and he enabled them to reach academic heights they had never previously dreamt of. It was my good fortune to attend his German classes for GCSE and A level, and to learn from a remarkable teacher who gave of himself without limit to his pupils. When one of my tutees left Eastbourne College (three years after Dr Waller had left the school) I asked him about his teachers. 'They were all terrific,' he said; 'but one was completely different, in a class of his own. Dr Waller's lessons were unbelievable. I've never worked so hard or had so much excitement before or since.'

Nick Pendry
(staff 1975 – present)

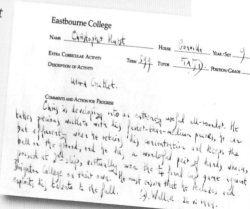

Chris Waller's report on Christopher Hurst.

A Nobel Laureate

Eastbourne College is one of the few schools that can boast a Nobel prizewinner among its alumni. Ours is Frederick Soddy, who was a pupil in the early 1890s and was much encouraged in his study of the sciences by his chemistry teacher at the College. He attended the University College of Wales, Aberystwyth, and then went to Oxford from where he graduated in 1898 with first class honours. He went on to work in Canada with Professor Sir Ernest Rutherford on radioactivity, and it was while working with the radioactive element radium that he observed that the alpha particles it was emitting were in fact the element helium, recently discovered in the solar spectrum by Bunsen and Kirchoff. This was the origin of the whole new concept that elements, once thought to be unchanging, could decay into new elements. Rutherford went on to split the atom, but Soddy concentrated on the fact that certain elements could contain a varying number of neutrons within the nucleus, which meant that they could have different atomic weights

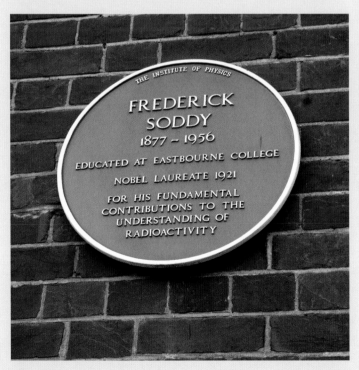

THE INSTITUTE OF PHYSICS

FREDERICK
SODDY
1877 ~ 1956

EDUCATED AT EASTBOURNE COLLEGE

NOBEL LAUREATE 1921

FOR HIS FUNDAMENTAL
CONTRIBUTIONS TO THE
UNDERSTANDING OF
RADIOACTIVITY

but still be indistinguishable chemically. Soddy named these variants 'isotopes', meaning 'same place', and it was for this work that he was awarded the Nobel Prize for Chemistry in 1921. He had been elected a Fellow of the Royal Society in 1910 and ended his professional life as Professor of Chemistry at Oxford. He died in 1956. His plaque is on the wall of the old Science Building.

Sport

Games were not compulsory during the early decades of the College's existence, and were organised almost entirely by the boys through a games committee. College Field could then be a quagmire in winter, with the lower end frequently under water. It also initially provided poor quality wickets for cricket; no century was scored on it before 1892. Improved drainage and maintenance during the last two decades of the nineteenth century enhanced the quality of the sports played there which after a while, as schoolmasters became younger and began to take over their management, became *de rigueur* for everyone. Michael Partridge (B46) remembers that 'in 1950, and probably long before, it was obligatory to pursue a sporting activity on five days each week. If no organised rugby or cricket was available, the "run round Paradise" was an acceptable substitute, though in Blackwater we had the fives courts which we often preferred.'

The first fives court was built in 1874, and when swimming and athletics were introduced there were several proficient exponents among the boys. The first blue to be awarded to an Eastbournian, Percy Robert Lloyd (B1883), was in athletics at Oxford in 1890. Carey encouraged athletics, as well as tennis and swimming; and under Nugee, in 1939, a sailing club was started, initially affiliated to the Eastbourne Sailing Club. Nugee also added golf as an acceptable sport, and the attitude towards playing games on Sundays relaxed and voluntary Sunday afternoon sport became a feature of the weekends, replacing the long country rambles that had previously been the norm. John Underhill, together with RSM Kent, started the Fencing Club in 1933: 'We got our first blue at Cambridge in the 1930s and in our first year at Radley we challenged Stowe, who were the champions that year, and won.' Christopher Kirk-Greene took over after the war and the club flourished for the next thirty-six years as 'sword in hand, I kept the youth at bay. Some did fencing simply as an alternative to mainstream sport. Others had a real inclination for it. Every year we had one or two able fencers, and in my last few years we made history when we had our first girl

Above left: Fives, 2006.

Above: High jumping, Memorial Field, 1951 (Michael Partridge).

One of the most outstanding sportsmen the College has produced from the era when it was possible for a man to achieve the highest honours in a variety of sports was Christopher Mackintosh (B17). He won his rugby Stag three times and swept the board at College athletics events, in 1922 winning seven of the ten events and going on to win the Championship Cup for the College as the sole Eastbourne entry in that year's Public Schools Championship. Moreover, at a time when tennis was not played at the school, he was one of the doubles team in 1921 that won the title at the Public Schools Lawn Tennis Meeting at Queen's Club; he later qualified for Wimbledon but went abroad before he could play. He also scored a century for the College XI against Brasenose College, Oxford, in his final year. At Oxford he gained full blues for rugby and athletics, and was promptly picked for the British athletics team in the 'Chariots of Fire' Olympics in Paris in 1924. In that same year he played rugby both for London Scottish and for Scotland against France, and was also the winner of the Kandahar Cup, a prestigious downhill ski race. Between 1923 and 1933 he was the outstanding British skier, alone able to compete on equal terms with the best of the Scandinavians and the Swiss. In 1931 he captained the British ski team, another member of which recalled that Mackintosh was the only man ever to have skied down the Cresta Run. After rugby, athletics and skiing, his fourth international honour came when he joined the British four-man crew at the 1937 World Bobsleigh Championships at St Moritz after one of the original members was injured. The British team won, with his strength and speed as the brake man being crucial. With characteristic modesty, he did not correct press reports of the victory which left the original team member's name on the team list.

Michael Partridge (B46)

Top: Denys Hopkinson, Sports Day, 1931 (Chris Hopkinson).

Above: Girls' First XI, 2004.

fencer, Penny Wynes, who was our secret weapon as our opponents never quite got over their surprise.'

After the Second World War hockey joined rugby and athletics as a sport played in the winter months, and soccer too later became available as an alternative to hockey. As facilities developed and improved a huge number of new sports were added to those available. The coming of girls – who frequently in the early days joined in with the boys at the traditional sports – added more, and the girls' teams are now highly successful in all sports at all ages. The astroturf pitches at Beresford, first laid in the early 1990s, have added yet more versatility to College sport. They are used for hockey in the winter and tennis in the summer, a sport which is increasingly popular with both girls and boys and is now the major girls' sport in the summer term. Netball too is very successful, particularly at senior level, and PE activities add to the ranges of games and sports on offer: these now include rugby, hockey, cricket, netball, squash, football, fives, rowing, tennis, rounders, athletics, swimming, water polo, golf, fencing, badminton, volleyball, basketball and general health-related fitness. Moreover, PE is now offered as an academic subject at both GCSE and A level, and is growing massively in popularity and take-up.

University College, Oxford, athletics team, Christopher Mackintosh in the centre, 1925.

RUGBY

For the first three years since its foundation in 1867, Eastbourne College played Harrow football, widely popular in schools at the time. This was a mixture of soccer and rugby in that the ball could be both kicked and caught as long as the catch was clean and the ball had not touched the ground. By 1879, however, the College was playing 'running with the ball', a form of rugby based on that played at Rugby School but with rules particular to each school that played it, including a feature called a 'rogue' that was peculiar to Eastbourne. Before a game against an opposing school the captains had to confer about which conventions would be followed, and it was to be some years before the rules were standardised by the Rugby Union. Early teams consisted of eleven players only, but they soon crept up to twelve and then fifteen.

There was an outcry in 1875 when, in response to the death of a boy at another school after a tackle, the headmaster announced that the school would revert to Harrow football. Despite mutinous boys and poor results in matches, his decision stood and Eastbourne became a soccer school until 1900, when the school reverted to rugby as the direct result of the appointment to the staff of E C Arnold, who waged a successful campaign to return to it. The new rules were drawn up under the same banner – ECFC – as has always been used for football of whatever code at Eastbourne. And it was not long before prowess was such that the school could claim its first two Cambridge blues – one of whom, Gordon Carey, was later to be headmaster – and its first international cap when Douglas (or 'Daniel') Lambert played for England against France. Carey also had had the distinction of being the first player to kick off at the new rugby ground at Twickenham, for the Harlequins against Richmond in 1909, a match in which four players were OEs; he repeated his kick fifty years later at the jubilee celebrations.

Ruari McLean (Crosby31) remembers the Drinking-In Ceremony, inaugurated by Arnold in 1917, which occurred at the end of term ceremony when the headmaster and staff had departed: 'Under the direction of Beefy Howell, the Stags solemnly recited *In hostium, et mei ipsius ni depugnavero, perniciem bibo,* which can be translated as "I drink to the destruction of the foe and of my own self if I have not fought to the finish." It was clear that at least half the members of the XV, who were not in the classical

> *I remember fair-haired John Bobby at full back, saving match after match standing alone with the opposition in full cry coming down the field at him; he had the safest hands and the coolest drop kick in the south of England. Gordon Crumley, my head of house, was brave and frequently dazzling in the centre. I remember [another] famous Radley match in 1954: Eastbourne scored over unbeaten Radley, after being just behind until the last minute of the last match of the season. The crowd on the touchline were hoarse and wild with delight. I watched the teams leaving the pitch: the College were unbelieving and completely exhausted; the Radley boys each looked like – in Terry Pratchett's words – 'the general who has just heard that his army came second in the battle'.*
>
> **Robin 'RC' Armstrong Brown (W51)**

sixth, didn't have a clue what they were saying. What they were drinking, I can't now remember… but it was an impressive ceremony, cheered by the rest of the school. In my third year I got into the First XV and received my Stag. On First XV match days the whole school gathered in Big School to sing the football song.'

Tony Morris (P59) recalls it too: 'My most uplifting memory of the College was the Stag ceremony that took place at the end of every rugby season. Following the headmaster's end of term speech he and all the staff left Big School, while every student remained seated. The First XV captain and remaining Stags from the previous season mounted the stage. Each new Stag was then called onto the stage one at a time by the captain. This was accompanied by tumultuous applause from the audience, especially for the player awarded the season's first Stag. Very nervously each new Stag held a beer-filled wooden chalice aloft and recited the rugby war cry, which I

> *During my time at the College two visiting rugby teams used College Field for their initial training on arrival in the UK. The first I can recall is the Springboks (shoulders, heads but no necks) and the second was the All Blacks. I have a vivid memory of the famous Don Clark of the All Blacks practising goal kicking with bare feet from halfway with a heavy leather ball on College Field in 1963, and still have a fixture card signed by the whole team.*
>
> **John Allan (S60)**

Below: First XV in Argentina, 2005.

have never forgotten. The cessation of that ceremony is a pity. Even though times have changed, the College is still a rugby school – one of the finest in the country. Once, when I asked why the ceremony had ceased, it was suggested that the First XV did not need it! Do the All Blacks need the *Haka*?' Michael Partridge adds: 'The cup was turned by Alan Gilbert (W12) from wood acquired by Arnold from HMS *Carmania*, a Cunarder turned First World War auxiliary cruiser. The drink in the cup was originally to be blood and milk, the blood to be supplied by the Stags. In the event, the contents were usually small beer, beer diluted with water.'

The award of the 'Stag' has for most of the College's history been formally restricted to members of the rugby First XV. Until the mid-1970s all regular members of the first team were awarded the Stag, but it is now an additional honour conferred by the captain under the guidance of the master in charge, an extra

Above: The Carmania Cup.

Right: Hugo Southwell playing for Scotland.

I remember particularly the friendliness of the school and the three years of unbeaten rugby success which our team enjoyed from Under Sixteen to First XV level. Over those times I made my closest friends, and ended up in a job that I love: playing professional sport.

Hugo Southwell (W93)

accolade on top of team colours awarded to exceptional members of the First XV who usually need to be performing at above schoolboy level. In recent decades the term has been used informally for the award of first team colours in other major sports; as Rupert Bairamian (S75) writes, 'My proudest moment was when I received my First XI cricket colours ("the Stag"). This was known during the season as "moose hunting" and was awarded to me as a result, I hope, of the odd endeavour on the field of play but mainly, I suspect, for the amount of drink I bought Nigel Wheeler during the cricket festival at Clifton in 1980. I passed on this technique to subsequent generations of Eastbournians who wear the Stag with pride to this day.'

One of the most celebrated rugby victories, remembered by all who were there, was that against Radley late in the Michaelmas term of 1944 while both schools were sharing premises. John Robbins (B44) says, 'I have never forgotten the thrill of that afternoon which made a terrific impression on me as a thirteen-year-old new boy.' Robin Harrison (P42) describes the match: 'During our wartime exile to Radley the annual

determination, of staff and boys, which helped to keep the College alive and well during those grim years of the war, when so few new boys were arriving and our numbers slumped to less than half. It was reported that Beefy was in tears at the end of the match. For the record the team were: K H Watson, R H Horne, G E H Wilson, D S Sams, A V Dunlop, D A Bell, R B Harrison, S Halstead, C C Brown, A D Mitchell, J M Williamson, G A Irwin, M J C Haines, A S Hunt, G G Sadler.'

Robin Harrison took over as master in charge of rugby from Beefy Howell in the mid-1950s, and the school's performance on the field continued to excel under him and his successors. When in 1984 David Stewart joined the staff to teach English and also to run the rugby, he made some changes to how it was organised, notably by dismantling the house rugby structure so that more emphasis could be placed on the school game, and also by changing the strip. The blue shorts gave way to white and the whole team was now to play in the same blue and white hooped socks, though many bewailed the loss of the distinctive Stag socks with their diamond tops. At this time also the traditional game between the College and the OEs had to cease for health and safety reasons.

David Stewart presided over a successful era in College rugby when numbers of boys became schoolboy internationals and two, Will Green (G87) and Hugo Southwell (W93) in the 1990s, went on to gain senior England and Scotland caps. In 1996 the First XV achieved their first unbeaten season since 1900 when rugby was reintroduced by Arnold, to be followed by another one in the next year, 1997, and yet another in 2000. Stewart attributes this golden age to a succession of exceptional captains, who not only played at a high level themselves but inspired their teams. He also feels that the College has an enormous, aspirational asset in College Field – a splendid arena right in the middle of the College and its daily life on which teams can strut their stuff in front of both the school and the town. For him and for others it is a potent symbol, at the heart of what the College tries to achieve in sport and in other fields.

Left: Eastbourne College v Epsom, October 1965 (Ian Ball).

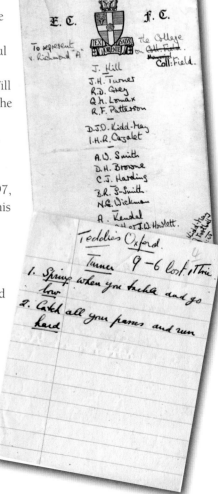

rugby matches between the two schools were great occasions, with the massed ranks of the Radley supporters on one touchline and the ever dwindling band of Eastbourne supporters on the other. That year the Radley XV were reckoned to be one of their best sides for years, and had been carrying all before them with comfortable wins over all their opponents. Eastbourne too were unbeaten, but the form book strongly favoured Radley and even more so when, in the weeks leading up to the match, we suffered injuries to three key players including our captain. It was a close-fought match, and our position worsened just before half time when disaster struck: one of our team broke his arm, and with no substitutes allowed in those days we faced the whole of the second half with only fourteen men, against a rampant Radley pack with the wind and the rain at their backs. Radley eventually scored a try, so it was 0–3. Then we heeled the ball under their posts and I passed to Bell who dropped a splendid goal into the strong wind – a score then worth four points! Fifteen minutes remaining and 4–3 to Eastbourne! I remember little of the rest of the match except our desperate attempts to keep our line intact against repeated Radley onslaughts. The cheering from the relatively few Eastbourne supporters completely drowned out the efforts of Radley and did much to help us to hold on to record an epic victory against all the odds. I have since talked to many people from both schools who played in or watched that match, and none have forgotten it. All agreed that it seemed to epitomise the spirit and

Team list and Beefy Howell's advice, early 1950s (Hugh Turner).

John Lush (left), Frank Quaife and the 1957 First XI (A J G Glossop).

CRICKET

Cricket was always the main summer game at Eastbourne and was played almost from the start. John Nugee, who had himself been proficient at the game in his youth, particularly fostered it and at his own expense engaged Maurice Tate, the Sussex and England cricketer, as a coach in the summer of 1939. Ben Lyte (G39) recalls sessions with him in the Wish Garden nets, when he would 'set out a single stump on which he placed a penny, which in those days would purchase a small but respectable chocolate bar and which he promised to any boy bowling who hit the stump. It happened that I had been long and well coached, so that he soon owed me a shilling – hence perhaps my immediate elevation to the Colts. But I never got the money. He could make the ball move in the air and break sharply either way without any observable change in his action. Claud "Billy B" Burton, Blackwater housemaster and head of cricket, devoted much time to

teaching us how a ball might be made to "swing" in the air – something which "Og" Arnold had apparently refused to believe possible.' Michael Partridge (B46) was captain of the Third XI in 1950 and 1951: 'We were known as the Erratics (Eastbourne's Rather Rough and Totally Incompetent Cricketers), and we used to play local villages and sometimes other teams like the London Symphony Orchestra.'

Nigel Wheeler summarises cricket at Eastbourne College from the early decades of the twentieth century to the present: '"Organised loafing" defines College cricket quite adequately and since 1919 three characters have been responsible for organising the loafing: Claud Burton (1919–50), John Lush (1951–76) and myself (1977–2006). They have been assisted by marvellous professionals such as Williams and Price in the 1920s and 1930s, and later Frank Quaife, Ted James, John Shepherd, Deon Kotze, Andrew Waller and many others.

The Eclectics – Eastbourne College Lads, Eastbourne College Teachers, Indifferent (or Illustrious) Cricketers – was founded by Claud Burton in the early 1950s, and developed gradually into the present Eclectics team, now drawn from staff members only, who play six Wednesday evening 20-over games against local village teams and two Sunday afternoon home fixtures on College Field.

The cricket is keen, with a wholly amateur ethos. The Eclectics' unique contribution to cricket – the Bucket – is pinned to the shirt of the first fielder to drop a catch and is then transferred to the next offender to do so. Many College stalwarts figure in the scorebooks (many now sadly lost), and recent headmasters have proved invaluable playing supporters. Our present head (an oarsman) required considerable persuasion before revealing a well-hidden expertise with the bat. He is on the list for next year.

Michael Mynott, Eclectics president and former school doctor

Eclectics v Perambulators, 1975.

'John Lush set up our cricket festival and Eastbourne was the first venue. Tonbridge, Clifton, Felsted and Winchester joined the host side for many years of competitive battles. It was Vince Broderick, the much-loved Winchester professional, who insisted on taking Eastbourne's fielding practice prior to the match against his own team in 1978 as he thought he could teach them a trick or two; he did and they won by 50 runs. Our first away festival saw us at Clifton in 1980 where NLW destroyed the suspension bridge barrier with the school van packed full of coaches and masters from the other schools as he erroneously assumed that the Clifton professional, Jim Andrews, in the van ahead had paid two fares for the crossing. Some years later Ed Giddins terrorised all the schools with his hostile bowling, and the Winchester master in charge warned that with the first intimidating bouncer by Giddins his side would abandon the game. A year later at Eastbourne Ed was so anxious to bat against Winchester that he locked his own team's no 5 in the loo, sauntered out to bat as the third wicket fell and made 93 including a six that landed in the bursary garden, a feat not seen before or since.

Our son, Christopher, was at the College (G98) from September 1999 until July 2003. He had a great deal of respect, in particular, for Dr Waller who taught him German and coached him in cricket. I remember watching him playing in the Under Fourteen XI against Ardingly in the final of the Lord Taverner's Trophy at Arundel Castle one year. Dr Waller could hardly watch at times, and was pacing up and down; he walked past us when Christopher was bowling, and I heard him say under his breath 'Come on, Chris, give them one of your yorkers' and he did. A few minutes later the same thing happened, and another wicket was down. I asked him if it was telepathy! They went on to win.

Jennifer Hurst

Top Left: Nigel Wheeler at his leaving dinner at Lord's, 2006 (John Thornley).

Left: Francis 'Tishy' Browne, the College's first Cambridge cricket blue, nicknamed Tishy after a famous racehorse which reputedly crossed its legs when running as he did when bowling.

Below: Angus Stewart, 136 not out, a score that cost Nigel Wheeler £86 after an unwise promise of £1 for every run over 50.

The Howell Pavilion.

My athletic experiences, with assistance from Michael (Hearty) Holland, led me to become an AAA athletics coach for thirty years. At the end of those years, I achieved a golden moment. One young athlete of mine, to whom I had taught biology, rugby and a bit of sprinting, was Jason Gardner who went on to become Olympic gold medallist in the 4x100 relay in Sydney 2000. He also achieved European gold in the Indoor 60m dash on three separate occasions and capped that by winning the World Indoor 60m title. My cricket experience helped me to reach a top coaching grade with the English Cricket Board, and I have spent most of my adult life coaching coaches how to coach. I sat on one of their advisory panels at Lord's for schools and youth groups. On my retirement from teaching, I became chairman of the Youth Committee for the Somerset Cricket Board and I had an input with Marcus Trescothick when I coached and managed the county Under Thirteen team in which he played. So John Lush, Ted James and Ralph Bryant, even the late Frank Quaife, can also claim that they did their bit for English cricket. I have played cricket with and against some famous cricketers, including a young raw recruit from Antigua – a lad of just twenty-two who was attempting to qualify for Somerset called Viv Richards. Others were Joel Garner, Brian Rose, Vic Marks, Peter Roebuck and, of course, the black sheep of the Somerset family, Ian Botham. But nothing was more memorable for me than when, as a sixteen-year-old novice fast bowler for Eastbourne College, I bowled against the Rev David Sheppard (later to become Bishop of Liverpool) who had been playing for England for quite a few years prior to this match. He opened the innings for the MCC on College Field and was a delight to watch – and moreover I had the honour of taking his wicket.

Pat Colbourne (S55)

'We toured New Zealand in 1988 with cricketers, two plays and a debating team. The sight of Eastbournians needing to finish the matches quickly so that they could prepare themselves to be dukes, fairies, lords and mechanicals added spice to the games. A month in New Zealand in March/April couldn't happen now; exams, timetables, manic striving for league positions would deny such indulgences. We visited Barbados on three occasions. In 1990 we shone rather better with the larger ball after Ben Miller led his team in a thrilling soccer match against the local sports coaches. Later, Simon Whitton (1996) and Tom Shepherd (2000) took hat tricks, and John Shepherd (professional 1991–7), back on his home island, ensured that we were welcomed at every rum house from coast to coast.

'Back home, it is College Field that is the centre of Eastbourne cricket, its small size ensuring some

memorable feats. Scores can be high: OEs once scored over 400 in a 55-over match, and the visitors' reply of 390, including two centuries, was not enough to prevent them losing. The tower, the library windows and Big School are popular targets for the big hitter, and Michael Birley offered five shillings to any boy who could hit what he regarded as the ghastly eyesore of the passage connecting the main school and the D&T Centre; it remains horribly intact. Some such big hits caused problems: the opening match of the 1977 season saw Trevor Smart clear Grange Road and hit the roof of the only house in the street not in the possession of the College. Tiles and ball landed at the feet of the owner as she worked in her garden, and she promptly marched off to complain to the bursar – whereupon Chris Kent dispatched a ball straight through her sitting room window. Then in 1980 Stephen Yorke hooked a ball through the Memorial Arch which travelled on down School House drive and landed among the tennis supporters queuing for the pre-Wimbledon ladies' championship. A somewhat worried American woman picked up the unusual leather object and suggested either that terrorists had struck or that the demise of English tennis was hardly surprising. Ah yes! Those golden days of summer loafing!'

HOCKEY

After the Second World War hockey began to be offered as one of the sports options at the College, initially however sandwiched between the rugby house matches and the athletics in the Lent term. Kem Bagnall-Oakeley was the first coach until John Lush

coaching First XI hockey. Under his aegis, and with help from many others on the staff, success has been phenomenal: the boys are currently (2005/6) Sussex champions at all levels and the girls champions at two levels, and none of the teams has been knocked out at any stage earlier than the semi-finals for the last five years. Moreover, they have on several occasions gone on to do well at regional and national level. Dusty Miller pays tribute to several tremendous captains, notably Bella Stewart, Ollie Smith, Jane Lyons and Amanda Price, and among both boys and girls in recent years several have gone on to be county and divisional players; the College can also boast two internationals and an Olympic gold medallist.

Top left: The first overseas hockey tour to Hamburg, 1968 (Brian Prentis).

Left: The Second XI v staff, 1971.

Below: Hockey on the Beresford astroturf, 2004.

took over in 1951, soon to be joined by Brian Prentis after he came to teach maths in 1955. Prentis took over the First XI in 1959, by which time the game had become well established, and it was not long before the teams started winning matches. A breakthrough came in the centenary year, 1967, when Eastbourne was invited to the prestigious Oxford Public Schools' Festival where the team won three matches and drew two. Then the following year the College represented England at an international tournament in Hamburg, finishing team of the championship. One of the players at the time, David West, became the College's first schoolboy international and later returned to the College to teach history and to coach hockey. David 'Dusty' Miller was another talented hockey player who is now on the staff, teaching chemistry and also

During my time at Eastbourne College I spent many hours training at, and travelling to and from, Wallers Haven learning to row on that narrow channel with fierce swans, angry fishermen and coaches taking their chances running along the rutted river bank. Our inability to race for anything over 1000m was always a limiting factor since that was the longest stretch of uninterrupted rowing that we could achieve. We spent most weekends leaving Eastbourne early on Saturday morning to drive to London to race on the Thames in various regattas. The commitment of the coaches, most notably Chris Alcock and David Hodkinson, is worthy of huge recognition and admiration. In the summer term of 1995 it was a great surprise to the men's First IV of James Henry, Nigel Sargant, Paul Steen, Ollie Dyer and Ed Winton (cox) that we found ourselves in the final of the Schools IVs event at the National Schools Regatta at Holme Pierrepont in Nottingham. As we approached the halfway mark we were a length down on the leading Lancaster Royal Grammar School and clear of the chasing pack. Our race plan hadn't accounted for any realistic possibility that we might win but, finding ourselves in a position to sprint for the line, we raised the stroke rate: with 500m to go we were a length down and with 250m to go we were drawing level. Our momentum, both psychologically and literally, put us in command and we continued to force the pace. It can't have looked pretty but the sensation of the crew working hard and together was inspiring and, as we crossed the line, we and Lancaster were virtually level. Neither crew could judge the result and we waited, gasping for breath, for it to be shown on the board. The result couldn't have been closer with 0.3s between the crews and Eastbourne College winning the National Schools Regatta for the first time.

Paul Steen (Pw90)

ROWING

David Hodkinson writes: 'Rowing was first introduced at the College in the summer of 1870 and took place on the sea. Subscriptions from parents and pupils raised money to have two boats built by a local boat builder at a cost of £19 each and these were stored by the Eastbourne Amateur Boat Club. At first there was plenty of enthusiasm but this proved short lived, partly due to the rule which required a safety boatman always to be present in his own boat, armed with signalling flags. By 1873 so little interest was shown that the boats were sold and the club came to an end. It was refounded in 1927 with a grant of £200 from the Council and under the guidance of the Rev E S Hunt, Truman Tanqueray and Robert Storrs. Initially intended as an alternative occupation in the summer term for boys who had no skill in cricket, it gradually grew, in spite of the sinuous nature of the river upon which they rowed, into a club which has three times won the Public Schools IVs at Marlow, represented the Youth of England against the Youth of Holland successfully in coxless fours at Henley and been National Coxed IVs

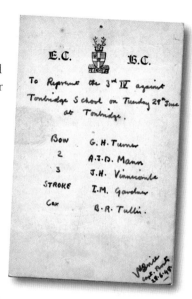

Top right: The Third IV v Tonbridge, 1949 (Hugh Turner).

Above: Rowing on the meandering Cuckmere, 1962 (Eric Koops) and (right) at Wallers Haven, 2006.

Left: Sheila Bett presenting prizes to the victorious Gonville First IV, 1963 (Eric Koops).

Below left: Colts IV, 1962 (Eric Koops).

Below: Alex Stimpson winning the 400m hurdles at the Sussex County Championships, 2005.

ATHLETICS

The College encouraged athletics right from the early days. The first blue achieved by an OE was in athletics (P R Lloyd, B1883); that exceptional sportsman, Christopher Mackintosh (B17), became an athletics Olympian; and Everard 'Tiny' Davis (Crosby26) represented Great Britain in the 1930s. The 1939 athletics team was one of the strongest in the history of the College; two of its members (Tony Chadburn and Alec Johnston), after distinguished service during the war, were picked for the 1948 Olympics squad though neither eventually competed.

champions at Pangbourne in 1966 and at the National Watersports Centre at Holme Pierrepont in 1995. Initially the club rowed on the meandering Cuckmere, but as the river became shallower and clogged with weed a new home was found on the Wallers Haven on the Pevensey marshes, where the club moved in 1967 and where it still remains.

'Despite not being recognised as a major rowing school during its ninety-nine years of existence the College Boat Club has produced an international rower, Ivor Lloyd (Pw64), and a blue, Kennedy Buckle (P26), as well as university boat club captains and officials and senior rowing club captains and officials. It has a long and proud tradition and continues to be "an alternative occupation in the summer term for boys who have no skill in cricket."'

If you were fortunate enough to be in the tennis squad, practice was held on the grass of Devonshire Park – a real joy, as the courts played superbly. We were coached by Chris Kirk-Greene and Donald Perrens. In the early and mid-1970s, one of the highlights of the hunting calendar was the annual point-to-point which the East Sussex used to hold at Heathfield. My older brother and I, both of whom had obviously left the seat of learning, decided to prepare a sumptuous picnic for the day's racing and socialising ahead. This proved too much for younger bro' Tristan who pleaded for someone to ring the school to say that he was too unwell to attend on that day and was thus also unfortunately unable to be part of the first six at tennis that afternoon. This was duly done and we set off in our ancient, very slow Land Rover which had a canvas hood open at the back and sideways-facing seats. Trundling up the dual carriageway towards the Boship roundabout at a sedate pace with Tristan in the back, we saw a Lotus Cortina car come up behind us. There weren't too many of those about, but there was one in Eastbourne that was white and green and belonged to Mr Kirk-Greene. As luck would have it this was the very vehicle being driven by Mr Kirk-Greene with other members of the tennis team on their way to their match. All Tristan could do was offer a foolish grin out of the back of the Land Rover. He duly returned to school, rather red-faced, on the Monday having undergone a miraculous recovery, and I believe Mr Kirk-Greene had the good grace not to mention the incident.

Morven Voorspuy (R64)

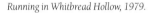

Running in Whitbread Hollow, 1979.

Athletics was the major sport of the Lent term for many years until hockey became an alternative, and is now mainly followed in the summer term when the College has fielded many successful teams for inter-school and county matches in all field and track events. The summer term also is when Junior Standards take place – an inter-house challenge for all those in years 9 and 10, when everyone has to complete five events, currently the long jump, the high jump, the shot put, the 100m and the 800m. And the last week of the Lent term is for College Sports, an inter-house athletics match when each house enters four teams, one for each of years 9, 10, 11 and the sixth form, to cover nearly every track and field event. The week culminates in a day of relays, including the Paalov which involves carrying a baton ten times round the track with a team of six; strategy and tactics play as large a part in this event as does running skill.

I was a member of Reeves House in the early 1970s, not an auspicious time for the house as we not only failed to win anything but occasionally never turned up on the sporting field. In an attempt to encourage us out of our lethargy the housemaster, Vic Ferris, promised a bottle of champagne to any house team that won a major sporting event. A couple of months later Vic was sitting on the bench that looks down to Whitbread Hollow during the school cross-country race as I ran up the hill towards him. His face was a picture as it dawned on him what I already knew. For in front of me were two members of Reeves in first and second places and here I was in third. On his way back to the school that afternoon, Vic must have taken a detour, for in house assembly he produced a bottle of champagne which the seven members of the winning team devoured.

Mark Pickett (R73)

Above: Running on the Downs, 2006.

Far left: Final 300 yards of the steeplechase, 1954.

Left: Sports Day 1931, Denys Hopkinson leading (Chris Hopkinson).

Right: Swimming sports, 1952 (Richard Terry).

Far right: Fencing team, 1983, with Chris Kirk-Greene.

Below right: College boxing team, 1954.

Bottom right: Verity Williams, 2006.

In my era Gonville was a good house to be in provided you were strong, good at sport and not overly keen on academic work. Everyone in the school had to do one run each week, but we were expected to go out twice; boxing in the Lent term was optional but not if you were in Gonville; summer evenings included walking up to the athletics track for 'standards' when house by house you tried to beat the standard times/distances/heights for the various athletic activities – again meant to be optional unless you were in Gonville…!

John Purchas (G55)

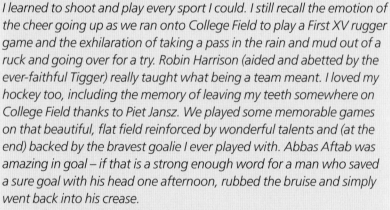

I learned to shoot and play every sport I could. I still recall the emotion of the cheer going up as we ran onto College Field to play a First XV rugger game and the exhilaration of taking a pass in the rain and mud out of a ruck and going over for a try. Robin Harrison (aided and abetted by the ever-faithful Tigger) really taught what being a team meant. I loved my hockey too, including the memory of leaving my teeth somewhere on College Field thanks to Piet Jansz. We played some memorable games on that beautiful, flat field reinforced by wonderful talents and (at the end) backed by the bravest goalie I ever played with. Abbas Aftab was amazing in goal – if that is a strong enough word for a man who saved a sure goal with his head one afternoon, rubbed the bruise and simply went back into his crease.

I also remember the glorious summer days heading out to the old rowing club on the Cuckmere. Messrs Binian and Holland passionately put us through our paces, and one day on the water I learned a lesson that has sustained me through the years. Somehow I ended up in the finals of the house Senior Sculling Cup. I was a total underdog against Jo Shubber – a wonderful athlete and character who was bigger and much stronger than me. I didn't stand a chance – I just wanted to row the course and finish afloat with my pride intact. We lined up and were off. Jo soon had a lead on me, and we were both going strong. I can still hear the booming encouragement from the bank. And then it happened. Jo 'caught a crab' and pivoted into the bank, and I shot past him as he struggled to back his way out and get going again. In disbelief I kept up a steady pace, watching this other scull tearing after me in a fury and I crossed the line first as stunned as everyone watching.

David Gould (B66)

The Corps

David Thomson (G55) writes, 'Eastbourne is not, nor has ever set out to be, a military school; yet for more than 100 years the Corps has proved to be one of the central pillars of excellence within the College. Indeed, it is the period immediately following the foundation of the Corps in 1896, and the close competitive contact thereafter with the leading schools in the country at the Public Schools Corps Camps at Aldershot, which mark the conversion of Eastbourne College into a true public school. From those days right up to the present, the Corps, under a variety of different names, has set standards that have made it pre-eminent within its peer group across the country. To James Shum Tuckett, the first commanding officer of the Corps, Eastbourne College owes an enormous debt of gratitude.

'Even today, the Combined Cadet Force aims to provide a disciplined organisation within the school where leadership and associated personal qualities can be developed. Uniform plays a part in any such organisation and here the modern practical camouflage uniforms provide a drab contrast with the greys, scarlet and blues of the early years. Judging from contemporary photographs, it is hardly surprising that at the beginning of the twentieth century cadets were on occasion caught wearing their uniforms to fancy dress parties.

'Annual camps figure large in the history of the Corps, though it is noteworthy that between the two wars these gatherings were as often as not cancelled because of outbreaks of infectious diseases either within the school or in the army itself. In much the same way that former inmates of Her Majesty's Prisons tend to say that prison was a picnic compared with boarding school, Guy Andrews (HB1899), writing of a camp in 1900, recalls "We slept eight in a small bell tent on palliasses and 'pillows' covered with coarse packing cloth stuffed with straw. The toilet and

Above: Field Marshal Viscount Montgomery with John Nugee, Speech Day, 1948.

Left: James Shum Tuckett.

96

Denys Hopkinson in army uniform (Chris Hopkinson).

Then there was the 'bugle band'. We were good, we looked good and it was taken very seriously. There were leopard skins for the three big drummers, the lead drummer had a silver drum, the lead bugler who called the tunes had a silver bugle and the drum major had a large mace. Everything was kept spick and span and well polished. We also had white belts with brass 'royal' clasps which had been presented to us. A favourite march was past the Cookery School, with the aim of getting the girls to open the windows so that we could impress them: we would first march past the building making as loud a noise as possible, turn sharply to the right at the top, do a smart about-turn and then march past again, by which time we hoped that the windows would be open and full of wonderful ladies waving at us. This was the moment for the drum major to hurl the mace into the air and – to our relief – catch it again.

Hugh Turner (P46)

As I intended to join the RAF for national service I went into the navy section of the CCF, not as an example of supreme logic but mainly because it was the slackest. I never regretted it. One of the best Field Days was a trip to Motor Torpedo Boats in the Solent which finished up as a full naval battle with potatoes as missiles at close range between the two boats. At 35 knots a potato explodes with some force.

Brian Tullis (P46)

sanitary arrangements compared very favourably with those encountered in Mespot (Mesopotamia) early on in the First World War to which they helped to inure me." Andrews would doubtless have been pleased to know that his description would have been equally accurate of Corps' camps in the late 1950s.

'Though other demands on pupils' time have led to the demise of the band, in earlier days the Eastbourne College Corps of Drums regularly swept all before it in annual competitions, winning the Public Schools' Cup twenty-six times and being allowed to wear the king's colours on their bugle

Top: Guard of Honour for the Prince of Wales, later King Edward VII, 1899.

In 1952 the College was given a glider (right) to use, installed in pieces in the old pavilion on Memorial Field where we practised the rudiments of flying – though steering it away from the goalposts sometimes made for anxious moments. In the summer Corps camp that year three gliders were allocated to us and in the short space of a week we had, with the help of others from different schools, reduced them all to matchwood. How no-one was injured was a tribute to the design.

Adrian King (G48)

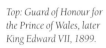

Corps of Drums formally and informally, c1975 (Roy Budgett).

lanyards. These results were all the more impressive considering that, in the main, both the drill and the musical instruction were undertaken by the cadets themselves. For fairly obvious reasons, shooting has always been considered an important Corps activity and here, without quite matching the success of the band, the College has also performed commendably.

Corps camp, 1890s.

For those of us at Eastbourne College in the early 1950s, the Second World War was still quite a recent, though fading, memory. R A (Tony) Henderson was a gunner who obtained his parachute 'wings' and still wore his red beret when he turned out for the CCF, of which he was for some time the commanding officer. To us he was known as 'Barrel' or 'Rajah', after his chest size and his style of speaking. He did not often talk about his war experiences, but one day he opened his desk drawer and showed us a hideous-looking iron and rubber weapon, which he had taken off a camp guard at Belsen concentration camp. He had been in the first contingent of paras to enter the camp and had discovered and disarmed the guard before he could do any further injury to the few surviving prisoners. Barrel was a fine poet in English, Latin and Greek, and an inspirational teacher. RSM Bill Strong (known to us as 'Arse M') was a fine figure of a man, with a commanding voice that could shake furniture and make young lads jump a foot in the air from 200 paces. The gym was his empire and boxing his favourite sport. Once a year he used to drill the entire Cadet Force at the annual parade and inspection: frightened birds used to scatter from their nests and the windows of Big School rattled. He had an interesting vocabulary, half Aldershot and half Rawalpindi, which he unleashed on young cadets when they lost the step or dropped their rifle.

Bugle-Major Ted Cherry was quite different. Small, round and rubicund, he had been in the Rifle Brigade and his prize possession was a beautiful silver bugle with all the battle honours of the 95th Regiment of Foot carved on the well-polished horn. When he put it to his lips it was as if a nightingale began to sing, and under his guidance the CCF band became one of the best in the country. His finest hour, however, came each year at 11am on 11 November when he played the 'Last Post' outside the chapel on Remembrance Day. You could hear it echoing in your eardrums for hours afterwards: his quavering high notes must surely have been heard by the angels in heaven.

The armoury and small-bore rifle range were the province of CSM Tony Watson, who was our instructor, armourer, coach and manager. For three years, because I was a member of the shooting VIII, I was his volunteer assistant, helper and hanger-on. In the summer the shooters used to go down to the full-bore rifle range on the Crumbles – a rag-tag group of about ten of us with Tony driving the truck and the rest of us on our bicycles. The Crumbles had a micro-climate of its own with sudden squalls and baking hot spells which made the targets swim before our eyes. The shingle made uncomfortable firing points and when we did 'fire with movement' we had to run across the shingle for 400 yards, swearing and sweating and firing as we went. Tony and his family lived not far away down Seaside Road and we used to drop in for tea and sometimes, when I was older, a pint; he gave me warm friendship and a family life which I rather missed in my barrack room existence at Blackwater.

George Low (B53)

> I was in the army section of the CCF and one year we had a night operation up on the Downs. Brian Jay and I were posted to protect a gorse bush from anticipated invaders coming from the Cuckmere valley. It was bitterly cold and raining torrents, so after a couple of hours – it was now 8pm – I suggested we should take a walk to the Eight Bells at Jevington. Since it was still raining at 10.30, the landlord suggested that we sleep in the bar and let ourselves out. We resumed our position at the gorse bush in the early hours, but seeing nothing but sheep decided to hitch back to Eastbourne – only to see the CCF parading in its entirety in Blackwater Road. We were able to melt in with the other cadets unnoticed – but were rather embarrassed when the Raeburn Cup, awarded to the best army cadet, was jointly given to Brian Jay and myself who were apparently the only cadets not captured on that operation.
>
> David Winn (S54)

Donald Perrens, 1972.

Above: CCF past and present, c1974 (from left to right): Bill Strong, John Underhill, Tom Rodd, Tony Henderson, Major General Goodwin, Forbes Wastie, Donald Perrens and Tony Watson.

Right: Admiral of the Fleet Sir Algernon Willis inspecting the Corps, 1955, with Lt Col Tony Henderson in attendance (Peter Rowe).

'It was during the Second World War that the single-service Officer Training Corps became the Junior Training Corps; then, in 1948, the Corps assumed its present title of Combined Cadet Force, and the Royal Navy and Royal Air Force sections came into being. On 15 June 1956 the Corps celebrated its Diamond Jubilee, with the parade taken by Admiral of the Fleet Sir Algernon Willis GCB KBE DSC DL (S02), the most senior officer the College has produced, in the presence of no fewer than seven of the original members of the Corps from 1896. The occasion marked the opening of a new headquarters, on Sears' Piece.

'Success for the Corps has depended over the years on small, dedicated groups of masters who, often

Inspection day, 1961 (Eric Koops).

The Civil Defence section of CCF would have been bussed out to the training facilities, like this one below, which I am pretty sure had tunnels and underground cellars. Most of our training involved inching stretchers out from impossible positions – unnerving for the 'casualty' – and the precariousness of the facilities did not seem to bother us or the authorities very much. I note we wore 'ammo' boots in those days, before the army was issued with moulded soles. The leather studded soles were fine for parade grounds but could be fairly lethal when clambering round rubble.

John Maclean (Pw58)

with little personal military experience, give of their time to lead and train the cadets. Perhaps the heyday of the Corps came in the twenty years immediately after the Second World War when the wartime experience and leadership of men like Lt Col Tony Henderson MBE MC JP TD and Wing Cdr Donald Perrens DSO OBE DFC were backed by the youthful enthusiasm of masters returning to teaching after having completed their national service. Further to the contribution of the officers must be added the part played in the success of the Corps by former regular soldiers such as RSM Bill Strong and CSM (later Captain) Tony Watson BEM. These two remarkable individuals, plus today's CSM, Tim Lucey, provide continuity going back seventy years to when Bill Strong first joined in 1937.

'Though the Corps is not itself either part of the armed forces or a recruiting agency, there is clearly

Donald Perrens ran a very active RAF section of the CCF, including a bungey-launched glider on the Links field and summer camps at stations such as Wildenrath in Germany, which included flying in the jump seat of a Canberra. I am sure he will remember with pride the time the CCF could boast six qualified pilots thanks to the flying scholarship scheme. Unfortunately, the plan to put on a six-plane fly-past on Inspection Day did not come to fruition for lack of enough aircraft or accompanying crew.

Peter Lloyd-Bostock (B61)

The CCF parading on the seafront before the Duke of Edinburgh for the funeral of the tenth Duke of Devonshire, 1950 (Nicolas Hemes).

As I crouched on College Field in the darkness, finger on the 'big red button', I could hear the assembled school behind me, counting down with all the enthusiasm of a First XV rugby match – 'ten, nine, eight…'. The Blue Book clearly states that no pupils are to have explosives, and yet here was a sixth former about to ignite a quarter of a ton of fireworks from the rooftops of the College buildings… with the headmaster and 100 military top brass in attendance. It was the evening of 9 May 1996. 'Zero' came, and the tower erupted in a thunderous blaze of colour and light.

The story begins a century earlier, when in 1896 the College Combined Cadet Force was formed. Now the celebrations for the CCF centenary were reaching their explosive climax. The day had seen all the pomp the school could muster: two helicopter landings on the field, inspection of an extensive Field Day by invited military guests, a full parade of the CCF accompanied by 'beating the retreat' from the band of the Royal Marines, prizegiving in Big School, a sumptuous formal meal and a firework display to close the evening.

Somehow, John Little (CCF commanding officer) and Tim Lucey (CSM) had convinced both the headmaster and the bursar to hand over responsibility for the firework display to an enthusiastic sixth former from Craig House to whom, somewhat unusually, the local authorities had the year before granted a pyrotechnics licence. My display featured fireworks launched simultaneously from the field, the roof of Doc Ed's science lab and the roof of Big School, with as the centrepiece a 20ft-high representation of the CCF cap badge outlined in fireworks. The whole ten-minute event was a roaring success, and as the smoke cleared we were all pleased to see that neither the tower nor Big School were ablaze.

Of the same event, John Little recalls that 'the large number of distinguished guests at the dinner in the evening had to listen to GFW summarising the hundred years of the CCF by candlelight since the lighting in the dining hall for the evening had managed to blow the main fuse in the kitchens.' He also records that 'as the College was the torpedo training school HMS Marlborough during the war, it was with particular pleasure that we were able to secure affiliation with the latest Type 23 frigate HMS Marlborough in 1991. From the beginning this was a strong affiliation – nearly all the serving captains visited, and indeed on one occasion the ship anchored off Eastbourne and the captain and members of the ship's company joined us for supper, after which the band of the Royal Marines beat the retreat on College Field. We had a dispensation to fly the White Ensign from the tower for the first time since 1947.

Sam Woodward (C90)

CCF on College Field, Remembrance Sunday, 2006 (John Thornley).

'The Last Post',
Remembrance Sunday,
2006 (John Thornley).

I played the bugle in the Corps of Drums and was asked to play 'Last Post' and 'Reveille' at the Memorial Arch on Remembrance Sunday. There I was, aged sixteen, incredibly nervous and not a little afraid, ready to do my bit. Suddenly I realised that I was playing in memory of lads maybe only a year older than myself who had felt greater fear and nerves giving their all in defence of their country. Even to a cynical sixteen-year-old this thought brought great poignancy to the moment and is a memory that stays with me every year.

Mark Pickett (R73)

Three years ago, while 'tramping' in New Zealand, a flightless native bird rustled out of the undergrowth and started to peck at my boots with its long curved bill, as if wanting to eat them. That was when I decided to chuck these fetid and by now leaking old boots and buy a new pair. I had owned and worn the old pair for hiking in Sussex, Northumbria, Yorkshire and Australia since the age of thirteen, having had them resoled a number of times. I used them regularly from 1965 until 2002, which adds up to thirty-eight years' continuous service. They were my College CCF boots. Is this a record?

Mike Scott (Pw64)

The evening before Field Day we trekked out to Og's Wood for our practice expedition, but in the early evening it snowed very heavily. At about 9.30pm Forbes arrived (we hastily hid our cigarettes and beer, although I am sure he knew we had them) and told us that we had to return to College as Field Day had been cancelled. We expressed considerable disappointment as we had come so far, and assured him we would be OK. He bravely took the decision to leave us there to complete our task (no mobile phones in those days). The next day, after a fun night in the snow, we returned to College, having completed our expedition and missed lessons – much to the annoyance of many of our peers who had had no Field Day.

Tim Wood (G&C66)

something of an umbilical cord between the CCF and the military. For many the drill, the seemingly pointless discipline, the unappealing uniforms, the boots that are a pain to clean may all serve to deter the potential recruit, but for others the Corps has been the first step in long and successful military careers. Despite its relatively small size, ever since the 1920s the College has been among the top thirty providers of cadets to Sandhurst, and the contribution of Old Eastbournians in both world wars and in other lesser

I entered the navy section and was issued the 1918 uniform: the white summer tank-top vest (to be ironed with a convex V down the front) and blue winter jersey, the jumper, with silk ('for picking up greasy cannon balls, lad') to be folded and ironed until one inch wide, and lanyard ('for whistling to attract attention when drowning at sea, lad'). Then the extraordinary 'jean' collar, tied around one's body under the jumper, with the collar pulled out and folded ('to avoid pigtail Macassar oil staining the jumper, lad'), to be ironed in the shape of a W, with three white stripes ('for Nelson's victories, lad'). Then the bell-bottomed trousers ('easy to slip off in the water, unlike pongos' (army) trousers and gaiters, lad'), to be ironed with a vertical inverted crease down each side, and with alternately folded and ironed horizontal creases down the length – five for short people ('for the five oceans, lad') and seven for taller people ('for the seven seas, lad'). This was topped off with the hat, with band sporting a tiddly-bow.

Jeremy Lovitt-Danks (W55)

RN section returning from HMS Vanguard, *July 1951 (Keith Norman Smith).*

Harry Watson ironing his kit, 2000.

campaigns has been significant. There were 164 Eastbournians who gave their lives in the First World War and, though overall national losses were to be dramatically lower, the College lost a further 163 of her sons in the Second World War. During these major wars there was not a campaign on sea, land or air in which Old Eastbournians were not present, and the decorations awarded to former members of the school serve as testimony both to their courage and to the importance of their contributions.

'Apart from the uniforms, the Corps today differs from its predecessors in many ways, not least because the school curriculum offers a range of alternative voluntary activities. Cadets join after their first year and, though they may volunteer to stay longer, are only committed to one compulsory year; female cadets abound and adventure training plays an important part in the modern CCF programme. Activities include sailing, mountain biking, archery, canoeing, clay pigeon shooting and many others, as well as camps in the midst of challenging terrain. The

centenary in 1996 was marked by a spectacular fireworks display, and at the time of writing there are Old Eastbournians serving across the world with all three services.'

CCF Field Day, 2006 (Tim Lucey)

Duke of Edinburgh Award Scheme

before attacking the Lake District for the qualifying expedition; one memorable group yomped east to west for fifty miles with no slope seeming too steep for them. Some gold participants have gone further afield on expeditions to the Rockies in Canada or sailing in the Faroe Islands. For a while the numbers involved, the availability of courses and increased academic pressures resulted in the decision to offer only direct entry gold….' More recently still, as David Miller reports, the Bronze Award again became available.

Eric Koops (G59) remembers the start in 1960 of the Award Scheme at the College: 'I attained my Gold Award in 1961 after successfully completing a fifty-mile expedition over four days in Snowdonia. I received my award at St James's Palace in December that year; I believe it was only the second presentation ceremony held there since the award scheme had started in 1956. Later, I greatly enjoyed helping to organise the scheme at the College for those doing their Bronze and Silver Awards. I took one group to the New Forest during the Easter holidays, and checked up on expedition groups at weekends along with Forbes Wastie or, when he was not available, Michael Birley. Little did I know then that, twenty-five years later, I would spearhead the setting up of a worldwide organisation with the support of His Royal Highness.'

John Little was involved more recently and oversaw the rapid growth of the scheme: 'We soon had over 200 participants working at all three levels. All too often in the summer term five Bronze expeditions were out on a weekend navigating their way round the South Downs. Some did try to avoid too much trekking, but Doc Ed soon found out about the taxi! Silver expeditions tended to involve Cornwall, and those going for Gold used Dartmoor and the Peak District for practice

World Challenge expeditions have also formed part of some Duke of Edinburgh qualifying challenges, after it was

suggested in 1989 that an expedition to Ecuador might be attempted. John Little again: 'Due to an outbreak of cholera in Ecuador, the first destination was changed to the Himalayas. Since then there have been many expeditions across the globe, some of them achieving firsts – for example, we were the youngest team to climb Nairamdal on the borders of Mongolia, China and Russia, and the first non-Russian team to reach the summit of Ala-Kul Kyry in the Tien Shan mountains of Kyrgyzstan, though an approaching thunderstorm meant that our time on the summit was cut short.

'Weather and transport have played an important role in these expeditions. On one occasion roads and bridges were washed away and when we eventually arrived back at our transport it was to find that it too was in the middle of a river. Teams have ventured along the most dangerous road in the world, have watched a plane taking off with all their kit on board and experienced the dubious comfort of trekking on Mongolian ponies through raging glacial water. As well as the mountains of central Asia and South America, we have experienced the jungles of Borneo and the Amazon, and have worked within local communities including the ECHO project in Lima, Peru. We have learned that the only true international language is football, with matches being won or lost with all the locals out in support. And it is not all work – there is always time for r&r whether it is chilling out on the beaches of Venezuela or some retail therapy in the markets of Ulan Bator (anyone for a Kalashnikov?).'

Opposite top: Shaving on expedition in the 1960s: Eric Koops and Andrew Bazergan.

Opposite bottom: Duke of Edinburgh with Tim Wood and others, c1970 (Tim Wood).

Above left: Bolivia, 1999: on the summit of Murarata (John Little).

Top: On the Ala-Kul glacier in Terskey Alatau, Kyrgyzstan 2004 (John Little).

Above: In the Lake District, 2004 (Tim Lucey).

Chapel

Today's chaplain, Chris Macdonald, writes: 'The College chapel was opened and dedicated as an Anglican chapel in 1874 by the then Bishop of Chichester. It has since been enlarged to meet the needs of a growing school community. Built in red brick and now with plastered walls, the architecture of this beautiful and much-loved building is typically Victorian, and yet it somehow has the feel of a medium-sized parish church. The wooden pews are not original and have come from Worcester Cathedral, and the ambience and colour of the place were further enhanced in 2000 by the lovely kneelers, embroidered and donated by friends of the College led by Mary Bush, wife of the then headmaster. The building

Above: Chris Macdonald with College porter Peter Sanders.

Left: The chapel before the addition of the chancel and transept in 1889 and north and south aisles in 1929.

> *I always enjoyed chapel – the singing, the formality, sometimes the peace and quiet – and was in time confirmed. The Rev Alfred Bird was chaplain in my time. It is something that I look back on as having given me a certain stability in life, especially when all is not going particularly well, and to give thanks when it is. I continue to be a regular worshipper and when out and about always try and visit the local church and cathedral. Marvellous places, full of history and often an opportunity to sit and think and pray for a few minutes. Perhaps Eastbourne College gave this to me?*
>
> Richard Browne (B49)

Choristers outside chapel, 2006.

contains some beautiful stained glass windows, many of which have been given in memory of former pupils and staff of the College. These and other memorials to the many OEs killed in the wars of the late nineteenth and twentieth centuries make the chapel in some ways a rather poignant place, a feeling enhanced by the plaques remembering other students, staff and OEs.

'The fact that the chapel can comfortably seat only about 350 people at a time means that it isn't possible to accommodate the whole school community together; yet this does mean that services have a more intimate feel than many larger school chapels, and it is possible for a speaker to make eye contact with nearly everyone. All members of the College community have access to the building and can go there any time they like, to pray or reflect or simply to have some space. In a busy and vibrant school, where there is always something going on, it is a place where people can get away from it all and be on their own or with friends.

'Chapel services are within the central tradition of the Church of England. The College has a rich choral tradition and an outstanding choir, with some parents and members of the local community regularly attending services. Sermons are kept short, working on the principle that if you haven't struck oil in six or seven minutes it's generally best to stop boring. Some evening services are created and led by the students themselves, with different houses, and occasionally the school Christian Union, putting on services. Collections are taken at Sunday services to be donated to a variety of good causes, some of which are suggested by the students themselves.

'One of the highlights in recent years was when the BBC broadcast a College chapel service live on Radio 4 on 19 January 2003 to an estimated audience of two million (the fourth time the College has provided chapel services for the BBC). It was the outstanding quality of the choir that led to this accolade. The theme of the service was the "Challenge of Faith", and it was conducted by the chaplain with contributions from ten different pupils who either led the prayers or talked about their experiences of trying to lead Christian lives with all the pressures on teenagers today. And of course there were stunning contributions by the choir. We received nearly 200 letters from all over the country (and beyond) congratulating us, one of which was from the renowned broadcaster Canon Eric James, who wrote

to say that it was as good as any service he had heard broadcast in forty years.

'About once a year a wedding service is held in the chapel as former pupils return to school to get married here, and from time to time OEs bring their children for baptism. Indeed, when OEs visit the College, the chapel is often the building they want to visit most. In some cases this is because the building has changed comparatively little in recent decades. More often old

Top right: The west window.

Right: Bishop Walter Carey.

boys and girls comment on how the College chapel and the various chaplains sowed seeds within them that only grew and ripened in later life. They often comment on how they didn't much like having to go to services when they were at school, but how much they have grown to appreciate what they learned there in later life.'

The Rt Rev Bishop Walter Carey, formerly Bishop of Bloemfontein in South Africa, was a charismatic and memorable College chaplain from 1936 to 1940 and again from 1945 to 1948. Anecdotes about him abound. He was a larger than life figure who became chaplain purely coincidentally after attending a religious event in Big School unconnected to the College, and being asked to lunch by the then headmaster, Gordon Carey (no relation). It emerged over the meal that the bishop was suffering from ill health and was in the midst of somewhat anxious

*A sevice in chapel
(John Keeling).*

cogitations about his future. When Carey said impulsively 'What about a school chaplaincy – here, for instance?' the bishop – somewhat surprised, and after thought – accepted the post. He introduced himself to the assembled school in chapel on his first day with the words, 'I'd better begin by saying that I'm not, as most of you probably imagine, the headmaster's grandfather or something of that sort…'.

He was an Oxford rugby blue, so added coaching and supporting the rugby teams to his duties. He was particularly involved with the Third XV, who became known as the Tigers after he had commended them for 'fighting like tigers' at a match in 1938; Brian Mulvany then decided to formalise the team name and set up the Tigers Club in 1939. Michael Girling (P33) remembers Carey well: 'That he was a rugger blue, smoked cheap cigarettes and was generally somewhat eccentric in approach endeared him to many of us. I remember one evening service when the preacher was billed as the oldest Old Eastbournian. As the bishop escorted him to the pulpit steps it was obvious that he would have difficulty mounting them. Whereupon the bishop

pushed him up, saying in a loud voice, "He and I were in the Ark together."'

Dermot Hoare (B44) has another memory: 'His sermons were legendary: in the winter life was like a game of rugby with its goal posts and touch lines; in the summer life was like a game of cricket with wickets and boundaries. What would he have used as a parallel with girls in the school, one asks! He deplored

> *I must add that our school chaplain had a great influence on us all. Geoffrey Evans (or 'Rev Ev' as he was affectionately known) was always gracious and generous, not least when in the fifth form I shocked myself by breaking the senior cross-country record. Rev Ev supplied the RE class that evening with celebratory beer in very charitable amounts. We were all convinced that our school chaplain should without hesitation be canonised. Needless to say, the English lesson that followed with Keith Budge saw impressive acting of the parts of Enobarbus, not to mention Antony and Cleopatra, thanks to the Party Seven Eucharist.*
>
> **Stephen Gray (Pw79)**

My father Peter Phillips (School House housemaster, 1959–74) was a gentle giant known affectionately by the boys as 'Brute', whose sawn-off squash racquet was known as 'Percy the Persuader'.

I was a very young and shy eleven-year-old when we went to live in School House in 1959. Every time there was a knock on the door I would hide behind the curtains. Dad's study was located at the foot of the stairs and most evenings there would be a long queue of boys waiting to have an audience. Sometimes I waited an eternity for the queue to disperse so that I could venture downstairs. By the time I was fifteen things had changed a little. My older sister Derry was at boarding school, totally opposite to me, always chatting up the boys. Big sister organised a blind date for me with one of the School House boys, Tony Ling. We met one Sunday afternoon on the promenade (in bounds). Now, forty-three years later, we are still together and have returned to Eastbourne. We married in the College chapel in 1971 (left). Our two sons, Daniel and Andy, were both educated at the College and of course were in School House. Sadly Dad died in 1986, but he would be very proud of his grandsons and their achievements. Now there is a great-grandson Freddie, born in 2006 to Daniel and Kate, and who knows, maybe he will go to the College and keep his great-grandfather's spirit alive.

Stephanie Ling, née Phillips

boys coughing during his sermons and entreated us to suck sweets rather than cough. By chance the *Daily Mirror* heard of this and printed an article under the banner "Bishop tells boys to suck sweets in church", and the next day a crate of Meggazones (the then well-known cough sweet) was delivered to his house.'

His hair-raising driving was legendary. As Dermot Hoare also recalls, 'On one half holiday he kindly drove me to Canterbury to see the cathedral. My belief in God stemmed from that drive for, even though I couldn't drive, I could see he was an appalling driver; swerving from one side of the road and then back again, shooting across road junctions and crossroads with never a sideways glance and gesticulating wildly with both hands as he talked. Only a God could have saved us that day!' Anthony Bryant (Pw45) has a similar memory: 'Two of us were walking along Compton Place Road on our way to the Memorial Field to play rugger when the bishop drew up driving his Austin. We were asked if we would like a lift, and we thanked him and climbed aboard. As was his custom he had a cigarette in one hand while the other held the steering wheel. The road in question has rather a high pavement on one side and the wall surrounding the Saffrons cricket

Chaplain Chris Macdonald christening Rebecca Lamb, daughter of Gonville housemaster Anthony Lamb, in the chapel, 2003.

ground on the other side. The trouble was, he would turn round to speak to us. We were wondering which obstacle would be our downfall, the pavement or the wall. In the event we arrived safely, although we fell out of the car rather than actually climbed; as the other players were walking we just had time to settle our nerves.' And Maurice Wyles (P44) recalls that the bishop 'put his trust in God while driving, and his passengers certainly needed faith. Lifts offered to his "Tigers" could be hazardous as he vigorously turned the steering wheel to demonstrate the wheeling of a scrum.' He has another memory too: 'A service to commemorate the fallen of the Second World War was held late on a Saturday morning. The Tonbridge XV, our opponents on that day, arrived in time to join us in chapel. At the conclusion of the service Bishop Walter prayed for a good match, and victory for the College. *The Tonbridgian* recorded that facing Eastbourne was one thing, but Eastbourne plus the Almighty proved too much.' His support for College rugby was unceasing. As John Congdon (P44) recalls, 'He took a keen interest in the First XV, and once – since he could no longer walk – drove his little Austin Seven on to the pitch at half time to tell the amazed College side how they could win the match. This didn't go down well with the rugby staff, nor with the headmaster, and he was cautioned not to do anything like that again. But had he felt strongly enough, we all knew that not for one moment would he have hesitated.'

The bishop also had robust political opinions. Michael Clark (Pw42) remembers doing his utmost to avoid nodding off during a sermon at the time when the Cold War was hotting up, and being abruptly jerked awake by the bishop roaring in a thunderous voice 'Molotov! I could spew him out of my mouth.' He also, as Maurice Wyles recalls, 'drew himself up to his full and impressive height, put his hands behind his back, put patriotism before charity and refused to greet Hewlett Johnson, known as the Red Dean for his Communist sympathies, with anything other than a curt nod.'

It is clear that he is remembered with huge affection, and that he had a lasting effect on the lives of many of those who knew him. John Congdon again: 'Without any doubt he was one of the great influences on my life. Not least because of him, I moved forward to ordination. He taught me that being a Christian should be fun. And through his amazing personality, warmth and genuineness of faith, something of the spirit of Jesus himself shone through and touched me

Confirmands with, from left, Cliff Comyns, Chris Macdonald and the Bishop of Lewes, 2006 (John Thornley).

and many others of my generation. He was, quite simply, an amazing man.'

Hair-raising driving seems to have been rather a speciality among College chapel staff. Cliff Comyns was, between 1975 and 2006, a much-loved assistant chaplain who did much of the administrative and organisational work associated with the chapel. He recalls that Ron Johnson, chaplain 1985–99, hated being driven by him: 'One day when he was in the car I cornered too quickly and bumped a traffic island. "What was that?" I asked innocently. "Probably St Christopher getting out" was Ron's reply!' As he also says, 'I only remember happenings if they are amusing – everything else disappears. On one occasion, just before a Leavers' Service, Ron walked into the vestry sporting the most appalling haircut which he uncomfortably hoped no-one would notice. I started the service by welcoming everyone to this special event, and pointing out that the chaplain and I had made an effort – we were both wearing clean surplices and Ron had had his hair cut. His first words to me after the service were to cast a grave shadow of doubt on the legality of my parents' marriage.' Cliff also remembers with pleasure his stint as a tutor in School House: 'One evening I had locked up and was about to get into my car when a girl appeared who had gone out with her boyfriend and had "miscalculated" the time of her return. When I told her that she would certainly be in trouble because the only way in was by ringing the bell, she smiled and produced a mobile phone. It was not long before her friend appeared in a dressing gown and let her in.'

Charitable activities

In 1906 the headmaster, F S Williams, encouraged the establishment of the Eastbourne College Mission in Bethnal Green. This started as two boys' clubs, run by a warden and staff with the help of London OEs and funded by individual annual donations and chapel collections. The clubs organised concerts, cricket and football matches, swimming galas and other activities including an annual camp. There was also an annual visit to Eastbourne where the club members would swim, play sports and be entertained to tea. Much of the organisation was in the hands of OEs, and College boys participated. David Stinson (S34) remembers cycling from his home in Beckenham to the camp at Kingsdown on the Channel coast in Kent, and other OEs, notably John Maccoy (W35) and John Millard (W45), recall being part of teams of boys visiting the Mission giving gymnastic exhibitions and helping with lessons. From the 1920s the club was based at St Simon Zelotes church, and after it was destroyed by a bomb in 1944 the Mission, soon to be known as Eastbourne House, continued to flourish at St John's church.

Len Herbert, now in his eighties and living in Australia, was one of the East End boys who benefited from the Mission: 'I can't estimate how much influence your Mission had on my early development, but I am sure it helped in giving me a fulfilling and useful life.' And Arthur Grove remembers camps in 1936 and 1937 at Westham and Whitsun visits to Eastbourne which would close with tea in front of the pavilion and music from the bugle band.

Members of the College engaged in other charitable activities too, with masters in the 1930s taking groups of boys to work with the unemployed in Dowlais, Stockton and Durham. And in the 1960s the Social Commandos were formed to work in Eastbourne, visiting those who needed help with household jobs or gardening, taking old people out in wheelchairs or just chatting over cups of tea. Working parties were arranged to decorate rooms for elderly townspeople, and others visited a home for the blind to read or play music, or again just chat. The Bethnal Green Mission closed in 1967, partly because of the difficulty of recruiting staff and help and also because of the increasingly heavy academic demands on

College pupils. But charitable work continued unabated. In the 1980s Forbes Wastie and later David West took parties of boys and girls to St Botolph's crypt project in London to help at this day centre for the homeless, and groups of pupils continue to take part in charity work both locally in Eastbourne – for example at the hospital or in charity shops – and further afield. Fund-raising for specific charities includes a range of sponsored activities under the aegis of the Charity Committee, formed in the 1980s as coordination and management support, though students often also set up their own projects. A more recent initiative is ECHO (Eastbourne College Help Overseas), which was the College's charitable millennium project and currently supports three programmes: nurseries in Lima, Peru; a secondary school, Tiger Kloof, in South Africa; and orphanages in Poland. As well as providing financial support, the College encourages gap year students and those on overseas challenge expeditions to visit and work at these projects.

Bella Stewart at a nursery school in Lima, Peru, 2006 (Maddie Eckert).

Music

The early years of music at Eastbourne College were interlinked with St Saviour's church in South Street, where on Sundays boarders attended services; this lasted until the opening of the College chapel in 1874. There was a succession of music masters in the early years, until in 1887 Frank Gillett, organist of St Peter's church, was appointed; he was to stay at the College for the next twenty-seven years. He set the school song ('Exaltemus, o sodales') to music, as well as the first rugby football song ('Now we'll sing you a song of the grand old game') written by E C Arnold in 1901. Graham Jones, the current director of music, in his history of College music written in the summer of 2006, quotes Gordon Carey's tribute to Gillett after his death in the 1930s: 'Gillett's organ playing… was grievously faulty but he was a most efficient choir trainer and, in charge of the school choral society, he managed, somehow, every December, to achieve a creditable performance of some fairly ambitious musical work.' Graham Jones adds that with these concerts, which featured a choral society of up to eighty singers and were usually held in the Town Hall, Gillett was the first of several key players to bring the then growing town into College musical life and see the importance of integrating the two for their mutual benefit. Carey concludes that Gillett was 'the kindest and most lovable as well as one of the wisest of men.'

Music at the College did not have a high profile during the First World War and afterwards, relying on a number of visiting instrumentalists and assistant masters with no-one to coordinate what they were doing. Allom's centenary book records that George Peacock 'with little encouragement from above, managed to keep a chapel choir in existence', with Elsie Reed as organist; she was to play a prominent part in music both at the College and at Ascham until

String quartet by the Memorial Arch, 2005.

her retirement in 1963. Arnold did not give music a great deal of support during his headship though, paradoxically, one of the boys at the time was the future eminent musician Ralph Nicholson (G21; composer, conductor and professor at the Royal College of Music), who observed in his autobiography: 'Our housemaster Mr Morres, who was very fond of music, sometimes allowed me to slip away from prep to go down to Devonshire Park to a recital by someone like the great violinist Fritz Kreisler.' He went on to comment, 'there must have been hope for the future as the facilities at the College were good. There was a modest little lady called Elsie Reed who taught the piano and played the organ in chapel… but I, naturally, felt the best hope for instruments was the teacher of violin, W J Read. He was a splendid player

Massed choirs and orchestra rehearsing in Chichester Cathedral, Graham Jones conducting (John Thornley).

The sound of the whole College singing has an impact which is simply physical, and is so powerful it can be dangerous. You may get used to it and start to think everywhere does likewise. But they don't. On my elder daughter's last Speech Day, in 1986, I persuaded my father to attend, and have three generations of Eastbournians on College Field together. The day started with the Speech Day service in All Saints' Church: it is always an emotional moment, and for many present it is the end of their schooldays. My father was beside me and Susan was in the choir. The organ led us into the first hymn and more than five hundred voices gave it everything they had: it was like a blow. I saw my father flinch, and he seemed shaky all morning. Later he said, 'It was that first note, like a trumpet call. It shook me rigid. And I started thinking how long it had been since I had heard that sound, those voices – nearly sixty years.' Powerful medicine – prescribe with great care.

Robin 'RC' Armstrong Brown (W51)

and teacher, and I learnt a lot from him during my five years there and we became firm friends.' The 1920s did see new music facilities in the tower of the Memorial Building, which would remain the centre of musical activity until the 1950s, and Ralph Nicholson returned in the 1930s to lead the violas or second violins in choral and orchestral concerts in Big School.

In 1931 Gordon Carey appointed the first full-time director of music, J S Lowe. Carey had resurrected the choral society as well as reviving the orchestra, and the first house music competition was held in 1934. More pupils were going on to study music at tertiary level, the music society was vibrant and the level of music appreciation and participation within the College had deepened considerably, with several masters – Bishop Carey, John Belk and Robert Storrs among others – involved in music-making. In 1938 Peter Temple became director of music, though he was soon to be called up, and John Alden took charge during the Radley years.

Temple returned after the war, with 'Jack' Phillipson, and they faced the challenge of reforming the orchestra which had become enfeebled during wartime. The late 1940s and early 1950s record the rejuvenation of music generally, both orchestral and choral. Many pupils were learning the piano and other instruments, and the Corps of Drums was flourishing. Moreover, several boys went on to study music and to make their careers in it, including Ian Sykes (later Ian Fraser, whose highly successful musical work, including collaborations with Julie Andrews and other stars, has won him eleven Emmys). The music room was still in the tower, as Brian Polden (S48) remembers: 'Piano teachers were "imported" souls whose lot was to suffer the endless stairs, seasonal temperature fluctuations and ill-regulated practice pianos that had been craftily secreted almost beyond earshot at the top of the tower. It was a mystery as to how they had got there.' But there were now plans for a new music school, consisting of a concert room, two teaching rooms and ten practice rooms; it opened in 1955.

There were several joint productions with town musical societies, and both orchestra and choir were increasingly augmented by players and singers from Moira House and Eastbourne High School. Chamber music concerts now took place, and a junior orchestra was formed. The new headmaster, Michael Birley, and his wife both sang in the December 1956 concert as members of the choral society, and a jazz group was

If music be the food of love, we had a fair sized larder. Despite the wartime privations, the aura of old-established values and traditions remained intact, including the College song which few of us liked or sang properly. The chapel, of course, was a fulcrum around which much else revolved – for me, organ, piano, choir and the lighter-hearted Glee Club. In the choir voices broke and former angelic-sounding trebles and altos were banned for a year before being voice-tested to decide where, if at all, they now fitted. In having to sing a new part everything that had been second nature before had now to be unlearned; either that or stick to what one knew and merely sing it an octave or two lower down – an inspirational technique that could generate at least seven-part harmony where only four was called for, thus embellishing the entire rendition and encouraging the distraught choirmaster to think about early retirement.

The organist was often in trouble because the lusty congregational singing was too much for the organ as it then was, buried away in its alcove. Solution? Hang a microphone in front of it to catch the sound, including wind noises from creaky bellows and mechanical clatter from moving parts. Result? Unintended 'noises off', distortion and pronounced hiss. Moreover, the instrument's mechanical tracker action was falling to pieces; notes became stuck down allowing the appropriate pipe, or pipes, to continue sounding. Solution? Incarcerate an idiot volunteer – me – inside the swell box near roof level to grab the offending non-returning parts. One was inspired to assist the sound output by whistling the tune as loudly as possible, thinking – wrongly – that one could not be heard above the pipework. The hapless organist was thus offered the luxury of an additional stop he didn't know he had. The result was predictable: congregational mirth, a disconcerted player and a reaction from the ecclesiastical quarter that was less than holy.

Brian Polden (S48)

Who can possibly forget John Walker? He was an institution in himself. Single-handedly he would take the entire school (masters included) through the glorious complexities of the 'Hallelujah Chorus' or 'Zadok the Priest' in preparation for Speech Day. His rehearsal sessions were memorable in themselves: his passion, his humour, his outbursts and – finally – his praise ('Right! I think you've got it. At least, I think that will have to do. Thank you everyone.') And so we would congregate on the morning of Speech Day, with blue cornflowers in our lapels, to sing the rousing chorus that we had rehearsed as a school.

Colin Brezicki

Above: The Corps of Drums, 1951.

Opposite below: John Walker and the choir, 1971 (Brian Sawyer).

Right: Giles Colclough at the organ, 2006.

started. By 1961 the house music competition had to be divided over three terms to accommodate the different individual categories.

In 1965 John Walker arrived as director of music, and the following year the choir combined with other musical groups in the Congress Theatre to sing Orff's *Carmina Burana* with professional soloists and an orchestra of professional players assembled for the occasion. Future concerts would now routinely engage well established professional orchestras. The Glee Club had been revived in 1962, and in 1967 the Folk Club was born. The centenary festival week in May that year began with two concerts involving twelve local schools (both

singers and players) and reached its climax with a performance of *West Side Story* in the Congress Theatre which attracted ten minutes of ovation after the last performance, and countless curtain calls. By the early 1970s there were ten visiting instrumental teachers covering brass, cello, double bass, guitar, piano, violin and woodwind. An annual musical (with cast from the lower sixth) was now part of the regular programme, initially conducted by Walker and directed by Philip Le Brocq, with the later involvement of other staff members such as Graham Jones and Andrew Boxer. A decision was taken to cease house music competitions and house concerts began to replace them. Performances in the Old Time Music Hall format began (to raise money for College choral society productions) and summer holidays saw the College close-harmony singers go to Cornwall with John Walker to sing and raise money for charity. Charles Halliday remembers 'singing a duet with Andrew Wicks in a Powell House concert. Andrew, now a

It's the wall of sound when a hymn starts that gets me every time. I remember it so clearly from College days, and yet it still surprises and stirs me whenever I return to a service where College pupils are singing. Anywhere else a communal hymn sounds thin and weedy in comparison. I remember my first Speech Day when trumpeters and pupils playing other brass instruments and drums were brought in – just in case the sound wasn't loud enough already. The congregation seemed to ignite, rugby heroes singing along with delicate third formers, united in a chorus without embarrassment and singing as loudly as possible without any feeling that it wasn't cool.

Vicky Henley (N75)

professional singer, was once head chorister at Chichester Cathedral, and after the concert Simon Langdale remarked to me that it must have been like batting with Hobbs!'

Graham Jones joined as assistant director of music in September 1976, and shortly afterwards the music facilities were improved by the addition of a building now known as the new music school. By the early 1980s there were, among other events, three orchestral concerts a year (one in St Saviour's), an annual visit to Chichester to sing evensong in the cathedral, an advent and Christmas carol service, sometimes a choral concert, regular sung chapel services, summer musicals and music club concerts.

Summer 1991 saw the retirement of John Walker after twenty-six years. A tribute to him said that 'his influence was mostly felt in the chapel where he was concerned with decent though unfussy observation of the ritual and encouraged the choir to sing reverently but with heart. He would never acknowledge the second rate. His music-making was never precocious, his performances never pretentious.' He was responsible for innovations like brass and percussion in the Speech Day service as well as many arrangements particularly for the choir, and he left a magnificent legacy of congregational singing. Graham Jones now took over as director of music and David Force was appointed College organist and assistant director of music. The summer musical gave way to one produced biennially at the end of the Michaelmas term and now involving all year groups, and high standards in choral singing were sustained, augmented by broadcasts on national radio, the production of CDs, an additional visit to sing evensong, this time at Winchester Cathedral, prep schools singing with the College choir and roadshows which included the swing band. These activities developed into annual prep school days each term, one for choral, one for jazz and one for strings. Practical music-making was increasing and there have been many masterclasses, often given by past pupils who have gone on to successful musical careers and return to perform and inspire. The choral concert became an annual event, involving the College choir and other singers (pupils, parents, friends) and now accompanied by the Eastbourne Symphony Orchestra. The ESO had been founded in 1979 by, among others, the College's then deputy head John Evans (concert manager, later replaced by John Thornley), Alan Gardner

John Walker with the Cornwall Singers (Vicky Henley).

(housemaster of Wargrave) and Graham Jones. So continued the tradition, set by Frank Gillett in the early 1900s, of College music playing a part in the musical life of the town. In 1999 the choral concert moved from the Congress Theatre to Chichester Cathedral, thus extending the College's musical presence into the further reaches of the diocese.

After the College returned from Radley in 1945, there was a great need to renew the music programme. A couple of things stick in my mind. The orchestra was very small and had no violas. Mr Phillipson said that if someone was willing to learn the instrument, he would give them a viola. I guess my hand was the first one he saw, and to this day I still have my viola, although as it and I grow old together, it gets played less each year. As a thank you, I took a picture of the Memorial Building, developed and enlarged it and gave it to Mr Phillipson. When we visited him twenty years after I left the College and he was at Ascham, the picture, suitably framed, hung in his office.

I was also a member of the choral society and a predicament was how to get the female voices where they were needed. The solution was to enlist girls from Moira House who would sing the upper parts. It now seems quaint, but at rehearsals and performances there was always a row of teachers or empty chairs between the girls' sections and those where we sat. How things have changed!

Peter Homburger (S42)

The 1995 academic year saw full coeducation, which was to have an inevitable impact on musical activity including a greater take-up of academic musical studies. Recent years have seen a huge variety of musical activities of all sorts and at all stages in the pupils' school career. Current staff comprise four full-time and nineteen part-time teachers. Other staff are involved too, and academic music results are increasingly impressive, with music technology – supported by new recording and sequencing facilities (provided by a generous OE) – a popular choice. Music is firmly at the heart of the College, academically, socially and as a valuable and much-loved out-of-class activity.

Left: Music technology lesson, 2006.

Above left: Brian Polden at the organ, c1971.

Above: Roydon Tse receives a masterclass, 2006.

COLLEGE SONGS

The Eastbourne College school song, the *Carmen Eastbourniense*, Arnold's rugby songs and the new millennium hymn are all part of the long musical history of the College. They are reproduced in full in the Appendix, with first verses and chorus given below.

The *Carmen* arrived with Bayfield when he became headmaster in 1895. He had composed much of it during his days at Malvern and he now added some verses appropriate only to Eastbourne; an English version of the Latin was also produced, and the song was set to music by W S Bambridge, though Frank Gillett later wrote a new tune for it. It has not been sung for many years.

John ('Bouncy') Barratt, nicknamed for his walk, was one of the music teachers and ran the Glee Club (for broken voices only), which gave me my lasting love of madrigals. I also sang in the chapel choir and choral society, and was allowed to sing down the parts as my voice broke – I don't think that would be approved of today. A group of us were taken to Glyndebourne for dress rehearsals in 1957/8, an experience which I would appreciate far more today than I did then. One or two masters would take one or two of us to concerts at Devonshire Park. I remember on one occasion there were two ladies knitting away behind us during a performance of Rachmaninov's 2nd Piano Concerto. One remarked to the other, 'I do like a little bit of piano with my music, don't you?'

Keith Dawson (B53)

During my time at Eastbourne I studied piano and organ, although I was a classics scholar until my last year. Peter Tranchell had joined the music department, and I decided to drop the classics and take on full time music studies. Tranchell went on to write a West End musical called Zuleika. He was a bizarre character, particularly in his very eccentric manner of dress, including multicoloured dressing-gown sashes with tassels instead of a belt, which didn't go too well with the fur of his academic gown. I vaguely remember the strange music he wrote for one of the school plays, which included a 'jungle piano', a small wooden box with pliant metal bars attached which you twanged. One of my best friends was a fellow student, Hugh Turner, whose father was the concert master of the Hallé Orchestra. I have a strong memory of meeting the great conductor Sir Adrian Boult after a symphonic concert at the Winter Gardens. When I was introduced to him as an up-and-coming young pianist, his words of advice to me were, 'You do realise, dear boy, that music is a very precarious profession!' After I'd signed on to do my national service in the RN Air Service, I ended up in the Royal Artillery Band in Woolwich when the navy decided I didn't have the aptitude to become a carrier pilot.

Ian Fraser (Sykes, P47)

Exultemus, o sodales,
Iam cessare fas novales;
Paululum laxemus mentes,
Dulce domum repetentes.
Chorus   *Age, frater juxta frater,*
          Celebremus Alman Matrem;
          Quae nos ornate, haec ornanda,
          Quae nos amat, adamanda.

Ho! Comrades, hearts and voices raise
To welcome the dear holidays;
Away with books, tear up the scheme,
No thought of these to spoil our dream!
          Come, Alma Mater, let us sing,
          Till overhead the rafters ring,
          With her – 'tis hers – our glory sharing,
          With answering love her love declaring.

Arnold's second rugby song, with music composed by a friend, R E Lyon, is the one which OEs of the era remember roaring out with gusto in Big School before all home matches.

Our game is not for milksops with their namby-pamby ways,
It's a game for the ding-dong fighter with the pluck of the good old days.
We've work for the speedy runner, for the rover who battles alone,
We've a place for the lightweight bantam, we've a niche for the sixteen stone.

Chorus   *For it's devil take the hindmost when 'College' strikes the ear,*
          Charge home with a rousing tackle,
          Bang through, stretch 'em out, never fear.
          Fit via vi Unanimi,
          Vociferabimur,
          Fit via vi.

The College millennium musical celebrations included the commissioning of a new school hymn ('Christ, the dawn of our salvation') with words by Paul Wigmore and music by John Barnard, and a new carol with seventeenth-century words and music by Grayston Ives from Magdalen College, Oxford; he has also been commissioned to write an anthem for Speech Day 2007 as part of the College's 140th anniversary celebrations.

Christ, the dawn of our salvation,
Rising light across creation,
          Lord of earthbound years,
Be the light that lights our living,
Our receiving and our giving;
          Light our laughter
          And our tears.

Left: The swing band (John Thornley).

Right: Will Kunhardt-Sutton and Mel Heslop, 2006.

Drama

One of the lasting legacies of the exile to Radley during the Second World War was the development of drama at Eastbourne College. Radley had a strong tradition in this area, whereas Eastbourne did not; but the school's enjoyment of dramatic productions while away from home encouraged their continuation once they had returned. For many years Tony Henderson, Max Halliday and Brian Harral produced the school plays, with enthusiastic casts both on the stage and behind the scenes. The talents of actors like John Wells, Royce Mills and Vernon Dobtcheff were nurtured by these producers. Indeed John Wells owes his theatrical debut to Max Halliday, who caught him one day impersonating his 'maiden aunt' voice and, instead of punishing him, gave him the role of Mrs Candour in his production of *The School for Scandal*. Wells' performance was reviewed in *The Eastbournian* with the words 'It is hard to imagine this part played better…. This was a really funny piece of comic acting, missing no hint of a chance, but never overplayed.'

Dermot Hoare (B44) recalls, 'With early ambitions of being on the stage, another milestone I treasure was the restarting of the dramatic society with a production of what went by the now unacceptable name of *Ten Little Niggers* by Agatha Christie inside Big School and later, outside, a cut-down version of Shakespeare's *Twelfth Night*. The latter was somewhat marred by a fierce crosswind blowing up just as, with an orchestral accompaniment playing on a first floor balcony, I was at ground level trying to sing "Oh Mistress Mine". As

Julius Caesar *in modern dress, and its programme, 1961 (Martin Swain).*

Above: West Side Story, *1967 (Tony Hamilton).*

Right: Annie Get Your Gun, *1983 (Philip Le Brocq).*

neither could hear the other I shudder to think what the audience experienced.' Keith Dawson (B53) remembers playing Hermia in *A Midsummer Night's Dream* in the mid-1950s, with Michael Doust as Helena, 'Arty' Williams as Oberon and John Wells as Thisbe. 'Max Halliday was the director and very good he was too. I remember he was insistent that on stage "all arm movements must be from the shoulder".'

Jeremy Lovitt-Danks (W55) remembers productions such as *The Lady's Not for Burning*, *The Merchant of Venice* and *Shop at Sly Corner* among others. 'There were some pretty good performers – Branch, who was crippled in one leg, used it to tremendous advantage when playing tragic anti-heroes; Andrew McNeil, an expert on the American Civil War, excelled at filling rather haggish leading lady roles (no girls then at Eastbourne) and Tony (now Royce) Mills was simply a delight to watch, and still is! Mark Robinson as Antonio

I arrived at Eastbourne College in September 1969 and together with five other girls – Clare Underhill, Anitra Swallow, Christina Jackson, Mary O'Brien, Sheila Wadley for the first year and Lesley Pickford for the second – we were the first females at the College (there were about thirty others who belonged to Moira House and came down for lessons). The other five were all day girls and I was the only weekly boarder. As a result I was the only girl to go into the evening meal, which was a bit terrifying initially. We were housed in the original Tenby Lodge on the site of what is now Pennell, and our housemaster was Forbes Wastie. Looking back, I don't think the College knew quite what to do with us outside lesson times so we seemed to have a great deal of freedom. I remember an illicit visit to the cinema to see Easy Rider *and the odd visit to Frasco's, the wine bar in Grove Road. I also recall organising the props for the lower sixth play* Death of a Salesman, *and getting the local fishmonger to provide the ice for soft drinks during the interval. When we went to collect it he gave us some of the ice on which his fish had been lying. No-one to my knowledge complained that there was anything 'fishy' about the drinks. Most of our pleasures were innocent, though, and we managed to avoid serious romantic liaisons with the boys. We all did well in our A levels and five of us went on to university.*

Sara Cooke (Richards, TL69)

in *The Merchant of Venice* was not that hot at remembering lines. His technique with "dries" was not to stop and wait for the *souffleur*, but to make it up as he went along until he reached a line he did remember; thus "What stuff 'tis made of, whereof it is born, I am to learn; and then we went into the pub and met the others who had already ordered pints; that I have much ado to know myself." No-one except for the cast and agonised director noticed.

'Behind the scenes there were some real experts. The Blanchard brothers put up all the scaffolding to create the proscenium, wings and lighting spars, and the artists, under George Simpson, created all the scenery. I was recruited by the make-up department. My first production was the "Scottish play". The big challenges were the three witches, a bloody child "from his mother's womb untimely ripped" and thirty-two beards to be built up with gum arabic in thirty minutes. For the witches I found a book on horror film make-up; for the beards I schooled fifteen boys to apply base make-up and do the basic beards, with me adding the final touches at the end of the assembly line; for the child, I went into a nearby chemist's shop and asked for six pints of blood. The chemist became very enthusiastic and finally concocted a red liquid which stayed red under arc-lights (the real stuff goes black, apparently). The young man playing the child discovered, after his first performance, that the concoction had another quality – indelibility. Were his face and body red before the chemist came up with a winning solution! The

smell of the sponges, continually used to apply liberal doses of base make-up to the faces and bodies of sweaty youngsters, and then placed, unwashed, in an old suitcase for six months, stays with me still.'

John Little also remembers the behind-the-scenes challenges, though his first experience of drama at the College was when, 'a few weeks before I was to join the SCR, I received a telephone call from the chaplain welcoming me and inviting me to take the role of Lord Francourt Babberley in *Charlie's Aunt*. My true metier later was as a director: all my shows were technically challenging and involved some notable achievements. Examples are the flying bridge and scenery on trucks in

Above: A Chorus Line, *2004.*

Right: Dino Kazamia prepares to play Shylock, 2006.

Guys and Dolls, 1987
(Philip Le Brocq).

Oliver, the stage gauze and the melt-through to the carbon dioxide waterfall in *South Pacific* and the live television news insert (courtesy of ITV Westcountry) in *Jesus Christ Superstar*. I also remember the dancing, none more than *Sweet Charity* with its stylised Bob Fosse Pompeii Club or the vibrancy of *Rhythm of Life* where we were able to fly Nikki Atkinson from the pit to the flies.'

When Philip Le Brocq joined the staff in 1962 he continued and developed the tradition of drama at the College: 'I didn't realise till years later that the charismatic then headmaster, Michael Birley, nearly sacked me after my trial year for being "rebellious". This apparently arose from starting "Bounces" in Room 20 (now the Studio Theatre), directing *The Hole* by N F Simpson at a School House Christmas supper and even calling all my pupils by their Christian names. What is rebellious to one generation becomes old-fashioned to another! But perhaps my most heinous offence was to take a minibus-load of seniors, after exams at the end of term, to queue up for Olivier's *Othello* at the newly completed Chichester Festival Theatre. It was an unforgettable experience. We left at 5am and returned after midnight fulfilled with Shakespeare, Olivier and Maggie Smith, to be met by some very angry housemasters. I assumed (I never did

again) that the boys had asked permission to be out. They hadn't and neither had I – I was the "new boy" after all. The school had lost eight pupils for a day. I nearly lost my first job!

'It was the Drama Conference at Clifton in 1965 attended by three members of our staff that set the subsequent scene. Through Dorothy Heathcote's brilliant lecturing on her teaching life in Yorkshire, we learned that children grow through drama, and if one gets the atmosphere of a class right one can teach them anything – subject matter comes second. It was a Pauline experience for me.

'Chapel was the venue for *Christ in the Concrete City*, and also for a one-act play festival where *A Sleep of Prisoners* fitted in aptly. Girls, tempted down from Eastbourne High School, first appeared in *The Crucible* and *The Caucasian Chalk Circle*, the latter accompanied by dire warnings from Donald Perrens, housemaster of Blackwater, about the "suggestive language" being bad for the image of the school. Pinter's *The Caretaker* appeared regularly in a variety of College venues. In 1969 a junior production of *Teahouse of the August Moon* gave a group of non-sportsmen a chance to shine in the eyes of their peers. It also got a jeep and a goat on the stage.

In the Still of the Night, the 2006 Cole Porter revue written by Tim Marriott.

'The first revolutionary production in Big School in 1972 was *Romeo and Juliet* with a stage thrust into the audience, flaming torches and black leotards for all the cast. Live stereophonically sited drums accompanied the frighteningly realistic fights. Improvised auditions for all the cast took up the first weeks of rehearsal. Peter Brooks, Franco Zeffirelli and *West Side Story* were the guiding influences. Movement, music, dance had been added to drama, and have remained key at Eastbourne since. Then the Summer Term Musical was born. All the lower sixth girls were involved somewhere – we only had them in the sixth form then – and starting with a modest *Let's Make an Opera* with some adults, we moved through *Oliver, South Pacific, Salad Days, Free as Air, Oklahoma, Cabaret,* several versions of *Guys and Dolls* and *Carousel* and, when Big School was burned down in 1980, did *Annie get your Gun* at the Winter Garden. The old days of only one or two directors had long gone – with Andrew Boxer, Colin Brezicki, Colin Polden, the chaplain Ron Johnson and Nigel Wheeler with his alternative theatre in the Dell, Craig House Garden and Room 20. In 1980 *Daddy* by Mark Freeland was one of the first originally written plays staged and directed in Big School, soon after our son John died. There were many moving echoes in the text, and most of the cast had been his friends.

'There were staff plays too – Stoppard's *After Magritte* stands out – and staff pantomimes, Old Time Music Halls and end-of-term summer balls. The fire

was a boon! With the new Big School theatre we could have the orchestra in a proper pit underground, rather than surrounded by platforms; *Half a Sixpence* was the first musical in the new theatre, and it has been used in a wide variety of shapes since – promenade, platform, in the round. Lighting and sound have transformed the productions and our first, and lasting, theatre technician, Paul Turner, has perpetuated this transformation.

'In 1980 we took plays on tour: three one-act plays in the round to Tonbridge; *The Proposal* by Chekhov in which Eddie Izzard starred; Anouilh's *Antigone*; and Feydeau's *Dormez, je le veux*. Finally, in 1988, Nigel Wheeler and I toured New Zealand with a double bill of Stoppard's *The Real Inspector Hound* using all the touring cricket team and the *Hound* cast in Shakespeare's *Midsummer Night's Dream*. Original music by John Walker, late inspirational director of music, played by members of the cast, added a superbly atmospheric touch. The *Dream* was done indoors and outside, as the schools required. It was an amazing silver wedding celebration for us on 4 April 1988, to see it performed in the garden of friends at Lowry Peaks, North Island, with Puck weaving his final magic and the cast humming their way into the night. Stoppard and Shakespeare have never been quite the same since.'

Adam Mynott's recollection of treading the Big School boards brought back very happy, slightly hysterical memories. In one production, I played Hermione in Shakespeare's The Winter's Tale, *opposite John Davies as Leontes and Suzy Parsons as Paulina. In the last scene, I had to remain still as the proverbial statue for nearly fifteen minutes, wearing a floaty long dress that was like a red rag to a bull for Adam who was backstage – he may even have been the all-powerful 'stage manager'. Every performance, while John gamely wept over what Leontes believed to be a real statue, marvelling at attention to detail, my dress was practically floating over my head thanks to a fan that Adam and his cohorts used to switch on behind me. May I say, as a former 'thesp' to a TV reporter: 'Adam – may your cutting room floor be strewn with out-takes!'*

Claire Lathbury (N74)

Art

Art was taught at Eastbourne College from the beginning, though initially it was an optional extra provided by visiting art masters who charged fees. Prizes for writing and drawing indicate that it was taken seriously as a subject in those early years; however, Arnold had little time for it, despite his own preoccupation with the carving of wood panels to embellish Big School and his watercolour paintings of birds, and it was not until Gordon Carey's headship that a full-time art master was appointed. Ralph Simpson, who joined the College in 1938 and stayed until 1958, is remembered as having engendered a great renaissance of artistic activities. Simon Wood (Pw50) fondly recalls art lessons in the roof space of the Arnold wing, where 'Simpson introduced us to the skills of draughtsmanship, painting, printing, metalwork, architecture and art appreciation, often with illustrated talks. He was himself a fine draughtsman and produced many watercolours of the local countryside. He and his wife, Diana, would often take a group of us sketching. I remember one incident when I was drawing a figure in a landscape with a dip pen. Suddenly two small puddles of ink dripped from my pen and landed next to the figure. I was mortified. But when RS looked down at the paper, he smiled, said "All is not lost" and with a few deft touches of his fountain pen turned the puddles of ink into a poodle.'

Left: Sam Abbakoumov and his giant rabbit, 2006.

Right: Emma Apps painting a picture of the cloisters, 2006.

Below: Statement on the teaching of art at the College in the early 1930s (Keith Pinker).

THE TEACHING OF ART AT EASTBOURNE COLLEGE

IN THE REPORT on the School made by them last winter the Board of Education's Inspectors, in the course of an enthusiastic appreciation of the art work, wrote: "With such premises and so skilful a teacher there are the means to give as good an education in this direction as could be desired, and any time or money that can be found for developing this side of the school work will certainly be well spent".

Hitherto art has been taken as a voluntary subject, for which an extra charge of £1. 15s. a term has been made; but the lowest Form in the School have been taking the subject *en bloc* as part of their regular work, and for them the fee has consequently been optional (though very few parents have in fact claimed exemption).

In view of the admirable results obtained by the present Art Master, it is clear that, in the interests of general education, his work should be given wider scope. Unfortunately the School is not in a position to provide for the teaching of this subject without any extra fee; yet the difficulty is recognised of making it a compulsory subject and at the same time making an

Patrick Attenborough (W47) reports: 'In my last year an art sixth form was created for Christopher Harris, Stephen Howell and myself, plus another boy, but he was also good at sport so didn't spend as much time as we did on art. I think we had twelve or sixteen lessons a week. We would meet in the art room on a Thursday morning and agree with Mr Simpson where to go and what to draw. One rainy day we suggested St Mary's church and the Lamb Inn. "I suppose you want to sit in a pub, drink beer and smoke cigarettes. Off you go then!" Some afternoons we would pile into his shooting brake with his charming wife and lively spaniel and find a place in the country, in the shade, to paint and draw. At four o'clock thermoses of tea would appear, and when in season strawberries and cream. Ralph Simpson was a huge influence. He made us use all manner of materials for all manner of subjects, and was both critical and encouraging. Would any other public school have created a special art sixth form for four pupils in 1950? I doubt it.'

When Eric Jones came to the school in 1958 on Ralph Simpson's retirement, he introduced a pottery class, taught at that stage by 'Mum'

Henderson, Tony Henderson's mother. He recalls that 'in the 1950s art in some public schools was considered a Cinderella subject, but not at Eastbourne where Michael Birley and his staff always strove for a broad education.' Facilities, however, were a bit patchy until 1980 when a new Art School was opened by Sir Hugh Casson (S24), who was amusing about his 'undistinguished career' at the College at a time when someone who preferred to sit down and paint rather than open the bowling was regarded with some bemusement as an oddball. This was at the end of Marcus Lyon's tenure of the art department; among his memories are the discussion he had with Michael Birley about his wish to start a sixth form life drawing class at the College, which his opposite number at Moira House was keen for her girls to join: 'He misunderstood what I was asking and said, "Well, Marcus, in principle yes… but I am not sure the parents… you see, some of our boys do go out with the girls at Moira House…". I realised then what he was thinking. "Headmaster – I was not thinking of using the girls as models. There would be a professional model." So it was agreed.'

It was during Marcus Lyon's time that sculpture was started at the College, 'which really got going when my wife, Marion, joined me in the art room. But we had so little space for what could be a messy form of art, particularly casting. Marion did have one pupil who went on to become one of our top sculptors – Peter Randall-Page (C68), whom I met again recently. He sent me a note afterwards: "It was wonderful to meet you again after so long and to realise what a kindred spirit you are. The atmosphere you created in that attic art room at Eastbourne was a real haven for me – it started me on my journey and I will always be grateful for that." One of my best pupils was Jonathan Mills, who composed a picture of David Hockney and sent a photo of it to Hockney, who immediately invited him to visit him in Paris. When he got there Hockney said he wanted him to do a sketch of him there and then. This would have scared me stiff, but he took it in his stride and did an excellent sketch. Hockney was most impressed, and helped him to get into the Royal Academy School of Art.'

Lyon's successor, Ian Markland, built the subject up to such an extent that, from his initial group of nine O level and five A level students, within ten years there were three classes for GCSE and two for A level. As he says, 'The art department now has a fully integrated

John Bond sits for Charlie Hawksfield, 2006.

and valued place in the scheme of things, with a great many students going on to art-based courses after A level and many of them now enjoying successful creative careers.'

As ever perhaps, the art department has been at the cutting edge of innovation at the College, not least in terms of the teachers' dress code. Jayne Harriott, still running a very successful sculpture and ceramics studio at the College, remembers joining the art department in 1990, and not thinking twice about coming to school wearing trousers: 'It did not cross my mind as an issue; after all, putting up all those art

Above: Oil painting of interior of School House entrance by Katie Hunt, 2003.

Top right: Sir Hugh Casson (S24), President of the Royal Academy 1976–84, drawn by John Ward CBE, RA.

Above and left: Watercolours by James Fletcher-Watson RI RBA FRIBA (G27) who served with the Royal Engineers in India during the Second World War.

displays was not something one would do in a skirt with all those adolescent boys around. I had one joking comment about "always wearing trousers", which I laughed off, and carried on dealing with being one of only five women in a boys' school of 500+ with fifty male staff. Sometime later I noticed Stephanie Wooldridge in a smart pair of check trousers in Old Wish Road. When I commented on them, it became apparent that I had been the "guinea pig"; she told me that when in the late 1980s she had turned up in the dining hall for lunch wearing trousers, she was given a very definite look up and down by a senior wife, which she took to be a "what are you thinking of, wearing trousers" rebuke. She didn't try it again, but after I arrived in my trousers she and the other women waited to see if anything was said, and as it was not, it slowly became the norm. Though Forbes did draw the line at one of my colleagues repeatedly turning up in leggings.'

Angus Forrester, 2006.

The lighter side

NICKNAMES

Along with David Stone-Lee (R57) and others, John Templeton (B55) remembers the nicknames: 'Lunchtimes in Blackwater House were always interesting and informative as we were joined by various members of the staff. The most entertaining was Vincent Allom, always known as Vim by the pupils, who told us that for a master to be given a nickname by the boys was a sign of acceptance and respect. Our masters all had strong and individual personalities: we had Beefy, Bags and Bum; Eggnog, Hearty and Juggins; Notty, Piggy and Pot; Ratty, Shifty and Vim, and many more. I treasure their memories. (Eggnog was Brian Harral, Bags was Kem Bagnall-Oakeley, Bum was Brian Mulvany, Hearty was Michael Holland, Juggins was Robert Storrs, Notty was Ernie Northcott, Ratty was Cecil Wrenford, Shifty was William Bett. It is well known that John Underhill was Pot and Ronald Howell was Beefy.)

Jeremy Lovitt-Danks adds: 'Boys had an instinctive talent for awarding masters nicknames. One learned them as a new boy, and then as new masters joined they acquired nicknames too – but who exactly coined them nobody knew.

Above: School House dining room, 1962 (Tony Ling).

Below left: Forbes Wastie with head girl Lily Crockford, Speech Day, 2006 (Philip Le Brocq).

Beefy	Juggins	Little Man	Bags	Penders
Pin Up	Tommy	Bambi	Brute	Nick
Barrel	Monty	Hearty	Jumbo	Lenny
Jock	Geoff	Dusty	Starsky	Vector
Hutch	Stewy	Mr Plunge	Tauro	Stan
Lenny	Hoddy	Schlep	CJ	Budgie
Westy	Pot	Snake bite	JT	Chesty
Dickie	Thirsty Pelican	Binny	Jasper	Bob
Ron Jon	Teddy	Herby	Ratty	Dagwood
Max	Twee	Bubbles	Crippen	Rastus
Piggy	Billy B	The Ogre	Puffy	Shifty
Tippy	Tubby	Pa	The Major	Georgie
Charlie	Pimp	Goofy	Meaty	Foxy Jo
Harpic	Nicotini Baldini	Eggnog	Hairy	Terrier

The school slang was learnt though day-to-day experience or through the fags' test. I forget who 'wog's old man' was, but 'jolly door' was a little door into the back of Big School, the 'tucker' or the 'grubber' was the tuck shop, needless to say, and 'stodge' was the pudding at lunch, which arrived daily in a single pile, subtly differentiated by colour, odour but not always taste, and varied between treacle (patriotic pudding), raspberry, date and cocoa/chocolate. It was warming, but slowed one down somewhat when playing rugger afterwards. The oddest expression of all was 'ike' meaning cheek; 'Bloody ike, Smith!' was a condemnation of some rough handling in the cold showers.

Jeremy Lovitt-Danks (W55)

'They invariably fitted the victim perfectly, some of them true, some wicked, some abstruse. Their origins were usually obvious – physiognomy, initials or names, disposition, peculiarities: 'Goofy' Godden's came from his teeth; 'Pot' from his shape; 'Ratty' from his disposition; 'Bouncy' and 'Bunnyfoot' from their walk; 'Shifty' because you could never tell where he was looking…'.

Forbes Wastie has his own take on the subject: 'With a name like mine, Granville Forbes Wastie, I have always been in the firing line, with people confused about my first name and often wanting to make me double-barrelled. How much better to have a nickname! I happened to have three sons at the College, JFW, JCW and WGW, as did my brother, whose sons were LFW, CPJW and SGW. LF and JF were commissioned at Sandhurst at about the same time and

Wargrave House Supper, 1957 (Roger Blackburn).

together attended the Royal Engineers Young Officers course at Chatham. On the first parade inspection the regimental sergeant major walking along the first rank came upon LF. "What's your name?" he bellowed. "Wastie, sir," LF replied. A little further along he came to JF and demanded his name too. "Wastie, sir," came the reply. "Blimey," said the RSM. "Well in future you will be Waste of Time and you will be Waste of Space."

'The College has been equally imaginative (though in some cases less so) in producing these endearing soubriquets. Perhaps the most memorable was that given to Arnold, who was known by boys and staff as "Og". Do you remember those in the list on page 136 and can you give them their proper names? And do they stick in your mind, never to be forgotten?'

FOOD

For almost all of the first hundred years of the College, the individual houses catered for their occupants. For the first fifty years, indeed, housemasters ran their houses like businesses, attracting their 'clientele', providing all the facilities and keeping any profits for themselves. Stephen Foot, the first bursar, introduced the hostel system in the 1920s, which took several years to implement fully while housemasters operating the old system were still in office. But eventually all the houses were run by paid staff, and continued to provide meals on the premises. Menu books kept in

the 1930s by Millicent Storrs, the Pennell housemaster's wife, record the daily meals; see below for those served at the beginning of the Michaelmas term 1938.

A year later, at the beginning of the war, the food looks much the same, though porridge has replaced cornflakes at breakfast, and stewed rabbit makes a frequent appearance.

By the early 1960s a central kitchen was ferrying the food round to the separate houses; then in 1965 a central dining room was built and has been in

	Breakfast	Dinner	High tea
Fri 16 Sept			Sausage and mash Bananas
Sat 17	Cornflakes Scrambled eggs	Brown stew, peas Stewed pears, custard	Sardines on toast Oranges
Sun 18	Cornflakes Cold ham	Roast beef, cabbage Pineapple, custard	Cornish pasties Apples
Mon 19	Cornflakes, bacon and spaghetti	Cold beef, salad Ginger pudding, custard	Beans on toast Bananas
Tues 20	Cornflakes Fried eggs	Roast mutton, cauliflower Bananas, cream and jam	Kippers Oranges
Wed 21	Cornflakes Herrings	Boiled beef, carrots, onions Jam tart	Luncheon sausage Apples
Thurs 22	Cornflakes Kidneys	Fried fish, parsley sauce Apple turnover, custard	Sausages, beans Bananas

Dining hall, 2006, with long-serving chef George Norton.

operation ever since. Ben Delaunay, today's catering manager who comes from a long line of chefs in both France and England, joined the school as an assistant chef in 1972 and has witnessed many changes and developments during the last thirty-plus years. Today, lunch and supper are provided for everyone at the school, including the day pupils, and the boarders and living-in staff also get breakfast. In addition, food is provided for those going to away fixtures or to other external activities, including hot stews for those on strenuous outings like CCF field days. The kitchen staff is now some twenty-two strong, many of whom, like George Norton, the head chef, have been at the College for over twenty years. In the past the kitchens were idle during school holidays, but now with the premises being used all year round for external activities, they are busy all the time, closing only over the Christmas holidays for maintenance. They cater too for events like weddings, celebration dinners and staff functions, and provide appropriate food for charity events – curries for a charity Bollywood evening, for example.

Catering is a more relaxed affair now than it used to be, with the students being involved in decisions about the food; there are several choices available every day, including vegetarian options and a salad bar, and students with special dietary needs are catered for. The kitchens use local produce, cook everything freshly and are increasingly moving towards fully free range and organic ingredients.

Ben Delaunay is also a lifeboatman, and remembers one morning, after a late call-out to a stricken fishing boat, arriving almost an hour late to start breakfast. Still in his oilskins on a hot summer morning after a fruitless night at sea, he stood in the kitchen frying eggs for the hungry customers milling around him. Others have memories of the food too: Duncan Symington (P45) recalls 'a very tasty mince stew which, according to the housemaster's wife, was "horse", which was good and much anticipated. The whalemeat stew was not so good; it didn't smell very nice and tasted oily and tinny. Fish was served on Fridays which was difficult for me because my last two biology periods before lunch were devoted to dissecting dogfish that were kept for weeks in a drum of formaldehyde and smelt horrible. The fish smell on one's hands combined with the fish smell on one's stomach to make eating that fish on Friday well nigh impossible. But I also remember accounting for seventeen medium kippers one Friday supper since some of the others didn't like them, and then being told that my parents had unexpectedly arrived and that I could go to meet them at their hotel – where I sat down to a three-course meal. The capacities of youth!'

INDUCTIONS

Charlie Bostock writes about his own and other inductions: 'The first days at school can often be testing and there must be a host of memories for any boarders first starting at the College. My wife Clare used the new boys' tea party in Wargrave as a time to identify mothers who might need supporting during the difficult moments of parting. Chris Saunders recalls attending a new boys' tea party in School House where one new boy had locked himself in his parents' car and was refusing to come out. His housemaster, David Hodkinson, had persevered but without luck, and when the headmaster approached he was told in no uncertain terms to "f*** off". The situation was resolved eventually. In a similar situation, one Wargravian pupil could not be persuaded out of the car by either his parents or his housemaster (me); but where one Charlie B failed, another succeeded and the indefatigable Charlie Bush punctured the professional pride of an aspiring housemaster. The boy finished as head of house despite his ignominious start. Yet another Wargravian, having enjoyed his first year at school while his elder brother was in the upper sixth, decided that returning for a second year was all too much. With my eyes on the new year 9, my alarm bells did not ring sufficiently loudly at first when his absence at roll call was noticed. It transpired that he had simply taken himself back home.

'The first days of school can offer challenges for staff as well. One present assistant head is known to have cut his arrival as a new teacher to the College rather fine. Having rushed to finish his MSc, he arrived at midnight on Saturday night prior to term starting on Sunday evening. While the teaching on Monday passed off reasonably well, the fact that he missed his induction day became telling on Tuesday morning. In inimitable university student style, he didn't see a 9.03am arrival for a 9.00am start as a problem. However, on arrival at the biology labs, it transpired that all were full. It was suggested he make his way to P5 across in the Science Block. He ventured over there only to bump into the head of science, Dr Graham Jones. "You're a bit late, aren't you?" he quizzed. That's a bit stiff; 9.03am doesn't seem too bad to me, mused the crestfallen teacher silently to himself. When the door opened it revealed a small tiered lecture theatre with eight boys sitting in the back row. "Sorry I'm late, chaps," announced the new teacher with a spaniel-like enthusiasm; "I overslept." Wry smiles all around. "My name is Charlie Bostock. I am here to teach you a bit of biology. Where shall we start?" "Sir, I think this lesson has just finished." "What do you mean, it's just finished? What time did it start?" "8.30 sir!" The irony of my involvement in staff induction now is not lost!'

Powell House, 2006.

A poem called 'Utopia', probably by H F Matheson (master for forty years from 1884 until his retirement in 1923 and first housemaster of Wargrave), was published in *The Eastbournian* in 1897:

My nephew once invited me to visit him at school
To see the inner working of a newly-published rule;
'Twas graven on the mantelpiece, 'twas written on the shelves
'Take care of prefects and the rest must take care of themselves'.

I found that my young nephew was one of the elect,
Which was more than my experience had led me to expect!
But there he was to meet me. 'Ah! Uncle! Is that you?
I was just a little anxious for the prefects' lunch at two.'

This sounded rather 'thick' but was indubitably true,
The prefects lunched, with aldermanic luxury, at two;
They took their fish and cutlet, and washed some pheasant down
With a pint of decent claret that would cost you half-a-crown.

It seemed to me that after this the 'natural man' would shirk
(Much more the 'natural boy') his bit of after-luncheon work,
But, daring to suggest as much, my nephew coldly said,
He didn't mean to work again before he went to bed.

There were so many little things a prefect had to do,
(They had to ask the head for halves, design a cap or two,
To edit the school magazine, or take an hour's prep)
That really they must be excused their 'books' and 'prose' and 'rep'.

So having crushed his uncle he proceeded to insist
On dragging in his victim to join the prefects' whist
That wasn't quite a game at which a visitor would jump,
For no-one but a prefect was allowed to hold a trump.

I smoked the prefects' best cigars, I drank their 'special' port,
I watched a mild encounter in their 'special' tennis court,
Till, declining invitations to 'stay and dine with us'
I was driven to the station in the prefects' private 'bus.

> Of course back in the 1940s corporal punishment was completely accepted and considered normal by everyone. I recall on one occasion breaking a milk bottle in our common room and failing to sweep up the broken glass and put it in the waste basket. This sin earned me a flogging by the prefect who caught me – six of the best administered on the rear end with a gym shoe. I was tall and a member of the school boxing team, and I was flogged by a vertically challenged little prefect which seemed rather ironic at the time. After the punishment it was the custom to thank the prefect for the flogging to show there was no animosity between those administering justice and the felons, and that each was just doing his duty. Another punishment was awarded by Beefy Howell after I had failed to have my bible with me for the first lesson of the day. He decided that my memory needed to be improved, so I was told that I had to find Beefy on ten separate occasions during that day, spaced at no less than half hourly intervals, and show him that I had my bible with me! If I did not manage ten visitations that day, then it would be eleven visitations on the following day and so on. What with the size of the campus and the difficulty in finding Beefy as he went here and there, including refereeing a rugby game, I have never had such a busy day.
>
> Ian Sacré (W46)

PREFECTS, FAGGING AND PUNISHMENTS

Prefects were appointed from the early years, with the 'senior prefect' initially being senior purely by virtue of date of appointment. House prefects were introduced towards the end of the nineteenth century, and the senior prefect title was changed to 'head of school' in about 1913 and became a position appointed by the headmaster. House and school prefects, as well as the head boys and head girls, continue to be appointed in the upper sixth.

David Atkins (G49) sums up the situation as it was in his day: 'Two activities that, like the non-lamented bear-baiting, have been relegated to the pages of social history played a large part in the minds and bodies of many generations of schoolboys. Tom

Page one of the College Rules, 1931.

Brown was in there somewhere near the beginning, and I was there very near the end. Fagging formed a sort of relationship between the prefect and the fag which could vary between hero worship and loathing – the master and servant, separated by perhaps four years in age but by an enormous gulf in terms of school position. The fag normally carried out his duties for three terms, but his work could not begin until he had passed the "fags' test". There was no point in failing this hurdle in an attempt to put off the evil day, and very few failed more than once since then the second part of the equation would come into operation – beating. The test took place after the first two weeks of one's first term. Each new boy was provided with a "nurse", a boy one year into his career

> 'Boy! Come and take this message to Kidd May in Gonville.' Up the road I went, into Gonville and knocked on the study door. Inside I announced 'A message for Kidd May.' 'Well, give it to him.' But I had no idea which one was Kidd May. 'Boy, you had better learn who is who round here. And don't come here again without knowing. Do you understand, boy?' I was beginning to think that my new name was Boy.
>
> Richard Browne (B49)

Giles Battcock and Roger Blackburn in a new study in Wargrave, 1958 (Roger Blackburn).

I was fortunate in that I was in a room with only two beds, but I soon found that, each morning break, the two of us were thrown out of our room by a couple of sixth formers so that they could smoke out of the window, and night time was spent listening to the loud music played by a member of the upper sixth whose study was next door. As mere third formers we felt it easier to say nothing in case of reprisals. After we had been caught talking at night several times, a member of the lower sixth tried to punish us. After I managed to put up valid objections to all his punishments, we ended up taking him a cup of hot water at 6am.

Andrew Paviour (P86)

Housemaster's study in Craig House, 2006.

whose duty it was to prepare his charge for the examination. At least 400 facts had to be mastered – school rules, masters' names and nicknames, the positions of buildings and playing fields, in general everything that the prefects thought one ought to know. On the dreaded day, the candidate would find himself confronted in the prefects' study by four or five of these demigods. They would show their feigned contempt for the whole procedure by draping themselves casually round the room, and they would fire questions at random. If the new boy had mastered his brief, the questions soon ended; but a few wrong answers would arouse the interest of the interrogators and, smelling blood, they would make the questions more difficult and probably throw in the odd trick one too. Should the examiners be of such a mind, the fag-to-be would be informed that he had failed and told to report back in seven days. There was great pressure not to fail a second time, for not only he but his nurse would suffer – and no-one actually failed because the prefects needed the fags for their own convenience. This is not to say that the suggested suffering – or

abuse, as we would call it now – was not administered. A less than perfect second attempt was awarded a "pass with beating".

'Once one had become a fag, slackers who at the end of a week had not earned enough positive ticks from the prefects suffered the inevitable physical punishment. House prefects were restricted to the flimsy gym shoe, but school prefects were allowed to use the dreaded swagger stick, and a few well aimed blows with this fierce implement would draw blood from the delicate young buttock. On this sliding scale, masters would probably have used a cat o' nine tails.' John Purchas recalls that 'being beaten by a school prefect was another kettle of fish altogether, because they would beat with a swagger stick. I remember a particularly horrible instance of this at Gonville which the whole house had to watch. I will not mention names, but the Gonville boy could hardly walk and had to sit on cushions for over a week and be treated by the house matron.' And Cecil Bell (P33) remembers talking in the Reading Room and receiving a slippering: 'I learnt my lesson.'

A Pennell bedsit, 2006.

Uniform

Bashers on parade for the Sunday walk along the sea front (Peter Robinson).

enry Stones (S17) wrote a useful and fascinating account of the development of the College uniform, at a time (around the mid-1970s) when 'as the wearing of caps and other kinds of traditional headgear is no longer compulsory, this seems an opportune moment to recall the fashions of the past before they are lost to posterity.' As he records, the original uniform was 'black coats or jackets, trousers without pockets, black neckties, black felt hats or in the summer term straw hats of a pattern made for the College, all procurable in Eastbourne, with the College ribbon, and on Sundays the ordinary silk hat.' It seems that a regulation cap must have been introduced very early on, since it is recorded as being changed as early as May 1870 for one 'of a vastly superior shape and darker hue'; it was also noted in 1874 that some poor children in the town had been seen wearing old College caps with white ribbons, so it may be that the dark

blue cap with six white stripes radiating from the centre was introduced at this time. In the 1880s a bowler was being worn for chapel on Sundays, but at the same time the black and white speckled straw hat (known as the 'basher') was in use, and remained so for most of the next hundred years.

Caps for games were awarded from the beginning, for both school and house teams, and also crests worn on jerseys once a certain level had been reached; the ultimate accolade in the early years for the rugby Stag was a dark blue fez edged with a narrow white ribbon and with a white silk tassel; a stag's head was worked in white silk on the front.

By 1897 the variety of caps, straw hats, ties and other insignia worn by members of the College was such that a resident of Eastbourne wrote to the College to request a detailed outline, which was subsequently published in the June *Eastbournian*. There appear to have been at least ten different caps ranging from the ordinary school cap through the caps prefects wore to those awarded to the members of the various sports teams; in addition there were three different straw hat designs, four designs of blazer, four types of knitted tie and school crests in different colours according to the house to which the wearer belonged. School prefects who also held colours had a special tie too, and the stag emblem on the caps of those with first team colours developed a different design of antlers according to whether the holder played rugby or cricket.

Five Stags, 1931 (Chris Hopkinson).

Speech Day at the end of the summer term is traditionally marked by the whole school, and those associated with it, wearing the cornflower. The question arises – why? There is no real answer – it seems to be just one of those traditions about which everyone knows and yet nobody knows. The archives yield no reference to it, and asking senior OEs elicits the answer 'I remember being told' but no further enlightenment. An indirect clue is the name Cornfield Terrace, to the west of which, when the College was founded in 1867, was open country with nothing but cornfields beyond. An early letter to the Eastbournian *pointed out the futility of siting the cricket nets so close to the cornfields that cricket balls were constantly being lost there. When we remember John Clare writing of 'the vast sheets of cornflowers troubling the cornfields with their destroying beauty', it is worth wondering whether a casual insertion of one of the flowers in a buttonhole, perhaps during a cricket match, became a lasting tradition. Should anyone know the real answer, the editors of this anthology would be pleased to have the information for the records.*

Forbes Wastie

Today's uniform.

The Cornflower Ball, 1990 (John Gorrie).

The First World War imposed some simplifications on this bewildering variety of insignia, and in the 1920s it was decided that the differently coloured crest (a rose and the letters EC) on blazers should become a uniform white without the letters. Clothes rationing after the Second World War resulted in a motley variety of sports jackets, trousers and even suits being permitted. Meanwhile, the introduction of a wider range of sports had necessitated new insignia, until in 1959 it was decided that caps and straw hats would no longer be compulsory and that house ties would be introduced as well as new designs of ties for prefects and sixth formers.

When girls joined the sixth form in 1969 their uniform was simply a blue skirt, a white blouse and a jumper; the boys at the time wore either a green or a blue jacket of a standard design with grey trousers, a white shirt and a house tie. When the school went fully coeducational in 1995 the opportunity was taken to standardise both girls' and boys' uniforms, which are now blue blazers with the white Eastbourne rose on the pocket, white shirts, house ties and grey trousers for the boys and tartan kilts for the girls. Sixth form girls and boys both wear dark suits and white shirts; prefects are allowed to wear coloured shirts. There is no school tie as such; house ties are the norm in the lower part of the school, augmented by different ties for prefects, sixth form boys, scholars, and those awarded sports colours.

Staff

This book is replete with memories of staff from the earliest days to the present – headmasters, housemasters and their wives, teachers, office staff, the school doctors and San staff, cooks, cleaners, porters.... Some of them have offered their own contributions to the book in one form or another; others appear time and again in the recollections of those on whose lives they made such an impact. Whether it's a housemaster's calm forbearance, a teacher's classroom style, the soothing effect of a friendly welcome on a nervous new pupil, the mind-opening eureka effect when something really gets through... these are the things that are remembered when Latin tenses and logarithms have been consigned to the deepest recesses of the mind. Such memories run through this book; and it is noteworthy that Eastbourne can boast two teachers nominated for inclusion in the 1997 advertising campaign run by the Teacher Training Agency entitled 'No-one forgets a good teacher' (Andrew Boxer by Eddie Izzard (P75) and Donald Perrens by Michael Fish (R58)).

It is invidious to single out only a few of those many; but this piece is intended to celebrate them all through memories of only some. The whole book is a tribute in itself!

SUPPORT STAFF

The strength of the support offered to the smooth running of the College by the non-teaching staff cannot be underestimated. Memories abound: of Kitty James (wife of Ted, much-loved cricket coach) and Jane Mitchell who ran the tuck shop for a total between them of sixty-four years; of Bert Turner who joined the maintenance staff in 1926 and stayed until 1967, twenty-two of those years as head porter, and his wife who ran the masters' lodge, as well as Alan Metcalf, current head porter with over twenty years

service; of Douglas Sansom who retired in 1979 after thirty years as senior lab technician; of Bernie Larkin, gardener for twenty-seven years, and two long-serving head groundsmen Ralph Bryant and Cam Tate. Office staff too: Audrey Needes, who was the bursar's secretary before helping Robin Harrison with the OEA, Susan Aynscough, the bursars' PA for nearly thirty years and Sue Davies, who was PA to successive headmasters and still comes in to help in the archives office. Forbes Wastie wrote in 1993 of Pat Dive, head porter, who was retiring after twenty-six years, 'We've grown accustomed to his face, his military swagger, his wide-ranging conversation and the pride he takes in all things, whether it be the pristine condition of the College buildings, his own turnout or having solved

Four headmasters: from left, Simon Davies, Charlie Bush, Chris Saunders, Simon Langdale (John Thornley).

the *Telegraph* crossword by break time.' When 'Amazing' Grace Kempton left School House in 1977 after being the matron there since 1961, 'her boys' gave her a cake with sixteen candles and wrote in with fond memories: 'dear old matron, who patiently scrubbed my hair with olive oil for terrible dandruff.'

The first full-time school doctor was Colonel Goodwin, who tended to the health of the school from 1933 until 1947. He was succeeded by Grahame Boal who left office only when he died in 1958; Michael Birley wrote of him that he seemed to control epidemics by will-power: 'There's a case of measles (or mumps, or chickenpox…) in the San; isolated case; there won't be any more.' Robin Harrison remembers Dr Nick (Charles Nicholson, doctor from 1958 until 1972) as having 'an enormous drawer full of assorted pills to cure every ailment. I sometimes envisaged a boy arriving carrying his head under his arm being courteously invited to take a seat while Dr Nick burrowed industriously in his drawer for the remedy.' Michael Mynott, the next school doctor, specialised in sports injuries, and was a redoubtable sportsman himself, as were his four children who all attended the

Right: The medical centre, 2006.

College. Sanatorium matrons were known for their longevity; Miss Jessop from 1925 to 1940, and again from 1945 to 1949; and Doris Carmichael who retired in 1984 after joining in 1960.

Simon Langdale remembers the maintenance staff, among them Ted Goldsmith, clerk of works for over twenty-five years, who keep the infrastructure of the school running smoothly and are always on hand to deal with day-to-day running as well as emergencies: 'there were the inevitable crises: a phone call at 1am to say that the dining room was flooded after the combination of a thunderstorm and an exceptionally high tide had forced a wall of water back up the drains (breakfast was served on time in the morning).' And Jean Alder, widow of Lt Col Bernard Alder who was bursar and clerk to the Council from 1964 until his retirement in 1981, recalls that 'these men were the backbone to the smooth running of the everyday maintenance of the College and were well known to all the staff and boys. If you had a broken window, a blocked loo or a broken light you phoned the bursary for a call to be put out to the maintenance department and it was fixed that day. My husband always said that these wonderful men were the first to turn out to fight the great fire in Big School and help with the clear-up.'

Diana Wastie remembers the staff at Blackwater after she and Forbes arrived there: 'I inherited an old

I very much enjoyed the three years I spent as secretary to Mr Nugee. He had a rather brusque manner but at the same time had a sensitive and sympathetic side. I was full of admiration for the way he looked after Mrs Nugee, who had developed polio soon after they became engaged, after which for six years she used to travel to and from a clinic in Switzerland for treatment, only to be told at the end of that time that there was nothing more that could be done for her and that she would never able to walk. In spite of this tragic news they were married. When he became headmaster of the College, I think he was determined that she should take as full a part of life there as possible, and he used to push her around everywhere in a wheelchair. It was at this time that the lift was installed in the headmaster's house to give access to the first floor. When he retired in 1956, the boys' parents showed their appreciation by presenting him with an estate car which could accommodate Mrs Nugee's wheelchair. When Kenneth and I were courting, it was convenient, when the staff were in class, that I was allowed to go into the Common Room to deliver notes and information from Mr Nugee into their pigeon holes, and at the same time Kenneth and I could exchange notes in his pigeon hole (dangerous liaisons!). We started married life in the flat above the garage (now the staff computer room) next to the Common Room at the end of Old Wish Road.

Peggy Hindley

College exercise book passed down through various housemasters' wives dating back to Elizabeth Underhill. Our domestic staff included Bert, Ethel and Peggy. Bert the houseman worked well into his eighties, cleaning the ground floor and helping with the ancient plumbing system. He spent the afternoons in an old chair in a cubby-hole under the stairs, emerging in time to share out the daily bread and butter for the boys and to make tea in an ancient urn. Ethel cleaned the dormitories and very out of date bathrooms. Peggy coped with Number 12 (now Watt House), keeping her biscuits in the airing cupboard. They gathered in the maids' kitchen for a break each morning at precisely the same time – Ethel's strict time-keeping was so that she could continue her day's work as an usherette at the local cinema. Later on we had some very loyal and hard-working staff including Eileen, Rene and Sylvia. They took great pride in their work, despite the modest pay, and were always willing to help boys in trouble, to clear up after the untidy ones and to assist with various crises including floods and flu epidemics. Sylvia continued working for us when Forbes became second master and remained with us for twenty-eight years.'

ARNOLD AND HARRISON

These two men between them bestrode the twentieth century at Eastbourne College. Edward Carleton Arnold joined the staff in 1899, became headmaster in 1924 and served on the Council for most of the rest of his life until his death in 1949. Robin Harrison arrived in Pennell in 1942, came back to teach geography in 1953 and on retirement from the teaching staff in 1989 continued as secretary of the OEA until he finally fully retired in 2004.

Michael Partridge writes of Arnold: 'Known to the boys and staff as "Og", Arnold was a bachelor and an enthusiast with limitless energy who devoted his long life to the College and its boys. One of the chief characteristics of Arnold's nature was his striving always for the first rate; whether buildings for the school, the conduct of a prefect or the status of the school itself. He coached the First XV for twenty-seven years, and the cricket team also, and generated a remarkable record of classical scholarships at Oxford and Cambridge. In 1904 he refounded the Natural History Society and his enthusiasm and national reputation as an ornithologist persuaded many pupils to join him in that activity. Some of "Og's bird boys"

My winter of discontent was in 1977. I was teaching at Plymouth College and had just returned from job hunting in Canada during the Christmas break. At home, there was a letter from Simon Langdale inviting me to interview at Eastbourne College. The next day a letter arrived from Richard Bradley at Ridley College in St Catharine's, Ontario, offering me a place in their English department. What to do? I liked the Ridley offer, and I had enjoyed my visit to the school during the Christmas break, but I decided to go for the Eastbourne interview just to see what the place was like. Simon Langdale picked me up at the station and drove me past College Field with the impressive view of the tower and the cloisters and the playing field that looked like a putting green. The next morning I met some of the staff. Everyone was so unjaded. My previous experience of schoolmasters in England was of a rather dowdy lot, sharp enough in the mind but a little cynical and irascible. The Eastbourne teachers I met were excited about teaching, and the students I encountered during my visit were responsive and outgoing. Simon Langdale was a headmaster I wanted to work for; he made me want to be the best teacher I could be. Suddenly I was desperate for the position. I got lucky. Simon offered me the job.

It is not for me to say that those were golden years for the College, but they certainly were halcyon days for those of us who taught there. All my new colleagues were individuals, and most were young blades who cut a swathe through convention and for whom the students were the real curriculum. From them I learned most of what I know about teaching. The students were very special too. Sure, there were rogues and mavericks among them, but the great majority were receptive and talented and interested and did not mind being pushed. One of them once came up to me after a class and said thank you for the lesson (on King Lear, I think). 'Not sucking up, sir, 'cos I'd tell you if the lesson was bad, but this was a good one.' I also remember the night after our daughter was born, when Nigel Wheeler (who else?) surreptitiously altered the script at the last minute to include a scene where champagne was called for and a toast was proposed to the new father, which brought hearty applause from the assembled students and a lump to the throat of a happy and sleep-denied yours truly.

Colin Brezicki (staff 1977–88)

C. V. Temperley   R. Butler   C.R.B. Wrenford   D.E. Noel-Paton   H.C. Aldom   R.G. Howell   R.C. Storrs   E.S. Hunt   J.E. Bowman   H.J. Belk

J. Hall   T. Tanqueray   H.F.M. Morres   G.H. Peacock   E.C. Arnold   E.C. Lester   R.C. Burton   H.V. Waterfield   S.H. Foot
HM 1925-29

Senior Common Room, c1925

went on to achieve eminence in that profession. His first remark to the Council after his appointment as headmaster was characteristic: "I should like to say at once that as headmaster I don't intend to draw any more salary than I did as an assistant master; the balance will go to the building fund." His generosity to the College knew no bounds and we can count Og's Wood, the Mere at Hampden Park, ninety acres of marshland near Litlington and the "Cuckmere Bounty"

among his many benefactions. OEs of many generations will recall the figure, with its ample Victorian moustache, clad in a large-peaked flat cap and ankle-length Ulster, patrolling the touch line at First XV rugby matches long after his retirement and until the year of his death. An Old Eastbournian, one of Arnold's closest friends, spoke at his memorial service: "Here was a man, we saw at once, who accepted the fundamental decencies of life absolutely

When E C Arnold became headmaster, he determined to turn Eastbourne College into a famous school. He had already moved the school into rugger – then more obviously 'gentlemanly' than soccer. He demanded the frequent singing of the Latin school song, with its magnificent and, alas, now forgotten tune. The now seemingly monstrous rugger song was roared out in Big School as the new Stags were sworn in; and he shamelessly wooed the upper classes. He didn't much care for day boys, and his stern refusal to admit the sons of 'tradesmen' caused, even then, resentment in the town, and it was the softening of this policy by Gordon Carey that brought about the great rift between the two men. Under Carey, thanks in part to its First World War record and in part to Arnold's brilliant and prolonged public relations campaign, the College's national reputation stood highest. And although Nugee initially wanted to turn Eastbourne into another Radley, the evacuation turned him into the stoutest fighter for Eastbourne's individuality and independence, and he is rightly honoured as the saviour of the school. The post-war public silence about the merits of the school can mainly be put down to Birley's long and distinguished reign. But Eastbourne's record – in the armed services, the performing arts, academia and the best of big business, and in all the inspired changes in its ongoing life – deserves a greater fame. So too can we lay what is no wild claim to being the happiest school in England.

Roger Holloway (P47)

Left: Staff pantomime, 1980.

Top left: Cam Tate prepares the cricket square.

– truth, loyalty, courage, generosity. With that acceptance, came the obligation to live up to those standards. To Arnold, to accept standards and not to live up to them, was quite unthinkable."'

'Robin Harrison,' Michael Partridge also writes, 'has been a part of the College for over sixty years. He joined Pennell House at Radley in 1942 a few weeks short of his fourteenth birthday and within two years was playing scrum half for the First XV in that epic match in which the College beat the all-conquering Radley side by a drop goal to a try (4–3). Back in Eastbourne, he was head of house for six terms, two whole years, in 1945–7, and head of school in 1946–7. As Tony Henderson said in his tribute to Robin on his retirement in 1989: "There were giants in the earth in those days and… foremost of these giants was Robin Harrison. His astounding enthusiasm and versatility leaves me open-mouthed. Head of school, captain of rugger, cricket and shooting, CSM in the Corps, he continued to find time to play tennis and fives for the College, besides winning both the 100 yards and the shot putting in the athletics victory over Westminster in his final year." He left in 1947 and we, as small boys, looked with awe upon this paragon. At Cambridge he won his blue for rugby, playing at scrum half against Oxford in 1951, and graduated in geography in 1952. Then in 1953 he joined the staff at the College to teach geography. He ran the rugby from 1955 until 1974, was head of geography 1966–79, housemaster of Craig 1978–86, helped with junior cricket and ran

golf from 1973 to 1988. After he retired from the staff in July 1989, having already taken over as secretary of the OEA in 1976, he proceeded to continue in that role (which in those days included the editorship of the OE magazine) until his final retirement in 2004. He kept track of OEs, their whereabouts, activities, marriages and offspring in a wonderfully archaic rotary card index. He and David Winn did much to revitalise the association, while the annual reunions owed their tremendous success to Robin's careful planning and efficiency. OEs of many generations

Chris Saunders sat at the end of the pine table in our newly refurbished kitchen to talk about the impact on our family of Colin taking on the role of housemaster of Blackwater House. Momentarily I considered giving up the day job to become house matron until reality set in. Could I really see myself sorting the laundry and tending the in-grown toenails?

The challenge was to combine the roles of wife and mother, working woman and housemaster's wife at a time when in order to be taken seriously as adviser with the Industrial Society one downplayed the supporting roles behind the scenes. (I considered, however, that I did have first-hand experience when we hosted a conference, sponsored by Good Housekeeping *magazine, for women with partners 'wedded' to the job.) We looked on the boys as part of our small family; Becki, our daughter, was even heard referring to them proudly as 'my boys'. I did duty on matron's days off, usually a Friday and Sunday, and to the initial amusement of more experienced hands insisted we booked an evening a week when we would go to a local restaurant to talk to each other (the entry in the diary read 'Out with Wife'). The rewards? Although at times it felt as if we lived in a goldfish bowl, our house was large and gracious; although a small family, the numbers swelled to seventy-plus during the term time and it was fun to share Colin's responsibilities with him. But I continued, and still do, to value my role outside the house and College.*

Rosie Polden

malevolent glare so that, rather than attempt to chase it, they always decided they had something much more important to do elsewhere. But whenever Tigger appeared it would come up and rub itself against his legs, purring loudly. He never really became an "old dog", keeping remarkably fit and active until his final illness. And when he died, that wonderful man Ted Goldsmith, the College foreman of works, took him from me and buried him beneath an apple tree behind the cricket nets on Memorial Field.'

Robin Harrison with Tigger.

venerate Robin, and rightly so. Tony Henderson again: "Whatever he does, the College to which he has given so much owes him far more than it can ever repay."'

He is also remembered for his dog, Tigger: as he himself recalls, 'When I got married, Liz was often referred to as "Mrs Tigger", and I can honestly say that, in my thirty years as secretary of the OEA, I never got a letter from an OE of that generation which did not mention how well they remembered Tigger.' And in an article for the *Old Eastbournian*, he wrote: 'Many OEs will remember Tigger patrolling the touchline during First XV matches, inspecting all the other dogs and, presumably, making sure that they were behaving properly. When I was refereeing house matches he always seemed able to distinguish the final whistle from all the other whistles, and would shoot onto the pitch to greet me long before anyone else reacted. He also had an extraordinary empathy with other animals. The Phillips' family cat was a ferocious creature which would never let another dog within yards of it. It could shrivel them with a

Where we are; where we are going

A metaphor: I am in the business of growing trees. I aim to be Capability Brown, the nurturer and landscaper of lasting monuments within a far-ranging and forward-looking design. Trees need the long view; they need to be well nourished right down at their roots, encouraged to grow straight and true, not forced or twisted into unnatural shapes. As a recent newcomer to Eastbourne, I am all too aware of the strong oaks that are the result of my predecessors' tenures as headmasters of the College; some of those that Chris Saunders and Charlie Bush planted are only sturdy saplings as yet, and I know that it is my successors who will see the fruits of my labours at Eastbourne. The converse is what I am not – a grain farmer, interested only in this year's bumper crop, this year's profit or loss. Not that the annual harvest isn't essential too; we wouldn't have any food without it. But children are not seasonally gathered grains of wheat. They, like the mighty oak, need the long view.

Metaphor over. Of course we, like all schools, know that first-class teaching and high, uncompromising academic standards are the bedrock of an excellent school. We want our students to do well at GCSE and A level. We want them to get the qualifications they need to study at good universities and gain a solid grounding for the challenges life will throw at them. Results are important. Our place in the league tables is an all too public indication of the quality of our teaching, the commitment of our staff and the hard work of our students. We do and will always pride ourselves on our achievements in this area, applauding and taking pride in excellent exam results and high positions in the tables. In the same way, we cheer on our sports teams and rejoice when they bring home trophies and reputations as fearsome opponents. We delight in a beautiful choral evensong, the virtuosity of the string quartet, the joyousness of

the latest musical. And we marvel at the creativeness and ingenuity of those who excel with their brains and hands at art, and design and technology.

Yet I have a wider vision too – one that I believe I share with the majority of Eastbournians. My values are predominantly about being positive and active, untrammelled by unnecessary rules and conventions, outward-looking, willing to question and to take risks. The pursuit of excellence, the willingness to participate fully in school life and pride in achievement and performance are some of those values; and so are doing the right thing with integrity, being courteous and kind, enjoying the thrill of

Simon Davies with two of his prefects on Old Wish Road, 2006.

A Greek lesson with Spencer Beal, 2006.

creativity, taking care of those who look after us and our environment. As I have set out in my values pamphlet, I believe that an Eastbourne College education develops pupils academically, broadens their experience outside the classroom, inculcates moral values and prepares them to play a full and effective role in society. My job, as well as that of all my colleagues on the staff, is to support our students in achieving all their goals and to treat them as we want them to treat themselves and others.

When I came to this school I was excited by the buzz I felt, from teaching staff, support staff, parents, friends of the College and most of all from the students themselves – a buzz that can only come from mutual respect and understanding. Then, on reading the contributions to this book from so many old pupils, I

Next year will be our tenth and final year as Eastbourne College parents, and we just want to say a few words – of thanks, really, and of our reflections as proud parents. As much as we greatly appreciate that all three of our children have excelled academically, for us boarding at Eastbourne College has been about so much more than that. It's been about a well balanced, all-round education within a happy and nurturing environment. It's been about a spectrum of supportive relationships. It's been about delivering back to us three wonderful adults, as well prepared as they can be for the future, and who all agree, for different reasons, that they couldn't have gone to a better school. Eastbourne College definitely has 'The X Factor'!

Sandie and David Heslop

was thrilled by their loyalty to and delight in their alma mater. Society and education have changed immeasurably in the last 140 years, and even more in the last thirty, so for many the College is a very different place now from when they were here. But some things remain constant. As one OE from the 1940s wrote, 'We lay what is no wild claim to being the happiest school in England.' I am tempted to make the same claim today.

Simon Davies

OLD EASTBOURNIANS

The Old Eastbournian Association was officially launched in January 1895, although for many years previously old boys had organised informal reunion dinners and matches against College teams. The OEA has been in existence ever since, promoting social functions among its members, offering considerable financial support and acting as the link between the College and its alumni/ae. Various charitable, social and sporting offshoots have grown up from time to time, as well as links with OEs at university and abroad. OE news was for many decades included as a supplement to the *Eastbournian* magazine, though the *Old Eastbournian* was published for seventeen years between 1922 and 1939 and is now in existence again, edited by Michael Partridge, OE and College archivist.

Individual reunion clubs also exist, for example the Mole Club, founded in 1962 by a number of School House boys. Peter Woods writes: 'Named after the nickname of one of the founders, the Mole Club had a very simple purpose – to encourage friends who had known each other while at School House to keep in contact by meeting once a year over dinner. The first meeting took place in a pub close to Victoria. As time progressed and the fortunes of the friends increased the meetings moved to more comfortable venues, and we now meet each January in a private room at a restaurant in London's West End. The success of such a dining club depends on having an organiser who is willing to put time and effort into making it happen. Christopher Dane immediately took it upon himself to be the secretary, and organised a meeting every year until his untimely death in 2004. In 2007 the club will celebrate its forty-second anniversary having not missed a single year. Members are: Robert Barrett, Bruce Bintley, Tony Booth, Chris Buckland, Nick Buckland, Mike Carpenter, Mike Dunning, Robert Gabriel, David Gast, Dougal Graham, Adrian Hall, Keith Kirby, James Lucas, Peter Mair, Richard Masefield, Peter Roach, Keith Ross, Tim Scott, Peter Smith, Hywel Thomas, Michael Valmas, David Winn and Peter Woods.'

The OEA is maintained through fees paid by its future members while they are still at school, and it organises dinners, sports fixtures, mostly against other alumni/ae associations, and careers conventions for current year 11 and sixth form pupils. It has reps all over the world and produces termly newsletters and the annual magazine to keep all its members in touch with the school and each other.

It was my privilege to become the secretary of the OEA in 2004 following Robin Harrison's twenty-eight-year tenure. Subsequently, in the light of the several thousand OEs as well as other friends whose lives the College has touched over its history, the College Council took steps in 2006 to harness all the goodwill engendered by this important constituency, and the Eastbourne College Society was born. As its first director, assisted by David Blake, our brief is to keep contact and reconnect with all former pupils, and also remain in touch with all who wish to keep abreast of what is happening at the College. The Old Eastbournian Association, the Arnold Embellishers, the archives, the Collegial Society (started in 2000 with the aim of organising events for friends) and all employees of the College are part of the ECS and it works closely with the Foundation Office.

John Thornley

GENERATIONS

Repeat business is a great testament in the business world today and the same is true of successive generations attending Eastbourne College. There are many examples of such multi-generation families, and the College is now sufficiently far away from the decision to admit girls into the sixth form in 1969 that we have the daughters of mothers who were here, not just the sons (and grandsons) of fathers. The following are only some of those whose families stretch back over the years.

The Cracknell family is one example: David Cracknell (G46), his sons Chris (G72) and Ian (G73), his grandson Edward, at present in Gonville, and his granddaughter Elizabeth who is in School House. The Ohlsons are another: Ken (G37) and his sons Christopher (G73) and Jonathan (G75); Ken's daughter's son, Francis Wynter, joins Gonville in September 2007. The Braithwaites can boast four generations at the College, with seven family members among the alumni. The three Lee brothers who were here in the 1980s had a father and a grandfather at the College as well as other family connections. The Yorkes too: brothers who were at the College in the 1980s and 1990s, whose grandfather and great-uncle were Howells, as were uncles and cousins of the next generation – a family association which goes back to 1919 continuously through attendance at the College, teaching there or serving on the Council. Stephen Yorke (B77), a current

Top: Staff children after Big School walk, 1981, with Chris Saunders.

Three generations of the Cracknell family.

governor, was moreover head boy when Big School burnt down in 1989 – and slept through the whole thing. There are many more – the Lovitt-Danks, the Caffyns, the Copps, the Winns, the Partridges, the Sibrees, the Underhills… just some of the many families whose names recur generation after generation.

BUILDINGS AND BENEFACTORS

Eastbourne College has never been a wealthy or well endowed school. Indeed at times during its history it has been perilously close to bankruptcy, and it survived its early years only through a combination of bank loans, the generosity of the Dukes of Devonshire and the input of successive headmasters. Then in 1901 came the first of what was to become a succession of generously supported appeals and individual donations from Old Eastbournians, when they paid for the South African War memorial windows and tablet in chapel. In 1909 funds were raised for the school's first assembly hall, later called Big School, and after the First World War a massive appeal was launched for what was to become the Memorial Building in commemoration of the 164 old boys who had died in the war.

Later appeals and benefactions from OEs enabled the College to make further purchases, including Reeves House (now Craig House) and Nugent House, both named after the OE benefactors whose generosity had made the purchases possible. After the end of the Second World War, the OEA provided a fitting memorial to the 163 of their members who had died by raising money to buy Memorial Field, in the 1950s a College Endowment Fund supported both new building and renovations, and the centenary appeal in 1967 both reduced the College's debt and allowed further purchases and improvements. The squash courts and swimming pool were the result of further appeals in the 1970s. Then after fire destroyed Big School in 1981 a fund-raising campaign led enthusiastically by OEA president David Winn raised £650,000. Big School was rebuilt as the College theatre within the carcass of the old.

Several old boys have been extremely generous to the College in their wills, and appeals have continued to be successful: in 1993 OEs supported the creation of the Ronald Howell Memorial Pavilion in memory of a much-loved housemaster; and in 1998 a shortfall in the funding for the new Science Centre and the new D&T department was once again met by OEs, parents and friends of the College. The forming of the College Foundation in 2002 was the response to the perceived need to raise revenue steadily over time so that major projects, scholarships and bursaries could be funded. Under this umbrella the Devonshire Society, the college's legacy club, was founded. Truly this is a school built by its alumni.

Michael Partridge

THE FOUNDATION

The Eastbourne College Foundation was formed in 2002 following the successful appeal which raised £1.3m towards the cost of the new Science and D&T Centres. Forbes Wastie was appointed as the Foundation's first director, with appeal secretary Christine Todd as its administrator. I succeeded Forbes at the end of 2004, although he continues to make an invaluable contribution in a consultancy capacity.

The Foundation is the main fund-raising arm of the College. Its primary function is to generate funds to enhance the fabric of the school and to provide bursaries so that talented boys and girls from all parts of the community can enjoy the benefits of an Eastbourne College education. The Foundation also manages and promotes the College's legacy club, the Devonshire Society, named after the founding family of the College, which has more than 80 members who between them have pledged in excess of £2.25m to the school in their wills. The 12th Duke and Duchess of Devonshire attended a reception at the College in May 2006 before the annual Devonshire Society lunch, which was followed five months later by the inaugural society gathering in the splendid surroundings of their home, Chatsworth, in Derbyshire.

Foundation receptions have been held throughout the UK, and in New York and Hong Kong. Closer to home, Royal Eastbourne Golf Club is host to the Foundation Golf Challenge every July, which

My lasting memory of the College is of my very first day, not because anything particularly dramatic happened but because it was one of the most overwhelming days of my life. I grew up in Malaysia and had only visited 'home' a few times before coming to Eastbourne to start boarding school. There had never been any question in my father's mind that I would be attending The College (Dad always pronounced the capitals), as he was the second generation of boarders and by now it was a firm family tradition. When the time finally came, Dad made the journey with me to get me kitted out and enrolled. The Lushes were running the school shop at the time and Mr Lush had, of course, taught Dad. Between them they conspired to make me look utterly ridiculous, dwarfed in clothes at least two sizes too large for me. We were given a tour of Gonville by the head of house, before being deposited in the hall outside the housemaster's office for a last chat before my father took his leave. I was now at a fairly low point, and it was a welcome relief to be put immediately at ease by my new housemaster, David Welsh, who told me that if I had any problems at anytime whatsoever, the door to his office was always open. However, as soon as we were out of earshot, Dad took me by the arm and earnestly told me that no matter what Mr Welsh had just said, under no circumstances whatsoever was I ever to think about entering the housemaster's office uninvited. He then shook my hand and departed for the plantations of Malaysia. Times had, of course, changed somewhat since Dad had been through the College, and needless to say I sat in David's office on many an occasion on the telephone to Malaysia. And I found too that Mr Harrison, who had featured a great deal in Dad's tales for his bullet-like rugby passes and his 'no-nonsense' teaching style, had changed not an iota since my father's day.

Philip Lee (G83)

attracts a convivial mixture of Old Eastbournians, current and former parents, pupils, staff and local companies. The 2006 event, for which the main sponsor was College bankers NatWest, saw eighteen teams of four players compete for the trophy and raise over £10,000 to provide a sixth form bursary.

In 2007 the Development Appeal is for music, the centrepiece of which is to be the new Birley Music Centre, named after Michael Birley (headmaster 1956–70) and his wife Ann. This exciting building will enable the College to showcase properly the impressive quality and variety of music taught and played at the school. The design includes a large recital hall and state of the art recording studio, both of which it is hoped will be widely used by the town as well as by the College.

Kim Deshayes

Right: Nigel Wheeler and his Millennium Globe, with George Eliot's words around the base: 'Our deeds still travel with us from afar, And what we have been makes us what we are'.

Left: Architect's drawing of the proposed new Birley Music Centre (Neil McWalter).

Appendix:
College songs

Carmen Eastbourniense in its full original Latin and English versions:

Exultemus, o sodales,
Iam cessare fas novales;
Paululum laxemus mentes,
Dulce domum repetentes.

Ho! Comrades, hearts and voices raise
To welcome the dear holidays;
Away with books, tear up the scheme,
No thought of these to spoil our dream!

Chorus
Age, frater juxta frater,
Celebremus Alman Matrem;
Quae nos ornate, haec ornanda,
Quae nos amat, adamanda.

Come, Alma Mater, let us sing,
Till overhead the rafters ring,
With her – 'tis hers – our glory sharing,
With answering love her love declaring.

Venditet Etona rivam,
Singularem Herga clivum;
Nobis magni maris fonts
Alluunt aeternos montes.

Of Thames let Eton boast her fill,
And Harrow glory in her hill;
Ours are the cliffs that Ocean laves,
Ours the sweet music of his waves.

Sive litus vis lustrare,
Sive iuga pererrare,
Fragrans ambit odor maris,
Spirat aura salutaris.

Whether we roam the sea-wash'd shore,
Or range the skyey uplands o'er,
Health's in the fresh breeze blowing free,
Health in the fragrance of the sea.

Forti fortes sic creantur
Matre filii, formantur
Sana mens et corpus sanum,
Nobile virtutis fanum.

Thus daily are renew'd our powers,
For Alma Mater's strength is ours;
Yea, fitter clime where will ye find,
To breed both healthy frame and mind?

Litteris, ludis studendo,
Artes, mores excolendo,
Si quid hinc nacti gaudemus,
Huic acceptum referemus.

Thorough in work and keen in games,
Nor yet neglecting Virtue's claims,
If aught of good we here have won,
Hers be the praise and hers alone!

Io! Vos, Io!
Undecemviri victores,
Vos, alipedes cursores!
Io, vos prudentes nare,
Vosque, robur militare!

Hurrah! Hurrah!
Elevens both a cheer for you,
Cheers for our hardy athletes too;
Cheers for our Gunners, gallant corps,
And for our swimmers one cheer more!

Gymnicos iam memoremus,
Studiosos collaudemus,
Omnes se, scholam clarantes,
Urbi orbi illustrantes.

Io! Da, Io!
Da patroni, da Rectoris,
Da senatus adjutoris;
Da memoriae priorum,
Da praesentum, venturorum!

Our gymnasts cheer; cheer them whose fame
Is to have earn'd a scholar's name;
A cheer for all who, winning glory,
Have graced the roll of Eastbourne's story.

A health! A health!
Here's to the President! The Head!
The Staff! All friends our weal who've sped!
To Old Boys' cherish'd memory,
To all Eastbournians yet to be!

Arnold's second rugby song:

Our game is not for milksops with their namby-pamby ways,
It's a game for the ding-dong fighter with the pluck of the good old days.
We've work for the speedy runner, for the rover who battles alone,
We've a place for the lightweight bantam, we've a niche for the sixteen stone.

Chorus   For it's devil take the hindmost when 'College' strikes the ear,
                      Charge home with a rousing tackle,
                      Bang through, stretch 'em out, never fear.
                      Fit via vi Unanimi,
                      Vociferabimur,
                      Fit via vi.

When the ball soars up from the centre, race under it while in the air,
If a 'three' gets it into his clutches, let him know, let him feel you are there,
Is it touch? Then out with it quickly, every man at the ball as it flies,
Come away the whole pack with a rattle, confound it what matters their size.

And now for a jolly good scrimmage, get hold of the ball to begin,
Whip it out to the halves and the centres, now a feint and a swerve and you're in.
What asleep! Brace up for the struggle, it has only just begun,
They will come with a rush in a moment, keep it up, keep it up or you're done.

If you're bottled on your goal-line, hang on to the ball if you can,
If you get in a stew or feel fuddled, barge in and bowl over a man.
Now we've reached the last five minutes, once more to our line they have come,
Screw up for a final effort, stick it out to the end and we've won!

The millennium hymn:

Christ, the dawn of our salvation,
Rising light across creation,
        Lord of earthbound years,
Be the light that lights our living,
Our receiving and our giving;
        Light our laughter
        And our tears.

Changeless noonday light of reason,
Proving truth in every season
        Of our changing heart;
As our founders caught your shining,
Worked with sight and faith combining
        Light our future
        At the start.

Christ, the star of contemplation,
In our every inspiration
        Shed your holy joy;
May our skills reflect your glory,
Lighting with the Gospel story
        All the talents
        We employ.

Christ is here! The sound of singing,
Advent bells their welcome ringing
        Echo down the years;
        Down two thousand years*
Dawn to dawning, choirs are raising
Songs of praise for Love amazing,
        For each day that
        Christ appears.

(*for use at millennium celebrations)

Nugent leavers, 2006.

List of subscribers

Ghazi Abbar 99–03
D Acloque 53–57
Jessica Adams 05–10
Sarah Adams (née Payne) 76–78
Douglas T Adamson 38–41
Furo, Boma and Ibiye Adoki 97–07
Sarah Aitkenhead (née Lyell) 74–76
Camilla, Harriet and Amy Aiton 89–94
Chris Albone 72–76
Peter L Albrecht 47–48
Jean Alder (Widow of
    Bernard Alder MBE, Bursar)
Anna Alexander and Family 99–04
Jaafar S Al-Hillawi 66–70
Faisal A Ali 84–89
John Allan 60–65
John B Alliban 39–42
David Anderson 57–61
Guy Anderson 99–05
Richard Anderson 03–08
Tim Andrews 82–87
Paul K Anthony 53–58
Joe Arch 99–03
Dr Robin C Armstrong Brown 51–55
John C A Arnold 51–55
Ann Arscott
Phillip Ashforth 68–73
Philip James Ashley 04–present
S B B Askaroff 73–75
David A Atkins 49–54
J M Atkins 43–47
Caroline Atkinson 94–96
Christopher L Atkinson 52–57
Edward Atkinson 77–82
Edward T Atkinson 79–84
Paul and Lisa Atkinson
    (née Chave) 94–99 and 95–98
Stuart Ayers 77–82
Mr and Mrs Mark Baddeley
Rupert R C Bairamian 75–80
Dr and Mrs Guy Baker
    School Doctor, 92–04
Charlie E Banister 88–93

Michael Barber 56–60
James and Alex Barbour 05–present
Mike Barford 63–68
P D Barford 59–64
Edward Barnes 01–04
Oliver Barnes 99–04
Phoebe Barnes 03–present
Satthaporn Barnes 06–present
Nick and Jonny Barr 99–04
Charles V G Bartlett 60–63
Michael Bartlett 57–62
Rebecca Bartlett 02–07
Kenneth B Barton 44–47
D Barwell 79–84
Robert Barwell 42–46
Jon Bathard-Smith 88–93
Sheila Batten Gonville Matron, 88–00
S Andrew Bazergan 58–63
Glen Beadon 74–77
J B Beatson 35–40
Hannah Christina Beck 06–present
Ronald Beck
Mrs C Beecroft
Nick Beecroft
David Beer Staff
In memory of Henry John (Aggie) Belk
    Staff, 24–26
Cecil L Bell 33–37
H Michael Benians 39–43
Jeremy Bennett 75–80
Anna Bentley 95–97
Ben and Harry Bentley 04–present
Charlotte S E Berry 02–07
Nicholas C Berry 94–99
Robert Bexson 70–75
Bob Bickersteth 77–82
Lauren Bicknell 95–97
G H Bilton 42–46
Edward Birkbeck 83–88
Stuart Birkbeck 77–82
Michael Pellew Birley Headmaster, 56–70
Alexander Bishop and Family 02–07
Mr and Mrs R J Bisson

Lief Bjornsen 04–06
Alistair Blackburn 84–89
Peter V H Blackburn 58–62
Richard Blackburn 51–56
Richard F Blackburn 65–70
Roger Blackburn 54–59
David Blake Staff, 06–present
Tim and Wendy Bluett
Richard Bones 50–53
A R Bonner 38–43
Charlie Bostock Staff, 89–present
Dominic Boulding 04–09
Ken Boulter 47–49
Harriet Bowers 05–07
G E W Bowyer 53–58
John Boyle 76–79
R G Brabazon 72–77
Chris Bradford 48–52
Sam Bradford 63–67
David J Braithwaite 64–69
Peter J Braithwaite 63–67
Nicholas Brewer 76–81
Philip Brice 70–75
Simon Brister 62–67
Penny Britt (née Wynes) 83–85
Philip Broadley 74–79
Anthony Brook 50–54
M M Brooke 37–41
Dom Brown 00–05
Maj G G Brown 38–43
Paul Browne 77–82
Richard G Browne 49–54
Dr Aleck Brownjohn 58–64
A C M Bryant 45–49
Molly and Fred Buchanan 04 and 07
Nick Buckland 59–63
James Bucknall 83–88
Nicholas Bugeja
J F Bull 57–62
P E Bullock
Mrs P Burbidge
Peter Burdett 39–42
Joel T Burgess 99–04

Lloyd J A Burgess	96–01	
Richard Burke	59–64	
Christopher Burt	47–51	
David G Burt	66–70	
David P Burt	88–93	
Peter A Burt	70–75	
Charlie Bush	Headmaster, 93–05	
Tom Butler-Manuel	05–09	
A M Caffyn	46–51	
Edward Caffyn	79–84	
Simon G Caffyn	74–79	
Simon Caldwell	75–80	
Sam Callaghan	01–06	
Reginald G Cambridge	48–52	
David Richard Candlin	49–54	
S D Cane-Hardy	00–02	
Richard Canham	61–67	
John Capaldi	74–79	
Ted Capper	48–53	
James Carragher	05–present	
Nicholas Carragher	05–present	
Andrew Carstairs-McCarthy (formerly Carstairs)	58–62	
Edward J J Carter	06–present	
Bill Castellan	53–56	
Ian H Cazlet	47–51	
Guy Chadwell	87–92	
Scott J Chambers	99–03	
Alexander Chan	03–present	
Adrian Chandler	70–74	
Subodh Chanrai	76–79	
Sunder Chanrai	69–74	
Clive Charlton	60–65	
Alison Charmain		
Steve Charnock	69–74	
Alex Chartres	92–97	
Harriet Chartres	91–93	
Michael Chartres	55–60	
David A Chesterfield	52–55	
Pinky Lee Ching Hing	06–present	
Sarah Chu (née Wright)	88–90	
David, Karen and Dominic Clark		
M T H (Shanker) Clark	42–48	
Tom Clarke and Family		
Brian Cleave CB QC	53–58	
Edward H Coates	04–09	
Patrick Colbourne	55–59	
Adrian Cole FRICS	58–62	
Dr Christopher Cole	29–33	
Jeremy Cole	68–73	
John Cole	72–77	
Miss Gemma Coleman	05–present	
Trevor R Colgate	42–47	
Brian Collins	46–51	
J Robert Alderson Colman	63–68	
Mrs P Colyer		
Claude and Charles Compton	98–06	
Jeremy Compton	77–82	
Tom Compton	86–91	
Cliff Comyns	Staff, 75–06	
Derek J Connolly	55–59	
Damian Conway	02–05	
Mrs Sara J Cooke	69–71	
Sam Cooke	97–02	
Ken Cookes (formerly Colsell)	56–61	
Lyndon Cooper	60–62	
Dr N I Cooper	67–72	
Nicholas Cooper	64–68	
Joyce and Don Copeman		
Copp Family		
Chris Corfield	Staff	
William Corke	00–05	
Simon Cornford	62–66	
Richard Cotran		
Wing Commander Patrick Coulcher	51–54	
Nicholas Coureas		
Charlotte Courtney	02–06	
Michaela Cowap	99–04	
Chris Cracknell	72–77	
John Crawshaw College Council, 81–present		
Steven John Crawshaw	74–79	
Neville Creed	69–74	
Helene Crook		
Richard Crook	65–70	
Crowther Girls	90–97	
Gordon Crumley	47–52	
Cumnor House School		
Alistair J Cuthill	52–55	
Mr and Mrs R Cutler	01–06	
Nick Darby	54–59	
P D Davidson-Houston	77–82	
Hugh Davies Jones, Council Member		
Matthew Davies	02–07	
Neil Davies	72–77	
Simon Davies Headmaster, 05–present		
Sue Davies Headmaster's Secretary, 73–99		
Brad Davis		
I Dawson	44–48	
Keith Dawson	52–58	
Lt Cdr P A C Day	34–36	
Richard L Day	46–50	
Stephen G de Clermont	56–59	
Nicholas Deane	80–83	
James Liam Deasy	83–88	
Benjamin P Deery	98–03	
Justin Denham	77–82	
M K H Denny	95–00	
Alison Deshayes (née Townley)	70–72	
Cathy Deshayes	99–01	
Kim Deshayes	Staff, 04–present	
A Devine		
The Duke of Devonshire CBE		
Geoffrey Christian Diamond	97–02	
James F Dickerson	65–66	
Dr D G Dickson	36–41	
Michael Dickinson	39–44	
Simon 'Dicky' Dickson	03–present	
Mrs H S Dixon-Nuttall, widow of Col J F Dixon-Nuttall CBE	37–41	
Christopher and Jenny Dodd	03–08	
D L Hudson	40–44	
Torin Douglas	64–69	
Adam and Ivan Dovey	96 and 98	
James A B Down		
Michael Drummond-Brady	42–47	
Pam Duffill	Staff, 95–07	
Mr and Mrs L S and C M Duggleby		
Fraser Dunk	04–present	
Stuart K Dunk	96–01	
C F K Dunn	42–47	
David J Durrant	77–82	
David Dyer	53–59	
John Earle	70–75	
Eastbourne Local History Society		
Jacqui Easterbrook	Staff, 81–present	
Rebecca Eaton	06–present	
Edgcumbe-Rendle Family	99–04	
R C Edmondson	Staff, 72–02	
Mrs S Edwards	Staff	
V C Ellison		
Dr Julia Elson (née Whiteside)	82–84	
John Elton MC	38–41	
Susanna Emsley (née Girling)	80–82	
Anna English	05–07	
J G Essame	40–44	
Katie, Amy and Josh Evans	01–10	
George Eve	51–55	
Mr and Mrs J C Everist		
Lucy Evershed (née de Moraes)	88–90	
Julian Evison	72–76	
Colin P G Farrant	69–74	
Alexander Farrow	03–present	
James Farrow	05–present	
Catherine Fellows (née Mitchell)	94–96	
Jeff Fendall	57–60	
Roger K Fendall	53–58	
Elizabeth Grace Fender	06–present	
Robert Fenwick Elliott	65–69	
Andrew C Ferguson	72–76	
Douglas W M Fergusson	66–70	
V W Ferris	Staff	
Carry Field	Staff, 95–present	
A M Fife-Miller	43–46	
Colonel J G Finney OBE	59–64	
A F Finn-Kelcey	56–60	

Dr Michael Fish MBE	58–62	Sydney Greet	34–38	Jodie Heslop	97–02
Hugh Fleetwood	58–62	John C Gregory	59–64	Mark Heslop	98–03
Kristian Fleming		Paul Gregory	62–67	Melanie Heslop	02–07
Mrs James Fletcher-Watson		Tom Gribble	93–98	Matt Higgins	77–82
Dr and Mrs A M Flett		R S Grover		Steven Higgins	74–79
James C K Fok	97–02	John Philip Groves	54–58	Isabella Highett	02–07
Sir Ian Forbes	60–65	Vicky Groves	06–present	James Highett	00–05
John C Ford	68–71	Jonathan Gunn	85–90	Annabel Hill (née Payne)	88–90
Charles Foster	99–04	Dr Michael Gurney FRCS	55–59	Michael S C Hill	54–57
Elizabeth Foster	69–70	Harry Guthrie	96–01	Noel Hill	40–45
Harry Foster	99–04	James Hackett	02–07	B M G Hillman	Parent, 81–83
John Foster	94–99	Francis Hadfield	62–65	M W E Hind	50–55
Lucy Foster	03–present	A D J Hall	49–54	Mrs M E Hindley	Staff
Mark Foster and Family	69–08	Alan Hall	42–46	Dermot O'Shea Hoare	44–49
Mrs Jane Fowler		Michael Hall	48–52	Michael Hobbs	69–73
A C Foxley	41–45	Oliver David Hall	46–51	Jake Hodgson	06–07
André François	94–99	Peter John Hall	50–56 (Prep), 56–60	David Hodkinson	Staff, 81–present
Dr Jeremy J Franklin	48–53	Robert C Hall	55–59	Thomas Holdaway	01–03
Ian Fraser (formerly Ian Sykes)	47–51	C F A T Halliday	Staff, 75–86	Richard Holliday	52–58
Mark Freeland	76–81	Christopher Hampton	00–05	Peter A Homburger	42–47
Tim Freshwater	58–63	Paul Handley	98–01	Matthew Honey	79–84
Jeremy Friend-Smith	49–54	Christopher Harding and Family	45–50	Paul A M Honney	51–53
Roy Galloway	53–55	Michael Richard Harding	35–38	Jan and Bill Hopkins	
Jamie Garratt	99–04	Trevor Hardy	65–71	Chris Hopkinson	65–70
Rory Garratt	03–present	R M Hargreaves	46–51	G Hornby MICE	44–48
Stuart Garratt	06–present	William P T Harper TD	62–67	Richard N Horne JP	39–45
M Iqbal Gelu	63–69	Hartnell B Harral	Staff, 47–81	Colin Hornsby	60–65
David George	64–68	Jennie Harrari and Robert Mumford		Mike Hounsell	76–81
Peter R Geyer	89–90	Mrs J L A Harriott	Staff	Antony Howard	
Charlotte Gibbs	99–04	David John Harris and		David Howell	
Georgie Gibbs	01–06	Benjamin Mark Harris		Diana Howell (Simpson)	47–57
James Gibbs	03–present	Elisa Harris	99–04	John Howell	53–57
R E Ginner	46–51	Mark Harris	95–00	Stephen G F Howell	47–51
M A Girling	33–38	Vivienne Harris-Jones (née Learner)		Felicity and Imogen Hudson	00–08
J Stuart Glass	35–40		72–74	Dr Mark G Hudson	84–89
Stuart Glenister	71–76	Michael Harrison	59–64	Christina Hühn	02–06
A J G Glossop	52–57	Robin Harrison	42–47	Robin E W Hume	36–39
Amanda Godman (née Graham)	70–72	D G Harry	49–51	John Hunnisett	59–65
David Godwin	Staff	Burton Hathaway	77–82	Katie Hunt	98–03
Cristina Hofmann Gonzalez		The Rev Andrew M J Haviland	78–83	Oliver Hunt and Louise Hunt	
Ben Goodberry	88–91	Anthony Haworth	50–53	(née Sloan)	87–92
Paul Goodenough	80–85	Francesca M K Hayward		Susie Hunt	00–05
C Goodman	02–07	Dr S R T Headley	28–32	Mr and Mrs T Hunter	03–09
John Gorrie		P M Healey	45–50	Hunter Blair Family	03–present
Oliver H Gosnell	50–55	B A Hebditch	47–50	Christopher R J Hurst	98–03
R David Gould	65–70	J R Hecks		Mrs E Hutchings	
R J Goulden	62–64	Lil Marie Hein	05–06	Peter Hutchinson	
Basil Gourlay	34–39	Nicolas P Hemes	51–55	Erica Hyder (née Pulford)	80–82
Chris Grant	02–07	Tarquin Henderson	74–78	Jonathan Hyder	77–82
Ian Caulfeild Grant	45–50	George Hendry	50–55	M C A Hyder	70–75
Robin G Graves-Morris	60–65	Ian Henley	70–75	Nigel Hyder	74–79
Philip M J Gray	40–44	Jim Henley	85–90	Alan Ifor-Jones	63–68
Rev Stephen Gray	79–84	Peter Henley	68–74	David Imlach	55–59
Green Family		Victoria Henley (née Crawshaw)	75–77	Nozomi Inoue	00–04
Harold Green	48–52	Philip Hepburn	61–66	Mr and Mrs T H Iqbal	03–present
William Green		J Peter Herz	78–80	Charles A L Isaac	90–95

F O N Jackson	55–58	Philip M Lee	83–88	Neil McWalter	55–59
Stephen Jacobs	63–68	Michael L Levene	56–61	G P Meanley	51–56
Alec James	46–48	Richard J Lewis	65–69	Jane Meanley	
Peter N Jamieson	60–63	Nathalie Lewis-Donaldson	01–06	Robert W Meek	94–99
Pieter J N Jansz	65–70	Toby Lewis-Donaldson	03–08	Jeremy E Mercer	96–01
D Jardin	46–50	Karen Liddell	94–96	John Carlos Mico	67–72
Michael and Andrew Jelinek	96–03	Richard Liddell	89–94	Stephen Middleton	81–86
Mrs V J Jennings	05–07	Paul, Matthew, Sarah and		Milo Mighell	44–49
Ayo Johnson	86–90	Nicholas Lindfield	87–present	John Millard	45–50
Nicholas Hope Johnson	71–74	Tony Ling	62–66	B H Miller	85–91
Dr Rodney Johnson	49–55	Alison Lingwood (née Gregory)	79–81	D C Miller	71–76
The Rev Ron Johnson	Chaplain, 85–99	John Little	86–03	E J Miller	01–06
Charlotte Lawson Johnston		Peter Lloyd-Bostock	61–65	J R St J Miller	72–77
(née Harvey)	98–00	John Lock	43–48	Charles C L Milligan	24–28
Eric Jones	Staff, 58–62	Emily Looke	94–96	Peter Milton Thompson	40–46
Graham Jones	Staff, 76–present	Jeremy C Lovitt-Danks	55–59	Sir Godfrey Milton-Thompson	43–48
Dr Julian Jones	90–95	Terry Lugg	60–65	Kelvin Miranda	87–89
Sam Jones	89–94	Martin Lulham	91–96	George Mitchell	03–08
Paul Jordan		Christopher Lush	73–78	James Mitchell	85–90
Devran Karaca	03–present	Mr and Mrs J S W Lush	Staff, 51–93	Carolyn Mole (née Deboo)	76–78
Maj Gen P R Kay CB MBE	35–39	William Lyth	67–71	Elisabeth Mollenhauer	05–06
Jeremy R Kaye	51–56	J G Maccoy	35–39	Richard Montgomerie	76–81
Jules Kaye	95–00	John Mace	47–52	Andrew Morgan	01–06
Stefan Philipp Keglmaier	00–01	Louise Macfadyen	04–09	Chris Morgan	04–present
D J O Kidd-May	45–50	Andrew Mackay	61–65	Peter Morgan	99–04
C J M Killick	99–05	Colin Mackenzie	59–64	Christopher John Morgan-Jones	57–62
Christian Kinde	00–05	D B Mackenzie	66–71	Allan Mornement	55–61
Christopher King	52–57	Natasha Mackey	04–06	A D C Morris	59–64
Martin King	63–74	Graham MacKichan	69–74	Johnny Morris	83–88
W M A King	48–53	John K C Maclean	58–62	Diana Moss (née Sparrow)	70–72
Miles Kirby	84–89	Rachael Macpherson (née Mackay)	87–89	Clifford Mould	56–60
C W E Kirk-Greene	Staff, 49–86	Christopher Mair	89–94	Ross Muir	78–82
Philippa C Kirtley		Gerald Malkin		Mrs Mary Mulroy	
Robert Kirtley	Staff, 65–95	James W Mangat	03–present	Matron Pennell House, 81–85
Rt Rev Mgr C J Klyberg	45–50	A J D Mann	45–49	Nigel R Mundy	50–54
John Knapp-Fisher	45–48	Luke March	65–69	C Andrew Murray	
Richard H Knight	58–62	R F Marchant	91–96	A S Muskat	65–70
Eric Koops	59–63	Tony Marcus	57–62	Adam Mynott	71–76
Michael Koops	67–72	Hunter David Mark	74–79	Dr Michael Mynott	
Adam and Matthew Kuchta		Sandy Marris	02–07	Medical Officer, 70–92
William Kunhardt-Sutton	02–07	M L J Marshall	38–42	Tim Mynott	68–73
Robert Lacey OBE		Claire L M Martin	96–97	A S Myrtle	46–49
Gilbert Lam	04–09	D H Martin		Tim Nelson	76–81
Y P Lam		Hazel Pauline Martin	98–99	Douglas Nethercot	26–29
M de L Landon	49–53	Sir Charles Beech Gordon Masefield		Jeremy Neville	66–71
Tim Landon	56–60		53–58	David D Newham	46–50
Simon Langdale	Headmaster, 73–80	Philip Mathew	42–46	Dr and Mrs J H Newton	Staff, 97–04
Jeremy Langridge	97–02	Imogen Maxwell	03–present	Jeremy Newton	64–69
Tim Langridge	95–00	Iona Maxwell	04–present	Major J D Newton	30–33
G R Langton	47–51	W D May	48–53	Christopher H Nicholson	60–65
Daniel and Chris Larkin	00–07	Paul Mayhew-Archer	67–71	John R Nicholson	65–69
George S Law		Michael J D McAra	60–64	Keith and Lesley Niven	
E M Le Brocq	46–51	Dr J F McGowan		Lt Cdr P A G Norman	33–38
Philip Le Brocq	Staff, 62–88	Colin McKerrow	47–51	Richard Norman	62–67
Sally Le Brocq		Sean N McLean MBE	84–89	Keith Norman-Smith	Staff, 48–84
Amanda Ledward (née Vokins)		A C McNaught		Julia Norris (née Fynmore)	72–74

Mark 'Henry' Norton	68–73	Colin Polden	Staff, 69–72 and 84–06	B N Salmon	79–83
David N B Nutt	51–55	David Pope	49–54	Nick Sankey	93–98
Martin Odell	62–67	Michael Pope	39–44	Prawit Sarakitprija	67–70
John Oecken	41–46	Chris Porter	74–79	Sargent Family, Charles Edward Piers	
N G Ogden	67–72	David Porter	78–83		91–02
K B Ohlson OBE MC TD	37–41	David I Powell	55–60	Chris Saunders	Headmaster, 81–93
The Old Eastbournian Lodge		Michael J D Powell	50–54	Cynthia Saunders	
Caroline J Oliver	98–02	Brian Prentis	Staff	Brian Sawyer	
Matthew Oliver	88–93	G H Price	59–63	David Sax	82–87
Simon R Oliver	97–99	John E Price	49–53	Friederike Schenck	06–present
Mark Oosterveen	93–98	Dr Meg Price		Ralph Schlüssel	00–05
J G R Osborn	47–51	D E Priestman		Gregor Schnuppe	83–88
Emma and Tom Osborne	06–present	Paul Prior	92–97	Michael Schnuppe	80–85
Dr David A Parker	Staff, 71–06	Alexandra Pritchett	95–97	Nina Schridde	
Gary Parrett		John Purchas	55–59	Sandra Schroeder	02–04
Desmond Partridge	34–37	Jack Putland		Clare Scott Dryden	80–81
Michael Partridge	46–51	Ian Quanstrom	72–77	Mike Scott	64–69
Tim Partridge	77–82	Jonathan Quantick	02–06	Robin C Scott	58–61
Eddie Pascoe	79–84	Timothy Quantick	04–09	Ted Seabrooke	67–71
William Patching	63–69	Ian Raeburn	76–81	John Seldon	49–53
Dr Richard G Paterson BSc MRCGP		Anthony Randall	52–56	Richard Seldon	84–86
	78–83	Christopher Ray	72–77	Mr and Mrs A P Selfe	03–05
David Patterson	45–49	Tom Reed	91–96	Tom Sewell	35–40
Andrew Paviour	86–88	Frederick R Reeve		Paul Seymour	69–75
Andrew F C Paynter	79–83	Angela Reid		Jeremy H Sharp	55–59
Lealand Pearce	00–05	Geoff Reynolds	57–60	Felicity J Shaw	08–
G J Pearson-Wright	67–72	Mrs R A Rhodes		Rebecca A Shaw	06–present
Alice Peck	03–08	General David Richards	65–70	John Shearn	31–35
Nick Pendry	Staff, 75–80, 84–present	Maj Gen N W F Richards	58–63	Rhiannon and Jack Shepherd	03–present
J A Penn	49–52	Nicholas Rideal	63–67	Jo Shubber	65–70
J G Penn	26–30	Jonathan Rider	06–present	Laramie Shubber	05–present
R A Penn	Staff, 76–05	Fergus Ridley Anderson	03–08	Salim Shubber	72–77
James C Penrose	66–68	Riley Family		D J R Sibree	69–74
Wg Cdr Donald Perrens		John Robbins	44–49	Alexander Simcox	93–98
DSO OBE DFC MA	Staff, 46–81	C Julian Roberts	76–80	Mrs Sara Simpson	
Dr Simon Petrides	74–79	Nigel Roberts	66–71	Tom (Simo) Simpson	01–05
Anthony L Philip	54–59	Clive W Robinson	68–73	Tom Simpson	05–present
John T H Phillips	65–69	David Robinson	50–55	Brigadier Ivan, John David and	
P C Phillips		Derek Robinson	60–65	Peter John Simson (three generations)	
Mark Pickett	73–78	Matthew James Robinson	05–present	Ms Maggie Sitto-Bjornsen	07–08
Peter and Janet Pickett		Peter Robinson	49–53	Hugh Skinner	98–03
Hugo Pickford	99–04	Thomas, Eleanor and Tania Robinson		Kate Skinner	04–07
Dr Christian William Pierce	89–91		97–present	Dr David Slavin	70–75
Kate Pierrepont	75–77	John Rodd		Roger Sloley	53–57
Tim Pilbeam	76–81	Katherine, Richard and Edward Rogers		Alex Smith	06–present
Jack Pile	02–07	R A G (Bob) Rogers	57–61	Darren James Smith	82–87
Nick Pile	94–99	Ted Roose		Dr David L Smith	77–81
Oliver Pile	95–00	J Keith Ross	58–63	Laurence and Christine Smith	
Christopher Piper	70–75	Vera Ross	45–77	Maria Smith	
David Piper		Peter Rowe	52–55	Mark Smith	86–91
Marian Piper	87–89	Guy Rudd	82–87	Michael R Snare	47–51
Samantha Pittman	95–97	Sophie Rugge-Price	91–93	Samuel Solt	06–present
Rowan Planterose	67–72	James Rushworth	85–89	Colin Soole	62–67
Christopher Plunkett	58–62	John Ryley	75–80	Hugo Southwell	93–98
Thomas Poffley		John Sabine	52–57	Magnus Spencer	80–85
Brian L Polden	48–51	F Ian Sacré	46–48	Ronald Spiers	80–83

Rev John A Stacy-Marks MBE	60–63
David Staddon	68–73
Chris G Stebbing	70–75
Jonathan Stebbing	63–68
William Stentiford	06–present
Robert Stephenson	53–58
David G Stevens MA	
David and Anthea Stewart	Staff
Alex Stimpson	01–06
Philly Stimpson	05–09
Michael Stone	55–59
David Stone-Lee	57–60
Fiona Storrs	
Ian Strange	60–64
Mrs Sally Ann Street	
Nigel C Strofton	55–59
James Strudwick	00–05
Anton Stumpf	76–80
Ian T Symington	47–51
L D Symington	45–49
Charles and Elaine Taylor	
Richard Taylor	53–58
Simon Taylor	59–64
J D Temple	49–54
B J Templeman	47–52
J F W Templeton	55–59
Richard Lionel Terry	49–53
Guy Tessa	
Anthony Thakerar	
Christopher Thomas	60–65
Meredith Thomas	
A B Thompson	66–71
A H Thompson	52–56
Claire Thompson	86–88
David Thomson	55–60
D Jon Thompson	62–67
Mr L Thorne and Mrs C Thorne	
John Thornley	Staff, 78–present
Sam and Lily Thornley	
Dr Ian Thwaites	56–61
Charlotte Tickle	04–present
Joseph Tickle	
D R Tillett	50–55
John Toby	54–58
Christine Todd	Staff
Jonathon Tomes	87–92
Hannah and Oliver Towner	05–present
Alistair Townley	70–75
Peter Townley	38–42
Jo Toy	Staff, 01–present
Paul Washington L Tremlett	57–62

Mr and Mrs L W Trevor	
Patrick James Trevor	06–present
Michael Tripp	52–55
Paul Tuckwell	72–74
Brian R Tullis	46–51
Adam J H Turnbull	05–present
Alice E M Turnbull	01–05
G Hugh Turner	46–50
J M F Turner	36–39
Philip T Underhill	50–55
Sophie Upfield and Callum Upfield	
	04– and 05–present
Nick Upton and Lydia Farmer (née Upton)	
David Urch	44–49
L E (Harry) Urena	67–71
Mackenzie J Urquhart	58–63
Mike Valmas	58–61
John 'Freddie' Venn	39–43
Philip Oswald Venn	38–42
Michael Venus	63–68
Daniel Vickers	83–88
E H Vickers	45–50
Mr John H Vinnicombe	44–49
Simon Vinson	69–74
G Q Vinson	40–44
Kathryn Vokins	
Susan Vokins	48–52
Trevor Vokins	
Morven Voorspuy	64–69
Michael G Wadingham	54–59
Christopher John Wainwright	76–81
Kirstie Jane Wainwright	77–79
Richard Wainwright	
Member of Council, 86–03	
E B D Waldy	64–69
Christopher H Walker	68–73
N C W Walker	74–79
Dr Cecil Walkley	44–48
Alexander Walsh	02–07
Dr Michael Walter	56–60
Declan Ward	04–09
Sam Ward	43–48
Forbes Wastie MBE	Staff, 61–98
Jeremy Wastie	76–81
Jonathan Wastie	78–83
William Wastie	83–88
Alistair R Watson	74–79
Patrick Watson	04–present
Rosie Watson	05–present
Guy Webb	02–07
Nigel Welby	64–69

Simon André Welham Grange	82–84
Sophie Weller	03–05
David Welsh	Staff, 78–87
David West	64–69
Willi Westenberger	05–06
Nicholas Weston	67–72
Fiona Wetzki	95–97
Harriet Wetzki	04–06
Richard Wetzki	97–99
Victoria Wetzki	98–00
Nigel Wheeler	Staff, 76–06
Mrs E Roger Henshaw White	35–39
Charles Thornton White	01–06
Jane and Stuart White	Staff
Lorna White	00–02
Roger Why	76–80
Chandu Wickramarachchi	05–present
N J Willetts	
Alan Williams	54–60
Gordon Williams	52–56
Brian M E Wilson	49–53
Crichton Wilson	50–55
Giles Wilson	83–88
Robert J A Wilson	77–82
Stanley and Jean Wilson	
David Winn	54–59
Paul Winnan	72–82
Mark Winston	77–82
Lottie and Arthur Wolstenholme	
	04–present
Christopher R Wood	64–68
S J Wood	50–54
Tim Wood	66–71
Sam Woodward	90–96
Mervyn Woolliams	59–64
Reginald Worsley	47–51
Andrew G Wright	
Andrew Wright	93–98
Tom Wright	01–06
M G Wyles	44–49
Peter Yapp	74–79
Dr R E Yorke	53–58
S D Yorke	79–84
S J Yorke	77–81
Ian Young	53–56
James Young	80–85
C F Zanetti	71–76

Index of names

Also available from Third Millennium Publishing:

Bryanston Reflections
Edited by Angela Holdsworth
In association with Bryanston School

Christ Church, Oxford: A Portrait of the House
Professor Christopher Butler

Downe House: A Mystery and a Miracle
Edited by Val Horsler and Jennifer Kingsland
In association with Downe House School

Durham Cathedral: Light of the North
John Field

Harrow: Portrait of an English School
Edited by Robert Dudley

Lair of the Leopard
Paintings of Sicily in celebration of Lampedusa's great novel
In association with the Francis Kyle Gallery, London

Newcastle University: Past, Present and Future
Professor Norman McCord

Oundle: A School for all Seasons
Edited by Stephen Forge with
photography by Julian Andrews

Sandhurst: A tradition of Leadership
Edited by Christopher Pugsley and Angela Holdsworth
In association with The Royal Military Academy Sandhurst

School Story: A Portrait of Cumnor House
Nick Milner-Gulland

St John's College, Cambridge: Excellence and Diversity
Edited by David Morphet

The Royal Hospital Chelsea: The Place and the People
Dan Cruickshank
Foreword by HRH Prince Charles

What it takes…to earn your place:
Celebrating the 150th Oxford v Cambridge Boat Race
Julian Andrews Foreword by Sir Stephen Redgrave

With a fine disregard: A Portrait of Rugby School
Edited by Catharine Walston

Forthcoming titles:

A Portrait of Lincoln's Inn
Edited by Angela Holdsworth

A Portrait of The University of Manchester
Historical Editor, Brian Pullen

The Guards: Excellence in Action
Rupert Uloth
In association with The Household Division

The University of Cambridge: An 800th Anniversary Portrait
Edited by Peter Pagnamenta